TURNCOAT

MATT COUGHLAN

TURNCOAT

How I Stopped Supporting Arsenal and Found a New Team

First published by Pitch Publishing, 2023

Pitch Publishing
9 Donnington Park,
85 Birdham Road,
Chichester,
West Sussex,
PO20 7AJ
www.pitchpublishing.co.uk
info@pitchpublishing.co.uk

A CIP catalogue record is available for this book
from the British Library.

ISBN 978 1 80150 464 5

Typesetting and origination by Pitch Publishing

Printed and bound in India by Thomson Press

Contents

Chapter 1

The problem with modern football

TURNCOATS, GLORY hunters, fair weather fans, hipsters, tourists. All disparaging terms used by real football fans to describe those who aren't dyed-in-the-wool, been-to-every-game-home-and-away, grew-up-around-the-corner-from-the-ground, always-get-behind-the-team, obsessives like themselves.

I certainly mocked school friends jumping on the Manchester United bandwagon, tutted at people leaving the ground early, and shook my head at day trippers more interested in taking selfies than watching the game. Now I was thinking of becoming one of them. After spending most of my life supporting Arsenal, I had fallen out of love with the club. Sixteen years as a season ticket holder were over. I was done with supporting a football team.

It hadn't always been this way. Things started out like a beautiful love affair. My infatuation developed after my best mates at primary school introduced me to

Arsenal. Fortunately, they didn't follow Liverpool, who were attractive, yet distant. Nor were they some of the few who followed West Ham, which was the equivalent of what you might go for at 2:00am if all the other clubs were taken.

Arsenal looked great in their red shirts with white sleeves. Even the name had a mysterious allure. I knew little about them at first. Small things like a catalogue for the club shop would be something I could stare at for hours on end. All I knew was they were doing well in the league and were about to go head to head with Liverpool in a title decider at Anfield.

It was May 1989. I was nine years old and therefore not able to stay up and watch the match. My parents had no interest in football, but they did like watching the news. I couldn't sleep. I waited for the news to come on to hear the result. I crept towards the stairs, peered through the railings and caught Michael Thomas's winning goal. I didn't appreciate the significance of the moment at the time, but I went to bed happy and could go into school the following week and bask in the reflected glory of supporting the champions. Lording it over the Liverpool-supporting Essex boys was particularly sweet.

A few years later, I progressed to my first date. I was adamant the setting should be against Brian Clough's Nottingham Forest, but a postponement and the rearranged fixture falling midweek put paid to that. I turned down the chance to see the 1991 FA Cup semi-final defeat to Spurs and more bizarrely, the last home game of the season where Arsenal were crowned champions and dispatched Coventry City 6-1.

After giving up on seeing Arsenal play Nottingham Forest, I settled for a home game against Liverpool in 1992. My dad took me and my brother to Highbury on a glorious spring day, with my brother supporting Liverpool just to be obnoxious. As a first date, it couldn't have gone any better. The art deco stands and bowling green surface looked stunning. Arsenal ran out comfortable 4-0 winners, with Anders Limpar chipping Mike Hooper from the centre circle to round things off in style.

A week later, we returned for the last game of the season at home to Southampton. It was to be the final match before the demolition of the famous North Bank terrace. My first game on the North Bank would be its last. I remember staying on at the end to applaud the team, after a 5-1 win in which Ian Wright clinched the Golden Boot award. As we made our way out of the ground, other supporters were hanging on for a few last moments, or chiselling away bits of concrete for a souvenir, and there was a clear sense of loss in the air.

With the ground being redeveloped, I had fewer chances to go to games. My dad started supporting Charlton to stop arguments between me and my brother over whether Arsenal or Liverpool were the better team, and then they both started watching the Addicks. My mum gamely took me to several Arsenal matches. She put up with the swearing and incomprehensible nature of one of the world's most simple and popular sports, mainly so she could swoon over Anders Limpar. Although, oddly, not because he was our only creative midfielder.

Being a lone Arsenal fan in what had become a Charlton-supporting household came with one substantial benefit when Arsenal faced Charlton in a pre-season friendly at The Valley in 1993. My dad arranged for my brother and me to be mascots for our respective teams. I got to meet the team who had won the FA Cup and League Cup the previous season and would lift the European Cup Winners' Cup. I remember in the dressing room beforehand, players took the mickey out of David Seaman for his indecisiveness, saying 'Mine, yours, keeper's, leave it' to him repeatedly. Paul Merson sang 'I'm a secret lemonade drinker' from an R White's commercial, which turned out to be the least troubling of his addiction problems.

In the warm-up I gave Seaman no chance with my first shot, so I could say I had scored against him. What I couldn't seem to do was lift the rock-hard ball off the ground. Seaman wasn't going to dive for a low shot and I couldn't just keep passing them into the corner, so I had to get them near enough for him to catch them, but still wanting to put a few away. I managed to score five past him this way, which is something I continue to boast about to this day.

Another up close and personal moment came when I bought a season ticket with my mate, Bisonhead, in 1996. Choosing our seats involved going through the marble halls and walking around the perimeter of the pitch to look at the seats. Getting so close to the pitch, even when it was unseeded, was a genuine thrill.

More thrills were to come when Arsène Wenger took over and soon delivered the Double. A Tony Adams piledriver capped a rampant 4-0 win over Everton to seal the title at a bouncing Highbury. This was followed by an FA Cup Final win over Newcastle United at a baking Wembley. Supporting Arsenal didn't feel like it would get any better than driving back from the game in my clapped-out Ford Fiesta with Bisonhead and his brother decked out in wigs and rosettes, scarves flapping from the windows, and a dubious cover of Donna Summer's 'Hot Stuff' recorded by the team blaring from the stereo.

Things did get better with more titles and cup wins. The fast-paced attacking football became turbo-charged, with Thierry Henry, Robert Pires and company delivering moments of incredible sporting prowess to dismantle visiting teams. They were a genuine pleasure to watch. From my seat just behind the goal in the Clock End, I was close to the action and felt part of something special. Not least when I was clearly visible on camera celebrating an Henry wonder strike against Manchester United, or when Kanu and I exchanged salutes during one of his goal celebrations.

I got to know a few of the regulars around me and we ended up travelling to several cup finals in Cardiff together, which was notable for one of the group falling asleep in a pub toilet and missing the first half of the 2005 final. Luckily, he made it into the ground in time for the penalty shoot-out win, which we didn't realise at the time would be the last trophy win for almost a decade.

Until this point, even the setbacks still felt like minor blips on an upward trajectory. The crushing defeat to Manchester United in the 1999 FA Cup semi-final replay was at least a pulsating encounter. Seeing two teams at the top of their game slug it out was pure sporting theatre. There was the euphoria after a deflected Dennis Bergkamp equaliser, sparking celebrations where I ended up about a block away from my seat having lost the contents of my coat pockets. Delight at Roy Keane's sending-off and Phil Neville's concession of a last-minute penalty was followed by despair at Bergkamp's easily-saved spot kick. And the exhaustion of extra time and mixture of despondency and admiration when Ryan Giggs capitalised on a series of defensive errors for one of the most overrated goals in FA Cup history.

A shock late turnaround in the final of the same competition a few years later, at the hands of Liverpool's Michael Owen, spurred the team on to another Double the following season. All the while, the attacking football made every home game a must-see event, especially so in the unbeaten 'Invincibles' season. The crowning glory would have been winning the Champions League in 2006. In the last season at Highbury, the team pulled off famous victories over Real Madrid and Juventus, before facing Barcelona in the final. It wasn't to be.

Arsenal moved into the Emirates and I chose my seat through a computer simulation, expecting to be sitting there until old age. I got to know a new bunch of regulars, who had a shared dislike for the referee Mike Dean and would come out with inadvertent witticisms like 'Get a fucking move on Howard, you fucking Tourette's cunt' aimed at Everton's procrastinating goalie.

The lustre of a shiny new stadium soon faded, and I was left watching the same old storyline unfold in a soulless concrete bowl. Moneyed clubs dominated the league and Arsenal lagged behind. Hope diminished and the team's defensive problems went unresolved year after year. Each season would see a bad run of form to end any trophy hopes, before the team would rally to finish fourth.

Fans expected better for their money. Things got fractious in the stands. The arguments between those who wanted Wenger out and those who continued to back him became more heated. My overriding feeling was apathy. I questioned the sacrifices I had made to make sure I was at every home game, and the guilt I felt for the ones I missed because of a badly planned holiday, a monumental hangover, or not realising a kick-off time had been moved.

I planned to make a clean break and not renew my season ticket at the end of the 2011/12 season. My last game was a 3-3 draw with Norwich City. Slack defending left Arsenal's hopes of a fourth-place finish, and Champions League participation, in the balance. This sounds spoilt. It wasn't a calamitous relegation, the club going out of existence, or some other major reason to stop going. It was the monotony of each season following the same pattern, the lack of ambition of the owners who continued to milk supporters for every penny, and the deteriorating quality on the pitch.

Going to games had stopped being joyful and became more of an obligation. Sure, true supporters stay with their club through thick and thin, and this was hardly thin. The problem was Arsenal no longer felt like a club to be part of. They were a business providing a service: an exceedingly expensive service at just under £1,000 a season for the cheapest seats; a service that no longer provided the customer with what they wanted. I didn't want guaranteed trophies. I just hoped that we would do our best to compete. Star player Robin van Persie must have felt the same way when he left that summer.

The new owner, who had bought into the club almost unnoticed during a period of relative success, appeared more interested in balancing the books than investing in the team. Wenger was no longer capable of recreating the magic of his early years, but it wasn't clear whether anyone else could propel Arsenal back into the elite under such financial restrictions. Even if the owner moved on, the best that could be hoped for was an oligarch, or leader of a dubious regime, interested in enhancing their image with some on-field success.

Elite football was becoming less attractive, with the super-rich asserting their dominance. The game was about amassing money, rather than bidding for glory. It prioritised the safety of a league finish over cup success, participation in European competition over trying to win a trophy. Television deals were more important than the fans. Games would be moved to all sorts of times, so the ritual of going to a Saturday game, with a 3pm kick-off, died out.

I wanted to watch games at Highbury, with its tight stands, its history, and an atmosphere that was better than the Emirates and sometimes better than a library. I wanted to go every other Saturday afternoon, with the odd midweek fixture for the special feeling of watching a game under the floodlights. I wasn't so worried about seeing one of Wenger's great teams. Even a dour George Graham side could provide moments of entertainment and would at least put in the effort. Like a lot of fans, I wanted to travel back in time to the game I knew as a boy.

It was time to move on. I wasn't looking to move on to a better, more attractive team to flaunt in Arsenal's face like Van Persie. I thought I might still go to the odd Arsenal match. In the end, once I had broken the habit, I wasn't interested in navigating the various membership and ticketing requirements for a midweek 'category C' match. The Norwich City game remains my last. I sold my old shirts and programmes and kept just the memories and the autograph book from my day as mascot.

I didn't even watch many games on television. The notable exceptions were FA Cup finals, which had always been the one game I was guaranteed to have tuned into since childhood. Arsenal's final against Hull in 2014 was a chance to end Wenger's nine-year trophy drought. I told friends I would be a picture of Sven-

Göran Eriksson-like calm watching it in the pub and not the ranting maniac they were previously accustomed to. This all went out of the window when Hull took a 2-0 lead. My celebrations at Arsenal's comeback showed I still cared.

The cup wins around this time papered over the cracks and the arguments pro- and anti-Wenger grew louder. I looked on, having made my decision a few years earlier and it was sad to see a great era peter out the way it did. My interest was piqued in the post-Wenger aftermath, even if it was mild annoyance when Unai Emery's second season unravelled. I wanted to get back into football, be part of the pub conversation again. I didn't want to go back to watching Arsenal, but I wanted to go to games once more.

I had enjoyed the atmosphere of games I had watched on trips abroad to Germany and Belgium. I was keen to find that authentic football experience of terraces, beer and communal singing back home. Going to Leyton Orient with friends had been fun, but they weren't my team and it was still league . I wanted to explore non-league football, which felt more like the authentic experience I was craving.

My plan was to play the field like a newly single man coming out of a long-term relationship. I intended to see clubs in the London and Essex area and hoped to find 'the one'. The question was: was I prepared to face the social stigma a divorcee would have faced generations ago and commit the ultimate taboo of switching my allegiance and becoming a turncoat?

Chapter 2

Why don't you support your local club?

THE OBVIOUS place to start when disillusioned with following a team in the Premier League is to follow the age-old taunt of 'Why don't you support your local club?'. I was keen to see if I could connect with my local team, Chelmsford City. This was only after finding out that Clapton Community had their game against London Samurai called off because of a waterlogged pitch. The Tons are famous for their continental-style ultras and left-wing politics and first attracted me to the idea of checking out non-league football. A trip to east London would have to wait. A look through the fixtures presented this far more prosaic option.

City were in the National League South, the sixth tier of English football, which is Step 2 in the non-league pyramid. I was vaguely aware of City's existence when I started going to Chelmsford as a teenager. Their old ground was visible from the train and they were sponsored by Red Card, a sports drink firm that advertised a lot in football programmes, but never seemed to be found in the shops.

After moving to Chelmsford in my twenties, I developed feelings somewhere between ambivalence and mild fondness for the place. In its favour are the county cricket ground, a popular parkrun, lovely cycle routes in the surrounding countryside, and reasonably good commuter links to London. The fact that two of these involve leaving Chelmsford is telling. Kirstie and Phil did place Chelmsford in their top 10 places to live in the country at one point, which was a matter of great local pride.

Naturally, the daily commute was joyless, and the city centre was becoming ever more clogged up with traffic. Schemes to build a new station and replace an ageing temporary flyover were subject to plenty of delay and local mirth. The city itself didn't have an awful lot of character, with the loss of City's New Writtle Street ground in the late 90s only adding to the soulless commuter-town feel.

The football team had plenty of history, with several failed attempts at election to the league in the 1970s, attracting a crowd of nearly 15,000 for a cup game with Colchester, and playing host to a brief spell of Jimmy Greaves's playing career. Much of this went unappreciated, and the club was allowed to move out of town for a nomadic period, playing in Maldon and Billericay. The Clarets eventually came back to Chelmsford, when they moved into the Melbourne Athletics ground in 2006.

The first game back saw almost 3,000 people attend and showed the huge potential of the club. A series of disappointments, such as seeming to lose in the play-offs every season since, saw attendances dwindle. The ground's location couldn't have helped, being out of town, and neither could having a running track. Locals call it 'the Gulag' and it's easy to see why when the wind blasts through the open space, taking any atmosphere from the crowd with it.

I've been to a handful of City games over the years. This usually involved a group of us meeting in the club bar to watch the end of the televised early kick-off. We would then miss the first ten minutes of the City game while finishing drinks. After taking up a position on the perimeter, we watched the antics of the mascot, Claret the Parrot, before deciding on when to beat the half-time rush at the bar. Drinks would inevitably overrun into the second half, before we caught a bit of the game. Eventually, someone would decide the last five minutes weren't worth getting any colder for and suggest we retreat to a pub.

It's fair to say the football wasn't altogether memorable, although I recall Ricky Holmes impressing on the wing, and being pleased to see him turn up playing league football for Northampton and Charlton. My only other memories are of Horsham fans doing a wonderful rendition of 'Close to You' by the Carpenters, with the title line replaced with 'HFC!', and of one City fan repeatedly screaming 'fat keeper' at an opposition goalie for a full 45 minutes.

Today's game appears no more promising. City are in tenth, five points off the play-off places. Visitors Eastbourne Borough are five points behind City in 14th and comfortably above the relegation places. The match has mediocre mid-table clash written all over it, but there's always the hope this is the start of a push towards more play-off heartbreak. Seeing former Bristol City and Reading striker Leroy Lita in the City squad prompts far more excitement than he probably deserves. Eastbourne's Sergio Torres sounds like he could be an exotic former World Cup star.

There's nothing exotic about the area in which City plays. There's a mini-market, where I once witnessed a checkout assistant require help to identify an apple, a flat-roofed pub and a bookmaker's. With some time to kill, the bookie's is the best bet. I take my time to make my selections on an accumulator. I think the technical term for the multi-team bet is a 'SuperDom' in honour of my mate, who is forever one result away from winning thousands.

I then turn to the greyhounds and spot the name Rockethall Ruby in the 2.22 at Doncaster. With the dog having the same name as my daughter, I put a few quid on at 11/4 and commit to putting part of any winnings into Rockethall's piggy bank. Ruby bursts out of trap six, like a rocket. I'm counting the winnings already, as she streaks round the track. On to the second lap, and her lead is steady. Maybe it's shrinking. I feel the sweat on my palms. The mutt seems to tire. It's being challenged as they go into the last corner. I can see the money disappearing, but the pooch holds on for the win and I savour the brief moment of sporting drama.

With a few extra pound coins in my pocket and the near-certain thousands on my SuperDom betting slip, I walk into Melbourne Park, where City share facilities with the athletics stadium. I pass a match on an adjacent pitch and slow for a glimpse of the action, which ends up being someone shouting 'Who wants it?' The ground's car park is full, which isn't a surprise because it's not a short walk from town. I pay £15 entry, which is £4 more than my last visit and it feels overpriced. I look to chase my losses and spend £1 on a ticket for the half-time draw. I decide against paying £3 for a programme, since I don't want to start another collection and I'm fairly sure I have a Thomson directory at home that will have all the ads I need for local businesses.

The club shop is located inside a shed. I'm not tempted to pop in and make the day-tripper's usual purchase of a scarf, despite knowing how cold the ground gets. I also get a first look at this season's current strip, which I haven't seen a single person wearing in town. The club bar is doing a brisk trade, and supporters inexplicably watch a post-match interview with José Mourinho despite the sound being off. The décor is a mix of some nice old memorabilia and flyers for various covers bands, and Sham 69, who all have upcoming gigs.

I take a seat in the grandstand and the announcer advertises upcoming after-dinner speakers and gigs at the ground, with the somewhat unnecessary clarification that the Beatles gig is in fact a tribute act. After some bad pop music, he then announces travel arrangements for a run of six consecutive away games. Most seem to involve a coach leaving the County Hotel at midday.

The ball boys are entertaining themselves with a hurdles race, using their stools positioned along the running track. City's manager Rod Stringer strolls onto the pitch in a flat cap and long coat. He surveys the ground and waves to the crowd, who are unmoved. The older fans filling up the stands look like they're here out of habit rather than enjoyment.

The speaker system blares out 'Right Here, Right Now' by Fatboy Slim as the teams come out to muted applause. The DJ, sensing he's got the mood of the crowd all wrong, soon plays a traditional 1940s tune, which may or may not be the club's anthem, 'The Waltzing Bugle Boy'. City in their traditional claret strip, and Borough in all blue, trudge towards the centre circle. City kick off and they play the first ball long into the left channel, which feels like it will set the tone for the match. City win a throw-in and look to work a cross. Borough clear and a brief game of head-tennis ensues.

Just two minutes in, I'm shaken from assuming I'm in for some classic Sunday league-standard football. The referee misses a push on a City defender. Borough arc through and one of their forwards fizzes a half-volley just over the crossbar. Soon after, Laurie Walker in the City goal is called into action. A Borough forward works the ball on to his left foot and rattles the bar before Walker saves smartly from the follow-up.

Sam Higgins is the next City player to catch my attention. A bigger lad with full beard, the burly number nine is easy to have an immediate affinity with. His perfectly weighted cross-field pass to the onrushing Chris Whelpdale soon dispels any imagined similaritie. Whelpdale feeds the ball to Shaun Jeffers, who finishes neatly, low to the keeper's right. 1-0 to City with only six minutes played. In the stand, the reaction is more Andy Murray winning a point than Marco Tardelli winning the World Cup.

Only 84 minutes for City to hold on to an early lead, like Rockethall Ruby did before the match. City have a Borough corner to negotiate. The low cross doesn't get beyond the first man, but the headed clearance goes straight back to the corner-taker. His next delivery is no higher, but evades the City defenders and Charlie Walker flicks it into the net. Eight minutes gone and it's 1-1.

Almost immediately after kick-off Borough's diminutive number 12 – I should have bought a programme – causes more problems for the City defence. He's brought down for a penalty, to the resigned moans and groans of those in the main stand, a sound that greets all but the most accomplished play in main stands the world over. A nearby fan confidently states it will go to the keeper's right. Laurie Walker can't hear this advice and saves the penalty, from his namesake Charlie, at an easy height to his left.

An entertaining opening ten minutes is followed by a series of misplaced passes and headed clearances. A lot of headed clearances. After hearing some arguments for banning headers in football to prevent brain injury, it makes me wonder what on earth lower league football would look like.

Some of the younger supporters are getting bored and start kicking the empty seats in front of them for want of something to do. An older supporter near me is reduced to checking what's being said about the game on Twitter. Then there's the light relief of the Borough keeper slipping on his backside whilst taking a free kick, which he promptly repeats. Not only is there a lack of quality football on display, it appears there's no Bovril on display either, much to the regret of the eldest of the three generations of a family in front. I make a mental note that I really ought to try Bovril at a game. It's certainly the weather for it, as the temperature drops inside the Gulag. The whistle goes for half-time.

The second half gets underway and Sam Higgins gives chase to a through ball in a similar manner to an overweight parkrunner desperate to finish ahead of a small child, and not quite making it. The ball eventually goes out for a City throw-in, deep in the Borough half. That prompts the first signs of life from those behind the goal to my right. A chant starts up. They give the advertising hoardings a whack. The attack fizzles out and so does the noise.

Events take a more exciting turn when the middle generation of the family in front has found Bovril for his dad. I resist the temptation to seek some out for myself. The game drifts along, like the middle overs of a one-day cricket game. Only without the warmth. The warmth one might get from a Bovril, perhaps. A half-hearted 'C'mon Chelmsford' chant does little for anyone.

Borough's Charlie Walker goes down with a head injury. Medics soon enter the field, followed not long after by two security men, one of whom I recognise as a doorman from the Bassment nightclub in town. He helps carry the stretcher as another young man's evening ends prematurely. Walker hadn't indulged in any minesweeping or erratic dancing to deserve this.

After a long stoppage and several mistakes, including an attempted clearance that is missed and bounces off a City defender's stomach, the main stand comes alive. People stamp their feet. City have won a corner. Or everyone is cold. Either way, the cheering soon ends. So too does Higgins' participation, subbed off after 70 minutes.

The break in play gives the announcer a chance to read out the attendance: 977. Around 20 more than completed parkrun in town earlier. The away support numbers about 18 people and is possibly all of Eastbourne's under-65 population. City try to build up a head of steam and pen Borough into their own half, but struggle to find a shot or cross. The referee awards Borough a free kick for a minor infringement and the home crowd is tetchy, sensing the game will peter out. The fourth official's board displays seven minutes of stoppage time. Normally, this would be greeted by fans urging their team to find a winner. This prompts the comments 'Can't you make it two', 'It's minus seven degrees here' and 'This lot ain't gonna score in seven days'. Classic terrace humour.

The moans are well-founded. City huff and puff. Borough break from a City corner. A long ball leaves a Borough forward one on one with Laurie Walker. It's Walker's turn to slip. He recovers, dives at the forward's feet and smothers the ball. Danger averted, and the match finishes one apiece. I check the full-time scores; my SuperDom bet hasn't come in. Manchester City and MK Dons have let me down in what must be a sign to move away from soulless, money-driven clubs.

I make my way out of this particularly soulless sporting area and head to the Rose and Crown to meet Dom, after whom the bet was named. Talk immediately turns to football, and it's good to feel more engaged in the subject again. I am the bearer of news on how the local team got on. Everyone is keen to know the score, but that's more or less where everyone's interest ends. There is at least more interest in the state of non-league football than the game on TV. The conversation moves on to the subject of money in the game, with mention of a player being on a grand a week at Salford, and the cost of an artificial pitch at Sutton, which is a valuable community asset, but would need to be replaced by a grass pitch if they want to be promoted into the league.

Chapter 3

Who's at home today?

NEXT UP I plan to follow City in their away match at Dulwich Hamlet. This isn't out of some new-found devotion to them, but more to cast admiring glances at Dulwich. The Hamlet caught my attention, being the club of choice for London hipsters.

With their fetching pink and blue strip, community ethos and specially brewed craft beer, they are worth checking out.

Since I knew the experience would be better standing with the home fans, I sought advice from my old boss, Graham, on how to fit in with the locals. He suggested that having a beard, wearing pink and bringing a small dog would ensure we would fit in seamlessly. Not having access to a small dog, I invite my mate Phil, knowing he would probably wear a cravat or something equally hipster. Phil plots a post-match pub crawl around some highly recommended pubs in what he describes as a 'slightly stabby' area nearby. He is then laid low with the flu.

In other news, I find out someone else wouldn't attend the game and that was City manager, Rod Stringer, who has been sacked. There seemed to be some sadness on the City forum that things hadn't worked out after a couple of promising seasons. Dulwich fans were incredulous that City had ideas above their station.

On the morning of the game, I fail a late fitness test, as I am coming down with something myself. By 2:00pm I feel well enough to get out to a local game. I look through the fixtures in the Essex Senior League and notice Hashtag United are at home in nearby Tilbury, where they ground-share. Hashtag came to my attention on YouTube. After watching repeats of Michael Thomas's goal at Anfield and random videos of three-sided football matches, this led their algorithms to introduce me to various freestylers, Norwegian five-a-side on laxatives, and Hashtag United.

Hashtag were formed by Spencer Owen, who set up a team to play exhibition matches, which were filmed and posted to his channel. He created a season around these games, setting targets for the team, as they faced groups of comedians, staff at football clubs and the like. As the team developed and viewing numbers grew, they took the plunge into the tenth tier of non-league football.

Hashtag duly won the league in their first season and were promoted to the ninth-tier Essex Senior League. I was familiar with this league after watching Burnham Ramblers' first team compete in it during the early 90s. Being in their junior ranks and wanting to watch all the football I could, I went along to see them play the likes of Southend Manor and Sawbridgeworth Town, both of whom I notice languishing in the current league table. Ramblers are no longer in this league, having been relegated at some point. This came as a surprise, since no one seemed to get promoted or relegated at this level, due to the vagaries of elections and ground grading requirements.

A second consecutive promotion would be on Hashtag minds, as they are sitting third in the table, with games in hand. There is a lot of hype around them for a non-league side and I am intrigued to check them out. I'm not expecting to have any affinity with such a new team. I imagine any sort of meteoric rise would be met with the sort of disdain German fans felt towards RB Leipzig. I had seen a few negative things about Hashtag on online forums, which seem to boil down to them not being a traditional club. Arsenal were a traditional club and fans took great pride in those traditions and ways of doing things. They had lost much of this in the modern world, with foreign owners, a concrete bowl for a stadium, a change of badge and a ragtag assortment of players who didn't seem to play for it anyway. Maybe tradition was overrated, and it was time to embrace a new type of club.

Hashtag are an interesting model for a club and appeal to those without roots, with their web content and e-sports team. The latter was of no interest. I don't understand the appeal of watching people play computer games. I am also slightly miffed that it is possible to earn a living from this, having beaten all comers at various early editions of *FIFA* games as a teen.

I'm not sure how much appeal there is in watching the Essex Senior League, either. I recall my mother's somewhat less than wise words of 'You won't notice the difference between Burnham Ramblers and Arsenal' to justify a cheaper and easier Saturday afternoon. I noticed alright, but maybe she was on to something. I resolved to be optimistic about the potential entertainment value and if nothing else, it would be nice to get some fresh air.

A drive to Tilbury was just about manageable during the early onset of man-flu. I've not had much reason to venture to this part of south Essex in the past, with my only previous visits involving cycle racing at the Ford test track, a parkrun across grim playing fields in Thurrock to complete all the Essex courses, and a family open day at a surprisingly nice nature reserve on the Thames Estuary.

Once I cross the A127, the locals' vehicle of choice goes from 4x4 to white van. Tower blocks and industrial units loom large. A takeaway advertises itself as the home of the Nutella pizza. It is a less-than-salubrious area. Luckily, not being the driver of a top-of-the-range 4x4, I'm not too worried about where I am going to leave my car. I fortuitously get parked behind one of the stands at the ground. In hindsight, it is probably more because of the low crowds at non-league games that means I find a space ten minutes before kick-off.

I join the queue at the turnstile (three people), pay a fiver entry and get a nightclub-style stamp on my hand.

The ground itself, shared with Tilbury FC, consists mostly of breeze blocks. Hashtag have added a teqball table, which seemed optimistic, expecting non-league fans, or indeed players, to have the skills to play this footballing equivalent of table tennis.

I head to the dilapidated grandstand, past as many cameras as you might find filming a Premier League game. Posters warn that filming is taking place and presume that I consent to be YouTube 'content' if I slip over, get a stray ball in the face, or eat a half-time burger sloppily. Thrillingly, other posters inform me the programme is free to download on Twitter. This is handy, since it's impossible to make out any of the names read out over the tannoy.

Hashtag are playing Takeley, which is most famous for being a crossroads on the way to Stansted Airport. They are in their all-red change strip, which looks identical to Middlesbrough's home kit, should they have fallen on even tougher times, and have some form of obscure local business sponsor them. Their goalkeeper even resembles Boro's former stopper Ben Roberts.

The Tags come out in the same colours as my old primary school team. Only, Adidas make their flash yellow and blue striped kit, sponsored by *Football Manager*. Straight away, they look like a much bigger club pitched into the classic cup upset surroundings of a bumpy pitch and adverse weather conditions. They even have 11 mascots coming out with them. I suspect an established non-league team might be antagonistic to the brash newcomers. The mascots file into the seats in front of me and turn out to be a local under-10s team. Normally, listening to kids shrieking at a game would be unwelcome, but at least they promise some semblance of atmosphere in a sparse crowd. They also act as excellent wind breaks.

Most of the early action comprises over-hit long balls. On the plus side, there isn't the usual array of old moaners in the main stand complaining about it, as such a new side hasn't gotten everyone accustomed to years of crushing disappointment. The four Hashtag 'superfans' behind the goal try to rouse everyone with some drumming.

From my vantage point I see Harry Honesty pop up from behind a pillar, jink past a floodlight post, then whip in a dangerous cross unencumbered by the wire mesh obscuring my view. Ben Roberts pads away the resulting shot, only for Honesty to float another cross back in. George Smith, with the goal gaping, heads the ball wide, in a passable tribute to Gary Lineker against Argentina in the 1986 World Cup.

The stakes are much lower today, but that doesn't stop tempers flaring in an off-the-ball incident. I don't see it myself, as someone had hoofed away the ball in the general direction of where my car is parked. The upshot is that a player from each side gets booked and my car is left unscathed.

Soon after, Honesty is left on the deck when an opponent backs into him while challenging for a high ball. The mascots, rather than berating the ref, which my youth teams would have done, ask 'Are you okay, number 11?' Honesty is soon back on his feet receiving the ball after a Hashtag defender goes on a run that's more Barnes Wallis than John Barnes, with the ball bouncing erratically at his feet on the lumpy surface. Honesty's cross is headed wide again by Smith.

A wayward clearance from Ben Roberts sends the ball high towards the main stand. The mascots are terrified. Who knows where it will land? The damage will almost certainly be filmed. An almighty crash of ball on corrugated iron. Children screaming. It's okay, the ball has just landed on the roof. More fuss over nothing, as the referee stops play after the ball brushes his arm and he needs to rub himself better. The mascots call for VAR on that one. Play continues and there's another example of lower-league quality as a Hashtag thigh clears a ball. The mascot's manager tries to explain the formations, but one of his charges points out Hashtag aren't playing three at the back, the right-back has just wandered forward. The mascots count five headers in a row at one point.

The referee is soon involved again, as players are squaring up. The mascots chant 'Beef! Beef! Beef!' Their coach, in clearly a forced attempt to sound responsible, tells them, 'We don't encourage that,' but secretly everyone is enjoying it. Apart from maybe the ref, who has his work cut out. Tellingly, no one is blaming him for his decisions, as both sides are putting in niggly challenges. The ninth tier really isn't a place to be looking for role models, but I am enjoying the game.

The superfans try out the alarm function on their loudspeaker. This alerts me to the fact that the queue for the tea bar is getting worryingly long. Next, joyous scenes of celebration divert my attention. There's been a nutmeg, much to the mascots' delight. The ball soon went out of play afterwards, but it's a sure sign Hashtag are on top. Just to underline their dominance, a mix-up between Hashtag's keeper and centre-half allows an innocuous ball into the box to trickle between them and into the net. No away fans celebrate, since there don't appear to be any. A split second later and the Takeley players realise they are 1-0 up and celebrate amongst themselves.

The half-time whistle goes, and I take in the half-time entertainment, which is joining the queue for the tea bar. This entertainment lasts well into the second half, where I get a delightful view of the first wind-assisted clearance of the half. After eventually getting served, I see another late challenge at close quarters. As much as I'm warming to Hashtag, I'm not moved to abuse the assailant. I tut and return to the grandstand with a lumpy hot chocolate and a Snickers.

I settle back into my seat and Hashtag have another free kick, this time in a threatening central position. Newby drives the ball low. It's low enough to be out of the wind. It goes through a crowd of players. It's close to the keeper, but Roberts can't stop it and Hashtag have an equaliser, greeted by jubilant celebrations from those around me. Hashtag keep pressing forward, putting Ben Roberts under pressure. He scuffs a kick straight at the onrushing Smith, but the chance goes. More chances come with a series of Hashtag corners that Samraj Gill swings right under the bar, forcing Roberts to do what he can to palm them away.

The mascots start up a chant of 'Oh! Hashtag United'. The game is livening up and even I'm moved to shout 'No, ref!' when a robust but fair tackle sees Takeley given a free kick. An hour gone and Takeley's number seven, sporting a topknot hairstyle, stands over the free kick. Right-footed, he bends it over the wall. Hawes can't get near it and the ball nestles in the top corner. Topknot celebrates arrogantly, which feels like a personal affront. Takeley have the lead again. From an undeserved free kick. Against the run of play. Hashtag haven't drawn me in so much that I can't acknowledge the strike was a 'worldie', but I would like to see an equaliser.

The sun sets over the Amazon warehouse in the distance. A stream of lorries continue along the A1089. Hashtag continue to send deliveries into the box, but there's no one there to receive them. Time is ticking away and there's another foul. It moves the mascots to chant 'off, off, off!' The referee is once again giving a few players a talking to. In amongst this, Takeley's number 10 walks over to a Hashtag player and head-butts him. All hell breaks loose. Players from both sides wade in. The mascots' manager and their parents are all at pains to remind the mascots not to do this in their game tomorrow. Despite the illicit thrill of a mass brawl and that I'll watch YouTube clips of Arsenal's altercations with Man United almost as much as I would the goals, it is just handbags. A player from each side is sent off. Takeley's number 10 deservedly so, the Hashtag player less so, seemingly selected at random to even things up. There's more urgency in Hashtag's game now. Both sides are battling hard. The mascots are willing Hashtag forward. Their coaches and a few other fans are willing them on too. Even I'm hoping they get the goal they deserve. Another corner comes and goes, with a wind-assisted goal direct from one looking less and less likely.

Hashtag win a free kick on the far side. It's too far out to shoot. It's a prime contender for being over-hit straight out for a goal kick. The Tags deliver the ball into a dangerous area. Someone gets a flick on. A Hashtag player tries a spectacular overhead kick right on the line. It's kept out, but then Tom Anderson bundles it home. The mascots go wild. Even I'm cheering.

Both sides have chances to win it in stoppage time, but the game ends in a draw and Hashtag move up to second in the league. I can't say I feel as euphoric as I might if Arsenal had snatched a draw late on, but it feels like I've done something worthwhile. If it were a first date, I would say it had gone alright. There were no butterflies in my stomach. I won't be bragging to my mates, but I am quietly content and interested in a second date.

I enjoy watching the highlights package on YouTube a few days later, which has very slick production values. In fact, it's a bit too slick, after documentaries featuring the likes of Graham Taylor, Peter Reid, Barry Fry and

John Sitton conditioned me to seeing a gaffer losing it on camera. Tags manager Jay Devereux is far more measured. Everyone's enthusiasm is great to see and there's a real positivity about the experience. It is not, as my mum would try to have me believe, in any way comparable to Arsenal, and maybe that's a good thing.

Chapter 4

Don't forget to Hashtag it!

LESS THAN a fortnight later I'm back at Chadfields, the home of Hashtag United, for a top-of-the-table clash with Saffron Walden Town. Hashtag are third with a game in hand over Walthamstow in second, and three games in hand over tonight's visitors, who are top. A win will put them back into second and in the driving seat, but with plenty of fixtures remaining there are too many permutations to count.

Tonight's visitors are the oldest club in Essex and one of the oldest in England. They are community-owned and based in a lovely rural part of the county, but with the sinister nickname of the Bloods. There's potentially a lot to like about them and I'm keen to check them out, as nothing in their long history has brought them to my attention before now.

I'm running late and as I know Walden will bring a large following, I'm worried about whether I will get parked behind the stand. Of course, a large following at this level is a coachload of fans and I'm parked up with less than ten minutes to go before kick-off. I have 12 people in front of me in the queue for the turnstiles though, and the queue for the tea bar looks like it will take the entire first half to clear. Again, it numbers around a dozen people.

I take my 'usual' seat in the grandstand, having worked out it has the least obstructed view, and savour the atmosphere of an evening game. The docks are lit up in the background. There's an extra sense of anticipation. The Hashtag mascots boo the Walden players as they go down the tunnel after their warm-up. I feel a distinct thrill going to an evening game, much like going to a gig. Whether it's the immediate escapism after work, or the atmosphere under the floodlights, I can't tell. The thrill exists even at this level, when the gig is more covers act in a pub than the Rolling Stones at Wembley.

The teams come back out of the tunnel. Walden are in red and black stripes, looking more AFC Bournemouth than AC Milan. The travelling support away to my left numbers around 100 fans. They see Walden kick off and create an early chance for centre-back Ross Adams, who can't direct his header on target. Walden continue their bright start, almost as if they are trying to capture my attention. Someone who captures my attention is a lone man screaming 'Tiger! Tiger!' in a section of the stand next to me. He has the section all to himself. The scene becomes less alarming when I realise he has a Walden training top on and is shouting at their left-winger, Tyger Smalls. It turns out this is the first team manager, Jason Maher.

Maher sips his sports drink as if his ranting will need all the energy it will give him. He goes to the front of the stand to bark orders at his team when they have a throw-in. Not everyone in the stand has clocked he is an official, so he receives some bemused looks. Smalls drills the ball towards the Hashtag keeper, as if to see whether he's paying attention more than anything else.

Someone not paying attention is a young fan in front, who traps her leg in a seat. Just as I'm trying to work out if there's a way of helping that doesn't involve accidentally breaking her leg, Hashtag's Tom Anderson brings the ball under control in the Walden penalty area. He hooks his foot round the ball and guides it into the top corner to make it 1-0 to Hashtag.

Maher looks anguished. The Hashtag superfans letting off the 'woo woo woo' function on their loudhailer can't help his mood. He takes an angry swig of his drink and shouts something. An older supporter nearby looks at him with concern. It feels like far too low a level of football to care that much, but then again, my under-11s manager once gave us the Alex Ferguson hairdryer treatment for not stepping up for an offside.

Hashtag look more composed after their goal, with Samraj Gill finding time on the ball. Maher exits the stand with purpose, knocking over a camera as he dodges past the smattering of fans. The game develops the feel of a band's lesser-known songs part way through a gig, where everyone is waiting for the hits. Walden then roll out one of Stoke City's famous hits, the long throw-in. Adams gets a head on it, but it doesn't bother the charts.

The game becomes increasingly bitty. I time how long the ball stays in play between restarts. Three seconds as a long free kick sails out of play. Two seconds between a goal kick and a free kick for a push. Five seconds when a Walden free kick stays in and is intercepted by Gill, before he's tackled for a throw-in. Eventually, there's a full 30 seconds of football as a Walden long throw is cleared and both sides try to gain possession before yet another throw-in.

Walden may not be proving to be too loveable in a footballing sense, but they have reason to be aggrieved after a shove in the back goes unnoticed. Their fans appeal for a penalty and I've seen them given. The half-time whistle goes soon after and Hashtag take a narrow and probably undeserved lead into the break. One of Walden's coaches remonstrates with the officials as they walk off and the Hashtag fans by the tunnel make a show of applauding the ref off, saying well done.

Now it's the turn of the tea bar to come under some pressure. The tannoy announces snacks will also be served from the main club bar. The Walden fans largely ignore these culinary offerings and trudge towards the opposite end of the ground. I sit and listen to the crackly ska music playing over the tannoy, which would probably make for a better gig than this would a game. Yet, I don't regret my chosen form of entertainment for the evening.

Maher comes out on to the pitch well before the second half is due to kick off. I assume their tactical plan doesn't require the full 15 minutes to reiterate. To my surprise Walden start the second half looking to keep hold of the ball. They work it forward to Gavin Cockman on the right flank, who waits for the overlap. The cross is cut out for a corner. Ross Adams is up from the back again and wins another header, but can't keep it down.

The game opens up and both teams have chances. A Walden defender inadvertently controls a through ball for George Smith. He faces the keeper and chips it left-footed, but the ball curls agonisingly wide of the post. At the other end Walden have another penalty appeal, as Smalls appears to be tripped on the edge of the box. The referee doesn't give it and leaves the away fans fuming.

Adams is soon left with another free run at the ball from a set piece, but can't convert. I'm shocked no one is marking him, but clearly not so invested in Hashtag that I feel compelled to yell at the defence myself. It's one thing doing so in a large crowd, but I didn't fancy being the equivalent of the lone drunken idiot shouting 'play Mustang Sally' repeatedly to a bloke at an open mic night.

Smith threatens to make it academic. A Walden defender misses a bouncing ball over the top. Smith shapes to shoot. The ball won't quite come down for him and he's either tripped, or falls over his own feet. No penalty given. Harry Honesty soon creates another chance for Smith, who thumps his header on to the crossbar. The tempo of the game is picking up.

A man passes through the stand to count the crowd; 274 are in attendance, unless someone moved during the count. Adams is busy at both ends of the pitch and he's up from the back for another long throw. Gavin Cockman takes it. From a standing position and with a ridiculous arch of the back, he hurls it towards the six-yard box. Adams wins the header. This time, he finds the target. He makes it 1-1 with around 20 minutes remaining. I kick myself for not making the sort of scene Jason Maher would have done to draw the Hashtag defence's attention to the threat.

Walden continue to threaten from set pieces. Adams wins another header, which is deflected wide, to loud claims for a handball. The referee gives a corner. Tim Pitman in the Hashtag goal is put under pressure by several Walden attackers and the referee awards the sort of free kick routinely given to worried-looking keepers. There's a brief chant of 'You don't know what you're doing' as the Walden fans continue to feel aggrieved.

Hashtag bring on Josh Osude to deliver a big finale, but his pace seems to cause more problems for himself than the Walden defence, with a Theo Walcott-like ability not to be able to keep up with his own feet. He lays off a pass for Smith, who can't get away a shot. Hashtag retain possession on the edge of Walden's box, but can't create a clear opening, before Walden clear and the final whistle blows.

As we leave the ground, a Hashtag volunteer thanks everyone for coming, which is a pleasant touch you don't get at the Emirates. I'm glad I went and feel like I'm getting drawn into the drama of a title race, even if the game didn't draw me into supporting either side. Tonight's protagonists will meet on the final day in what could be a title decider, or a damp squib. It's hard to tell, especially as Walthamstow finished the evening best placed, with fixtures to come against both Hashtag and Walden.

Chapter 5

A title race!

I STICK with the title race in the Essex Senior League and visit Saffron Walden for my next match. The Bloods are hosting Redbridge, not to be confused with Dagenham & Redbridge. This Redbridge were originally called Ford, who I remembered playing Burnham Ramblers in the early 1990s and looking impossibly exotic at this level, having a shirt sponsor I'd heard of, namely the eponymous motor company.

The Motormen had made the journey from outer London and so had I, taking a couple of tubes and my car from the office out to north Essex. It's no great surprise I didn't see any away fans making the same journey.

I arrive in good time for once and pay my £7 entry and £1 for a programme. Now I can read about the clubhouse buying a second-hand pool table, see a picture of the equaliser against Hashtag, and find out a bit more about the Walden players.

I enter the ground behind the goal and see a sign welcoming groundhoppers and an even more noticeable slope from one touchline to the other. I walk down the hill to the older of the two stands and pass several red portacabins housing a club shop, press room and small museum. In the corner of the ground is a clubhouse, playing loud music and having the feel of an over 40s night in a local pub you don't frequent.

I make my way to the stand resembling an old cow shed and take a seat on the repurposed railway sleepers painted in club colours and marked as individual seats. I am at the bottom of the slope and feel part of the action as the teams warm up in front and one player gives his keys to his mum for safekeeping. The ground is well cared-for and signs ask supporters not to litter, not to take glasses outside, and to mind their language. The last one might have been an issue at Arsenal games, but won't be a problem for me tonight.

The dance music being played over the tannoy drowns out the church bells in the distance, until the announcer gives a shout-out to Bloods TV, which is the bloke filming the game, and to the St John Ambulance. The teams are announced and there is no Tyger Smalls or Ross Adams in Walden's line-up. There is no sign of Jason Maher either.

Fewer fans are in attendance than I expected as well, so I double-check the programme to make sure that this isn't a minor cup game. It's not, and the referee gives a shrill blow of his whistle for the kick-off. Straight away, I'm taken aback when the first action is not a long ball into the channels. The language from the field is less surprising, with the first audible words of 'Fucking hell ref!' from Walden's Gavin Cockman not quite in keeping with the 'mind your language' signs.

The slope ensures much of the early action is right in front of me. I hear the crunch of two players going in for a 50-50 tackle. The Redbridge player goes in fractionally later and comes off worse. A random bloke wanders on to the field, with no physio bag. Given the club's Ford connections, I imagine him making a pained whistle through his teeth and saying he can probably get the right sort of bandage by next Thursday. Both players eventually continue.

Walden work their way along the bottom of the slope. Spike Bell, at right-back, plays the ball down the line to Cockman, who holds it up. He crosses, and the ball sits up for Julian Simon-Parson. The Town number 11 hits a low half-volley, which nestles in the bottom corner. The keeper has no chance and Simon-Parson celebrates enthusiastically in front of the smattering of fans behind the goal.

The restart is delayed, as the Redbridge number nine acts as temperamentally as my old Fiesta. He boots several balls away that don't have quite the right amount of pressure. Eventually, we get underway and a couple of Walden subs are dispatched under the main stand with a collection of balls to pump up.

Walden surprise me with some neat football before Redbridge win possession and counter. They break quickly and a through ball splits the defence. Their striker takes a touch round Nick Eyre, in goal for Walden, and slots it under him from a tight angle. It's

1-1 out of nowhere. The Walden announcer doesn't deem it necessary to mention the scorer's name and I've still to get into the habit of checking names off on the programme. Walden look to get back on track straight away, but a cross from the right doesn't make it all the way up the slope. Another Walden forward collects and squares to Simon-Parson, who bags his second to restore Walden's lead.

Walden continue to threaten down the right flank. Whether that's the slope sending much of the play that way or the efforts of Bell and Cockman, it's not clear. Walden aren't relying so much on Cockman's long throw tonight and look to beat Redbridge's offside trap with a through ball at every opportunity. Walden's Charlie Cole gets in on goal. He can't take the shot first time, but does well to lay the ball off to Carvill, who slots home to make it 3-1.

I buy some fifty-fifty tickets as Redbridge have their own chance to strike it lucky. Their number 10 lines up a free kick in a dangerous area. He curls his kick over the wall, but Eyre palms it over. The corner comes in low to Redbridge's exceedingly tall number six. He doesn't have the guile to dribble his way through a crowded penalty area, but he wins another corner. A supporter next to me implores Walden to put a defender in front of him. This is exactly what they do, and they clear it without fuss. Clearly, I should have alerted Hashtag to a similar set-piece threat the previous week.

As the half-time whistle blows, the smell of salt-and-vinegar-covered chips wafts through the air, and talk in the stands turns to promotion. Questions are asked about how much Hashtag are spending and how much of a blow to them it would be if they missed out. I feel defensive towards them, having built up a certain affection for them and respect for their model. I do some quick calculations on how the finances must stack up at this level. If around 200 people are paying £7 each, plus a bit more on food and drink, that doesn't seem like much to cover ground upkeep and player expenses. The inevitable sponsorship from a local builders' merchants must be key, along with individual player sponsorships and other fundraising initiatives. It's no surprise the music played over the tannoy is a somewhat eclectic selection of whatever is knocking around. We go from 90s dance classic 'Movin' Too Fast' to an actual classic, 'Hey Jude'.

Just before the second half kicks off, they announce the winning raffle number. It's in the same ballpark as my own tickets, but I can't find them. As I rummage through my pockets, Redbridge win a corner. I've potentially mislaid £120. The corner comes in. There's some sort of chance. The ticket is nowhere to be found. Redbridge lash the ball into the net. Still no ticket. Redbridge have reduced the deficit. It's not looking like I'll reduce the deficit in my bank account. Having once missed all the wickets in a day's play at cricket from various faffing around, missing a goal should come as little surprise, but isn't ideal without big screen replays, which I have to remind myself aren't a thing in non-league football.

Redbridge are revved up. Their goalscorer, number 15, a half-time substitute, beats several players on a mazy run. I'm none the wiser as to his identity as the Town announcer still refuses to acknowledge opposition goalscorers. Walden's defence is as lax as the possible owner of a winning raffle ticket, until someone does what can be best described as a slow motion spear tackle from Walden's rugby playbook.

The Motormen look to drive forward, but they leave themselves open at the back. Walden try to spring the offside trap. A through ball finds Cockman, who beats the keeper with a low finish to restore Walden's two-goal advantage, much to the delight of the scorer and several home fans behind the goal.

A Redbridge move breaks down and they commit a foul. Walden send the free kick towards where I'm seated. The referee obstructs Simon-Parson. He remonstrates with the official, incredulously asking him, 'What are you doing ref?' several times. What the referee was doing amongst those challenging for the free kick isn't clear, but he will not stand for this backchat. He escorts Simon-Parson away from the touchline, so those of us gathered there can't overhear the telling off, before play resumes.

Walden soon click into gear again, as Carvill gets to the byline and cuts back to Cole. He taps in a bobbled shot from close range to make it 5-2. Redbridge's number 15 is a clear disciple of the non-league mantra 'Keep talking' and tries to gee up his team-mates, saying there's plenty of time. I expect that time will be used to rack up Walden's goal difference, especially when Redbridge's number six clears with an actual toe punt, which I haven't seen since under-11s football.

The attendance is 151. Lower than usual and a supporter nearby says you can't blame people staying away in this cold. Someone who has been warming up is Walden substitute Nyanja, or Ninja, as everyone calls him. He comes on and looks to get involved straight away. A robust challenge from Bell leads to the sort of scene you might expect to see on a Friday night at kicking-out time. Nyanja is prominent in trying to provoke opponents. Others are telling each other to walk away. It just needs a girl with a shrill voice saying 'Leave it Dave, it's not worth it,' to complete the effect.

The officials take an age to restore order, much to the annoyance of everyone sitting in the cold. Yellow cards are flashed around. A fan next to me asks if I'm writing this up for the Beezer comic, which tells you both the average age of the fans around me and their views on the officiating. When play resumes, Walden contrive to miss several chances before sub Jack Isherwood is presented with a simple tap-in for 6-2. It could be 7 (seven) soon after when two Walden forwards bear down on the Redbridge keeper. This time, the ball isn't squared for the tap-in and a tame shot is saved.

Six minutes of stoppage time is announced, which is plenty of time for another goal or two, and for hypothermia to set in. My trembling handwriting reveals the only things of note in stoppage time were 'eeyore' calls aimed at Redbridge's number six, and at least one more occasion when Walden players queued up to score and managed not to. The match finishes 6-2.

Another large number is the one on the fifty-fifty ticket I finally locate in my pocket. I can't remember the winning number, but mine seems quite close. I go to the clubhouse bar to see if I can find out what it is. This serves as a good excuse to check out the bar. It has the feel of a local pub you might avoid if you are new to town, but could come to love after a few visits. Inevitably, I was a couple of numbers out, so after watching some FA Cup replay highlights, I drive home, which takes longer than I expected. The distance might be an issue if I want to take things further with the Bloods, but it's a nice place to visit and it could tempt me back.

I wait a few days and the highlights from Bloods TV drop into my YouTube mailbox. The video is less slick than Hashtag's. It starts with a title sequence that could be from a minor horror film with eerie music, a black and white shot of the church and 'Bloods TV' appearing in red text. Some of the following camera work is equally horrific, but it's great to see a replay of all the action. I'm grateful to the fan behind Bloods TV when I'm able to see the next chapter of the title fight unfold when Walden host Walthamstow. Having failed to find an excuse for a family outing to Saffron Walden, I settle for highlights of what was a narrow 2-1 defeat, which put Walthamstow in the driving seat.

Soon after, Walthamstow travel to face Hashtag. I'm tempted to go, but end up having to work late. Instead, I recreate the famous *Likely Lads* episode and try to avoid the score. The non-league version is much less eventful than Bob and Terry's attempt to avoid hearing the result of an England international. All I need to do is not go on either team's website.

After waiting for what feels like an eternity for the video to appear, I settle down one evening for the half-hour show. The tension builds through the usual pre-match interviews on a sodden pitch. Hashtag take an early lead through George Smith's composed finish, which he didn't look capable of when I've been present. It's soon cancelled out, but before half-time Albie Keith restores Hashtag's lead.

Both sides have had chances, but based on highlights put together by Hashtag, they are worthy of their lead. Of course, no one ever mentions the bias of the Hashtag commentators in the comments section. Jay Devereux delivers his usual measured team talk, and it's on to highlights of the second half.

I'm on the edge of my seat for this as Walthamstow create a series of chances on a pitch resembling something from a 1970s FA Cup upset. They hit the post. They force last-gasp saves. They must score. I regret not being there. I imagine the tension in the stand. I feel like I've missed a classic. The game moves into stoppage time. More chances for Walthamstow, but somehow the score remains 2-1. There are big celebrations at the final whistle, as Hashtag move into pole position for the title.

Chapter 6
Fancy a game?

I PLAN to stick to the ninth tier, and another fan-owned club for my next match. My friend Vicki talks fondly of Fisher from her work in helping community-owned clubs get off the ground. Vicki tells me she 'loves the fish', which could refer to the club or a large portion of haddock, it's not clear. Either way, I need little convincing to check Fisher out.

Fisher play in the Southern Counties East League Premier division, which is at the same level at the Essex Senior League, and have a fixture against Punjab United. Having seen names like London Samurai, Sporting Bengal United and FC Romania in lower leagues, I'm also intrigued to see a different type of community club.

I rope my dad into coming along, as a south London native, and all is going well until the combination of major pandemic and rail replacement bus service strikes. I suggest my dad might not want to come after all, given his age, which offends him somewhat. He is more concerned about the game being called off at short notice than any risk to his health.

When he hears the nearby Millwall game has been called off, his concern turns to the match being overrun by hooligans with little better to do. I suggest they're more likely to go to the pub, or go bear-baiting than watch a non-league team. He takes a rain check.

My concern is the pain in the backside of a rail replacement bus service, when a quick hop into London becomes a long-drawn-out affair. I look at some other fixtures. Dulwich Hamlet poses the same problem. Clapton Community is easy to drive to, but somewhat sensibly decide to play behind closed doors, expecting a large influx of fans from clubs with games called off. Hashtag don't have a game. Then I spot Chelmsford City are away to Dartford. Now, this isn't the most glamorous destination for a trip away. Dartford is mainly known for its river crossing, but I happen to know they have a modern ground built to high ecological principles and I'm keen to check it out.

The game is Robbie Simpson's first as permanent manager, after temporarily covering the role following Rod Stringer's departure. City have an outside chance of the play-offs and will need a decent result against Dartford, who are undoubtedly in the play-off mix. This sort of vain hope often justifies following a team.

I can't say that I am altogether excited by the prospect of watching City, but with all the uncertainty about whether they might postpone games for an indeterminate amount of time, I'm keen to watch a game while I can. A couple of hours before kick-off, I text to see if anyone wants to join me. I try to persuade Phil he's turning down the equivalent of tickets to see England in the World Cup Final, when we are all living in caves in six months' time.

The impending end of society as we know it doesn't feel so real at this stage and carrying on as normal hasn't been advised against. In fact, I'm confident that being outside and in a sparse non-league crowd is pretty low risk, especially as it's a short drive, rather than a drawn-out journey into London on trains, buses and tubes.

I park outside the ground, which has the appearance of a visitors' centre for a wildlife trust, with its stone, wood panelling and green roof. The obligatory adverts for local building firms are the only giveaway that this is the right place. After staying warm in my car and waiting for the queue for the turnstile to die down a bit, I pay my £14 entry, £2.50 for a programme and £1 for a fifty-fifty ticket. I have plenty of time before kick-off to walk all the way round the fully-enclosed ground, which is modern, but full of character. It must be all the wood. The giant carving of a supporter with arms outstretched is a delightful touch.

I check out one of the spacious bars, which are plain function rooms, but with a good view of the pitch. The bar would be a good place to watch the match from if I weren't driving. Instead, I try to pick one of the many good vantage points, before settling on a corner near the City fans. I notice the surface is in fine fettle and the City players are warming up with an elaborate passing exercise, which would have soon fallen apart at a lower level than this. I observe there are no players with a pub-goer's physique and I'm amazed how much better the sixth tier appears after solely watching ninth-tier football since my last City game. It's reassuring to spot my postman amongst the City fans, to keep that local feel.

The sun comes out as the Lightning Seeds are playing over the tannoy, which prompts some nostalgia for *Match of the Day*'s Goal of the Month competition. It feels strange that the regular rhythm of checking scores, catching match highlights and reading the back pages of the paper is about to be put on hold. I now realise I've rekindled some of my love of football, that most important of non-important things.

Government spending is viewed as a far more serious matter and I spot an advert on the halfway line saying 'built by a Conservative council' referring to the £7m spent on the ground. I can't help think Chelmsford would benefit from its own Conservative council helping the club find a decent ground closer to town. Football clubs often feel undervalued and I hope the developing crisis doesn't drive any more to the wall. I realise I haven't exactly supported my local team, but had they stayed at their historic old ground, or played anywhere other than an out-of-the-way athletics stadium, then myself and many others would flock to see them. I don't begrudge Dartford their new ground, as they've had an even more nomadic recent past than City and someone has booted a couple of holes in the council's advert.

While I get worked up about civic matters, I once again make the error of not jotting down the starting XIs on the team sheet in my programme. The ground is filling up nicely, the crowd no doubt swelled by this being the second-highest level of football taking place today. The Dartford fans behind the goal at the far end start up a 'We hate Chelmsford' song to the accompaniment of a large drum. City fans respond with 'We don't need a fucking drum'.

The game kicks off with quite a few fans making their way reluctantly back from the bar to familiar scenes of hurried clearances, throw-ins and head tennis. City fans are soon appealing for a penalty when there's a clear shove in the back. It's not given. Dartford create a couple of openings in front of their vocal supporters, who sing 'Can you hear the Chelmsford sing?'. The not-so-lyrical response would be: 'Yes, way more than I did when I last saw them.' I may not see myself as being a City supporter, but I won't stand for factually incorrect chanting, or 50-50 decisions favouring the home team.

Dartford's fans start signing 'Olé, olé, olé, Dartford!' which the football doesn't justify. Anthony Church turns smartly in the centre circle for City, but is tripped cynically before being able to break away. Players square up. Mercifully, this doesn't descend into a mass brawl that will add another five minutes of standing in the cold to the game. It's amazing how the appeal of a brawl can wear thin. There's a bit more control at this level. The level of fitness and defensive organisation is noticeably better too, as City chase Dartford back to the halfway line from a cleared corner. This almost feels like a league match, in terms of crowd, playing surface and perhaps a certain lack of charm.

I'm less inclined to give the referee the benefit of the doubt at this level, when three players fall over each other and the free kick once again goes to the home side. The ball is played into the box and it's flicked over an onrushing Laurie Walker. It falls to a Dartford forward for an easy tap-in. Under pressure from a recovering defender, he puts it over. The xG statistic for that chance would have been sky high, much like the finish. It's a let-off for City, who look like they might crumble if they concede first.

Leroy Lita is battling hard and shoves a defender into an advertising hoarding. The hoardings feature again in the game's big moment when the ball rolls under them. Dartford's burly keeper walks over and will not demean himself by climbing over to retrieve it. There are no ball boys. I am one of only a handful of fans nearby under 60. With the keeper's 'yes fella' instruction aimed squarely at me, here comes my big moment. I walk down the terrace as nonchalantly as possible. I pick the ball up. I throw it back to the keeper. Textbook. I realise an ambition I never knew I had, becoming a ball boy in a National League South game and not messing it up.

Some might argue a bigger moment comes soon after Dartford are awarded a corner. They swing the ball in, right on top of Laurie Walker. He stops it dipping in under the bar, but the rebound falls to Dartford's number nine, who taps it into an empty net. This leads to some sort of altercation in the stand as a few City fans decide they need a drink and go to the bar. They exchange words with Dartford fans that they pass and a couple of stewards need to calm things down. City look to respond at a corner kick of their own. Lita knows where to be and uses all of his compact frame to get on the end of it, but Dartford clear.

Dartford work the ball upfield. It's approaching half-time. A cross comes in. A Dartford player goes for a spectacular overhead kick and misses completely. Dartford recycle the ball and play it back into the box. They get a shot away under Walker, which is stopped by a combination of a defender and the post, before a Dartford player taps it into an empty net.

It's 2-0 and all over. City's season would have been in the balance had they gone in just a goal down. There's no way back now. At least that makes the decision for me on whether to swap ends with the City fans, or stay at the end nearest the car park for a quick getaway. 'Absolute shit' is the verdict of one of the City fans changing ends. I soon wish I had stayed in my car a little longer before kick-off as well. If I had got a fifty-fifty ticket about 70 numbers higher, I would have been £233 better off. I wonder whether it's possible to develop an addiction to football lotteries, after another near-miss.

Dartford fans take up their places around me, including some old boys worried City will come after them in the second half, which seems unlikely, and a ten-year-old going for the market-trader-cum-hooligan look, complete with ill-fitting flat cap. The young fans start some anti-Chelmsford songs, which irks me. The second half kicks off and one of Dartford's substitutes warms up in front of me. His routine seems to involve necking a can of energy drink. I'm not convinced this is ideal preparation, even for a non-league game.

Out of nowhere, City hit the post! This isn't as dramatic as it sounds. The low shot looked like it was going wide before gently bouncing back off the upright. Dartford look to regain the initiative and Garth Saunders skips past City's right-back and cuts inside to shoot past Laurie Walker and make it 3-0. It's all the sweeter for those Dartford fans nearby, who are still bitter about the way City celebrated a dramatic play-off result on a previous visit.

City look to respond, but there's no danger of me having to use the acting I once had to deploy in the Charlton end when Robin van Persie scored a stunning volley. The way I turned jumping out of my seat into muted applause, while saying 'it was a good goal, although he should have been sent off', may not have been Oscar-worthy, but was certainly good enough for a second-rate soap opera.

The ball goes out for a Dartford goal kick and I note the second-rate ball boy skills of a City fan, who gives the ball to the City attacker who couldn't keep it in and not to the goalkeeper for the restart. I'm not sure it's this incident or the lack of noise from the City end that prompts Dartford to sing 'Your support is fucking shit'.

I overhear a home fan say he's never been to Chelmsford and his mate replies, 'It's not a terrible place.' One for the marketing board to note, and sums up my own ambivalence. City's defence seems ambivalent to the threat posed by Dartford's number 11, who gets past several lazy challenges, before someone eventually brings him down for a free kick. There are more goals in this for Dartford if they want them. Luckily, City's defence isn't so bad that a simple through ball will open them up every time, in the way Saffron Walden opened up Redbridge. The Dartford subs warming up in front must expect the need for trickery, as their warm-up now appears to be more of a dance routine than any recognisable stretches.

Twelve minutes to go and the big exit gates open. The only other time I remember leaving a game early was a crushing Champions League semi-final defeat to Man United. I'd sat through a League Cup drubbing to the bitter end at White Hart Lane, not wanting to give them the satisfaction of seeing another supporter leave. The United game was different – it was finely poised at kick-off, only for Arsenal to be torn apart, with a Ronaldo free kick and a Rooney goal on the break ending it as a contest in the first half. When a spectacular comeback didn't materialise, it was all too much having fierce rivals taking such delight in our downfall.

People leave the ground. I'd rather not miss a goal, even if it is City gifting Dartford another, with a hospital pass across their own penalty area and a hasty clearance being charged down. Walker saves the low shot. Maybe there's something about seeing how players react in these circumstances that's part of the sporting drama. Maybe seeing disappointment after disappointment would make any eventual promotion all the sweeter.

Walker makes another save and City counter. It comes to nothing, so I head out of the ground. Home fans were going for a cigarette by the open gate when I thought they were leaving. I feel a little guilty, but I don't miss any action and am back home by 5:20pm. I text Phil to let him know he hadn't missed the equivalent of England in a World Cup Final, which must be a relief to him. 1,486 people attended, most of whom will have gone home happy.

I don't feel like I've wasted the afternoon, but neither is my first City away game any sort of significant landmark. They would remain that convenient partner I would resort to, while waiting for a date with these seemingly more attractive clubs. I would have a long wait, though, with much bigger concerns taking centre stage as the coronavirus pandemic unfolded.

Chapter 7

The game has gone

NOT LONG into the first national lockdown, I looked for football news, as a distraction from the actual news. There wasn't much beyond speculation on how and when the season would continue or be settled. One football story left me far angrier and more frustrated than it should have done. This was when the FA declared the season null and void for leagues below the sixth tier. I was disappointed the title race in the Essex Senior League was to end that way, having hoped to see Hashtag prevail. Hashtag were upset about how the decision was made and were one of several clubs who wrote to the FA asking them to reconsider.

I read about teams like Jersey Bulls and Vauxhall Motors, who had already won their leagues, being denied promotion, along with many other near-certainties, and felt that the situation wasn't resolved fairly. While no one was suggesting this was a priority, or that games should start up again, there was a solution on the table. This was already used to resolve promotions across multiple feeder leagues into a single division above and ended up being used in the third and fourth tiers of league football.

The much-touted solution was points per game. This settled a league based on points accrued divided by games played. It had the effect of evening out differences in fixtures completed. So Hashtag, who were two points behind Saffron Walden with three games in hand, would finish above them, as would Walthamstow who would finish second and potentially get promoted as well. Both sides signed the letter to the FA. I immediately warmed to Walthamstow at this moment and their Twitter feed revealed a likeable club, who weren't some mysterious nemesis out to deny Hashtag or Saffron Walden.

Of course, this solution wasn't entirely fair, as some teams would be worse off. It might lead to teams sitting above the relegation zone being relegated and others in the relegation zone pointing to an easier run-in that might have saved them. For me, it was better to reward teams whose efforts over the course of a large part of the season deserved some reward, rather than worry about those who had been performing poorly.

In my outrage, I did the only thing that I could. I signed a petition. It had no effect. I then wondered how many clubs at lower levels would survive the lack of revenue caused by shutdown. Finances were often parlous at the best of times. I hoped there would be fixtures to come back to, and tried to comfort myself that the teams I'd grown attached to seemed to have strong support that would see them through.

I continued to follow the fortunes of the clubs I had seen, and hoped to see, through their Twitter accounts. Hashtag provided some cheer with their regular updates, particularly when they announced they were taking on a women's team and setting up a youth division. I still wasn't desperate enough to watch their e-sports team, mind.

Nor was I desperate to watch any replays of matches, even those I didn't know the result of. Football isn't a box set to be caught up on. The joy is in the unpredictability and the spontaneous reaction of the crowd. The appeal of wanting to see the likes of Clapton, Dulwich and Fisher was more in the atmosphere and ethos of the clubs than the football on display. Clapton, in particular, continued to support vulnerable local people and be a superb model for community clubs.

Arsenal did a few charitable things to support the coronavirus response. Well, at least they didn't get caught up in controversy like Spurs furloughing staff, despite the scheme's intent and their owner's millions. Then again, both sides had players break basic lockdown rules, which further reinforced the distance between most ordinary people and the Premier League's pampered millionaires.

More homely updates came from Saffron Walden, who announced player baby news, free season tickets for NHS staff, and community fundraising schemes. If one upshot of coronavirus was the increased ability to work remotely, maybe I could consider moving closer, so the Bloods could become my local team. I saw I could even apply to work with Jason Maher, when Walden advertised for an assistant coach. Maybe I could pass as a Phil Neal 'yes boss' type, or I could yell at players to 'hit the channels'. A quick glance at house prices in the area put an end to this thought.

My current hometown club, Chelmsford City, drip-fed news of players being retained and released. Leroy Lita and Sam Higgins both left, along with an array of players who I less clearly recalled. It surprised me to see players coming in, giving the financial uncertainty surrounding the situation. I have to admit I fell into the trap of assuming clubs like City would always be around and wasn't minded to back the club financially, or as a volunteer. The connection just wasn't there, but listening to their chairman, Steve Shore, on City's *Claret Army* podcast gave me more of an appreciation of the challenges they had recently overcome and how they planned to be more involved in the community.

I looked at community-owned clubs like Clapton, Fisher and Dulwich and was tempted to become part of their fan ownership schemes, or buy something from their club shop. It would have been odd to do so for a team I had never seen. I had no way of knowing if I would want to get more involved in those clubs, or just be a day tripper.

I was keen to find a team to get more involved in, having found a few I would happily follow at a distance. I even toyed with following FC Seoul, when the Korean league started up before all others. They had former Arsenal player Park Chu-young in their line-up after all, but in the end I decided I would not be one of those fans who supports a team in another country.

One thing I missed was losing small amounts of money on a club's fifty-fifty draw. It was with far too much excitement that I bought several tickets for Dulwich Hamlet's online draw for the chance to win a modest cash prize, or match tickets. The club was donating its share towards King's College Hospital, so I was pleased to be doing some good. Although getting to choose what ticket numbers I bought from those remaining almost led me down the route of a particularly rabid contestant from *Deal or No Deal*. In the end, I went for the classic 'pick the next available number' strategy. I didn't win.

Big money interests of the Premier League always meant that top level football would return first. One of the first games after the easing of lockdown restrictions was Manchester City vs Arsenal. A lack of alternative entertainment led me to shell out for a subscription to watch the game on TV. I figured I would get the equivalent of seeing a favourite band playing an intimate acoustic gig. There would be the same quality, just a different pace to it.

I was quietly confident about Mikel Arteta's return to the Etihad. He steadied the ship after a turbulent period and looked like he had some clear ideas to improve the side. Surely, playing a rusty City side well adrift in the title race, in an empty stadium, would mark an upturn in an abysmal run of results away to the top teams.

There was some optimism as the City players didn't chase things down as quickly without supporter encouragement, and Arsenal looked fairly sharp. All this promise evaporated when the Gunners suffered two early injuries and were forced to bring on David Luiz. If employing circus clowns as central defenders had become a transfer policy over the last decade, then this was the Ronald McDonald entering the fray.

City put some moves together and forced Leno into a few smart saves before Luiz misjudged a through ball to let City in for their opener. After that Arsenal came nowhere near City's goal and just about got to half-time without going further behind. During the interval I drifted towards looking at the Twitter feeds of several non-league clubs, rather than reflecting on Arsenal's all too familiar capitulation away from home. The most thrilling part of the evening was Hashtag putting out a call for volunteers. I would not be any use to them on video editing, social media or coaching. Unless, of course, they just needed someone to put the cones out. I put my hat into the ring to help on the matchday programme and other matchday tasks.

In my excitement at the thought of getting more involved with Hashtag, I missed the start of the second half in the Arsenal game. They were now 2-0 down after Luiz had conceded a penalty and been sent off. It was another farce. It was frustrating. The result still rankled a little, but my mind was elsewhere. I was looking forward to non-league football restarting.

It didn't help that the subscription deal didn't cover many of Arsenal's subsequent games, so it did not draw me back into being an armchair fan. I would still follow online updates, willing the scoreboard to tick over in their favour. I even missed the FA Cup Final, which I could have watched, but settled for updates on the BBC website. Certainly, my mood was better after seeing the result, but the bond had been well and truly broken.

I wasn't even interested in following Dial Square, a self-styled phoenix club run by disillusioned Arsenal fans, using the club's original name. This would seem like an obvious team for a disenchanted Arsenal fan like myself to check out, but there were a few things that didn't feel right. This wasn't a true phoenix club like AFC Wimbledon, who had seen their club ripped from beneath them and moved to Milton Keynes. It wasn't like AFC Liverpool, set up by Liverpool supporters priced out of Premier League football. It wasn't even like FC United of Manchester, who were disillusioned with hardly the worst owners in the world, but at least had some laudable founding principles.

The Arsenal version was set up by Stuart Morgan. He was an Arsenal season ticket holder who was said to be fed up with the atmosphere in the vicinity of his seat in one of the most corporate parts of the ground. The club was going to play in Addlestone, with a long-term ambition to move to a ground in Woolwich. Addlestone was a curious location, being near the M25–M3 junction in Surrey. This would have been a long way for me to get to and the same could be said for the countless other potentially interested Arsenal fans from Essex, Hertfordshire and north London. The location became less of a mystery when it was revealed that Morgan had previously tried to set up a team, Addlestone United, so was presumably connected to the area and he hadn't seriously sought to start out somewhere closer to north London.

The long-term plan to move to Woolwich was equally curious. Arsenal never played in Woolwich despite their former prefix, with early teams playing in nearby Plumstead, before the move to north London over a century ago. Few fans would have a connection to the area these days either. My Charlton-supporting dad scoffed at the idea of finding any suitable land to build a stadium on in Woolwich too. So, this plan smacked of being a pipe dream to lure people into thinking the cause was like Wimbledon's, when in fact, this team would be stuck in Surrey for some time.

In fairness, Morgan moved quickly to open up a fan ownership model, but I was too sceptical of the entire project to look into it further. Even the kit, which soon went on sale, didn't tempt me. This was even though it was nearly identical to the classic Arsenal kits, after followers on Twitter predictably chose the designs that most resembled those kits.

The early focus was on revenue generation and there was little sense of the club coming together behind the scenes, with only sporadic news about random backroom appointments and no real chance for fan involvement. The Twitter feed irked me when it would bask in Arsenal's glory days, which undermined the point of a breakaway club.

Despite their faults, I was tempted to check Dial Square out. There was something appealing about being involved from the start with like-minded fans. It was then I remembered a decent amount of the disillusioned fans at Arsenal were idiots, more likely to argue with each other than form a nice community club. I watched highlights of their very first fixture on YouTube, a pre-season friendly against Bedfont & Feltham. Dial Square lost 3-1, having carried on the recent Arsenal tradition of atrocious defending. This did little to convince me to drive all the way to Surrey to watch football at an even lower standard than the Essex Senior League.

Meanwhile, I continued to follow Hashtag's pre-season on YouTube. Having had no prior interest in watching pre-season friendlies, the novelty of football returning, and games having been played behind closed doors made me all the keener to see the Tags. Their friendly against Frenford was at Hashtag's new ground-share with Bowers & Pitsea and I couldn't wait to get a look at where I hoped to see a few games next season. The ground looked in good nick. There were fewer breeze blocks on display than at Tilbury and the artificial pitch promised to make games less of a lottery.

Hashtag brushed aside Frenford, with help from the returning Jesse Waller Lassen. Normally I wouldn't be so keen to see a former Spurs player, but ever since I started to follow Hashtag, every video seemed to have at least one comment asking 'Where is Jesse Waller Lassen?' I imagined I could do a line of unofficial Hashtag t-shirts with that printed on them. As a prospective Hashtag fan, it felt wrong that I hadn't seen the player who had been described as 'a baller' in modern parlance. Of course, I could have trawled through the old videos to find footage of him, but now I didn't have to, and he was full of flicks and tricks, or more accurately, one particular flick.

Lassen looked good, as did new signing Toby Aromolaran. It was also good to see 'Jacko' back in goal after a long-term injury. Tim Pitman hadn't convinced me between the sticks and Jacko looked the better option. Having opinions about who Hashtag's best side was must have been some sort of sign I was becoming a fan. The squad was looking stronger and excitement about the new season built.

No one covered themselves in glory during Hashtag's next friendly against landlords Bowers & Pitsea, where a poor defensive display led to defeat, but the YouTube video did at least feature highlights of a better performance by the women's team and a game between the reserves and development team. So, the signs of the club's development were positive at least.

I got more excited about the new season. For the first time in a long time, I wasn't waiting on news of Arsenal signing the two or three players who would solve obvious problems and help them challenge at the top of the table. It amazed me to see Saffron Walden's pitch with grass on it. The pristine turf held the possibilities of attractive football under bright sunshine.

Clapton Community had won their battle for ownership of the historic Spotted Dog ground, which would be saved, although it needed work to get their turf looking pristine. Leagues started setting out plans for supporters to return. The FA Cup extra preliminary rounds were drawn. I waited with anticipation for the league fixtures to be released.

Chapter 8

First game back

AFTER NOT going to a match for several years until last season, the wait of a few months through lockdown seemed far longer. At last the time came when it was possible to go to games. I was spoilt for choice on who to visit. Would it be Fisher, who I planned to see immediately before lockdown? Would it be Clapton Community, who I had intended to watch from the outset, and their famous terrace atmosphere, which didn't appear entirely blunted by social distancing restrictions? Or, would it be one of the many other local teams, or community-owned clubs in the region? It wouldn't be any of the teams higher up the non-league pyramid, like Chelmsford or Dulwich, where the start of their season would be delayed. Once again, it was teams from the Essex Senior League that lured me in.

Hashtag and Saffron Walden were both playing in the extra preliminary round of the FA Cup, only a matter of weeks after Arsenal had lifted the previous season's trophy. This would be Hashtag's first appearance in the competition and, following their build-up videos, I appreciated how important the competition was to clubs at this level. Despite being a dozen ties and a million miles away from winning the famous trophy, there was still a sense of excitement about the prospect of going on a cup run, with the upsets it would entail and the prestige that would be gained. Not to mention the increased revenue from the prize fund.

I missed Saffron Walden's come-from-behind win against lower division Little Oakley, after working late. With capacity limited for social distancing, albeit at a number the crowd was unlikely to exceed, I didn't want to chance a sizeable round trip for nothing. I missed some heroic resistance from the underdogs before the keeper finally succumbed to a couple of tricky crosses. The silent slow-motion replay in the highlights video had the feel of a 1970s public information film, warning about the pitfalls of being a goalkeeper.

Hashtag also came from behind to win the following day, away to Park View. They played the game down the road from Spurs' ground. A combination of knowing that's an awful part of London to go to and Hashtag likely to draw somewhere close to capacity meant I settled for the highlights video on this one as well. There was a tinge of regret I was missing one of their games, particularly a historic first-ever FA Cup game. It was that sort of fear of missing out that drove me to get an Arsenal season ticket and almost skip helping move to a new house with my now wife to see a routine league game against Fulham. Maybe I realised there were more important things in life, or I just wasn't a Hashtag superfan yet.

I got the same thrill following updates on Twitter as I did as a teenager waiting for Arsenal's score to update on Teletext. I had to settle for Twitter updates on Hashtag's opening day win against Ilford in the league as well. It was perhaps inevitable then that my first game back would be a Hashtag one. I wasn't put off by them not taking me up on my offer to volunteer. After all, Arsenal had decided not to take up my goalkeeping services despite a scout seeing me save a penalty. I didn't hold that against them, even if Manuel Almunia was equally suspect on crosses.

I couldn't wait to watch a game again, and putting on trousers for the first time since March feels like I am dressing up in a tuxedo for a big night out. Instead, I am going to Pitsea on a cool September evening for a night at the Len Salmon Stadium. This is a shorter drive than Hashtag's previous ground share at Tilbury and I arrive in plenty of time to make sure I don't fall foul of the reduced capacity for their game against Hadley.

I park up at a nearby sports centre due to limited parking at the ground, and wonder if the gates will close before the game finishes. I spot a Hadley player who clearly has the same dilemma, so it won't just be me locked in. He also looks like the sort of no-nonsense player who will make sure we get out, gates or otherwise.

A short walk to the ground takes me through an estate of council houses and prefabs. Three teenage girls are pushing a road cone in a shopping trolley. I'm there 45 minutes before kick-off and there are quite a few people in the ground already. Most are from other teams finishing their training session on the artificial pitch. I make a contactless payment and scan the QR code for track and trace, the sort of identification measure long resisted by fans, but now the new normal.

Hashtag's home for the season is clean and modern. Even the tannoy is audible. I'm glad to be back at a football ground and take a seat in the main stand. I take in the pre-match entertainment, namely a stereo from the dressing room under the stand. Fans arrive, many wearing the much-hyped new kit, which looked smart. Certainly better than a random design I sketched. I thought they were missing a trick by not having a giant yellow hashtag on a blue background: a bit like Boca Juniors' kit, only more garish.

The ground continues to fill up and each new arrival has the ever-trickier job of trying to find a seat a couple of places away from a neighbour to maintain social distancing. Quite a few people seated nearby are involved in the club; a photographer with a giant camera lens, someone with the team sheet, and several people huddling around a laptop looking like they are editing highlights of the Ilford game.

Then it is the turn of founder, chairman and commentator, Spencer Owen, to arrive with injured player and co-commentator for the evening, Jamie Hursit. The duo take up a position directly behind me and set up for an introductory piece to the camera, which I try to stay out of shot for. Spencer and Jamie expect a tough game against tonight's visitors. The sides recorded narrow 2-1 victories apiece in last season's fixtures, with Hadley not entirely out of the promotion picture. They mentioned both sides had won 4-0 on the opening day and it was all rather slick and the sort of thing you expected in a match intro.

Off mic, Spencer briefs Jamie on the commentator's art. Apparently, the key thing is that if the action was between the Ds of the penalty box the co-commentator can chip in, but once play is near the goal, they should leave it to the commentator to describe the action and wait to be asked for a reaction.

There is a minute's applause before kick-off. No one, Spencer included, is sure what it's for. I think everyone assumes it's for the NHS and joins in. Then the lights in the stand go down, which reveals how dim the floodlights are. Hashtag start brightly in a 4-3-3 and the pace of Albie Keith on the right causes problems for Hadley, who concede a corner. Having live commentary behind me is a bit like playing in the school playground with the kid who insists on commentating while he plays. The lone Hadley forward Solomon Ofore gets on the ball in the box. Spencer highlighted him as their danger man before the game and is relieved when Hashtag clear. Spencer also calls the Hadley keeper's erratic kicking and I wonder how well Arsenal's owner Stan Kroenke would do commentating on a game. Maybe that ought to be part of the fit and proper persons test for owning a football club.

Hashtag's forward Toby Aromolaran, who had been impressive in pre-season, gets on the ball and bursts forward. He wins a throw-in, then a foul, but doesn't seem to get in on goal every time he's on the ball, as the highlights package made me think he would. Hadley look to get Ofore on the ball at every opportunity and he is almost in on goal when a strange bounce on the artificial pitch catches out a Hashtag defender.

After another foul on Aromolaran, Jesse Waller-Lassen stands over the free kick wide on the left. Hursit knows his team-mate has a good delivery on him and hopes Hashtag can score. Waller-Lassen whips it in right-footed to the back post, in a difficult area to defend. In fact, it travels to an incredibly difficult area to defend, namely the top corner. The over-hit free kick is unsaveable and Hashtag are 1-0 up, with the commentators obliged to ask whether it was a shot or a cross.

The Hadley defence struggles to catch Albie Keith as he breaks through a couple of tackles on the near touchline and plays in Smith, who can't keep possession. Off mic, Spencer and Jamie question whether there should have been a foul in a manner far gentler than most fans would. I suspect I will not overhear a Big Ron-style gaffe from them, which can only be a good thing.

Aromolaran isn't able to jink his way through the defence and it's the ref who shows a lovely bit of flair, letting a Hadley pass through his legs as they work it wide. In getting excited about Hashtag's wide forward, maybe I'm missing the real star in the making, the new Mike Dean that's refereeing the game. That, of course, is far too harsh on the man in the middle, as he's only missed a questionable high foot from a Hadley player having given one at the other end.

The yells from Jacko in the Hashtag goal get more frantic, as he opts for the familiar goalkeeper's tactic of trying to shout the ball clear. There is respite as Aromolaran pulls up with a hamstring injury. I don't need the commentary team to point out the tell-tale signs. Soon after, Smith receives a yellow card to match his shirt, a line I should thank the commentators for.

Aromolaran can't continue and has to be replaced by Harry Honesty. The stadium announcer is so worried about pronouncing the departing player's surname correctly that he gets his first name wrong. Pronunciation prompts much debate at half-time and I hear at least half a dozen versions held up as being the correct one. The commentators stick with using Toby.

Just before half-time Hadley win a corner. Hashtag have looked comfortable until this point. The corner is swung in and Alfano flicks it on. Ofore is on hand to tap into the empty net to make it 1-1 going into the break.

Spencer spends half-time dealing with the things a chairman at this level has to do, such as updates on Twitter, resolving pronunciation issues and chatting to various people involved in the game locally. His biggest gripe is how last season was concluded and there are no plans should further restrictions interrupt this season, or if teams fall ill. Even this early in the season, those he is talking to have tales of protocols not being followed and last-minute postponements.

For now, it's best not to think about the season being cancelled again and enjoy a game both sides are looking to win. Hashtag's chances of the victory are dealt an early blow as my apparent curse on watching George Smith play sees him go down injured. He's replaced by young Joe Gregory and suddenly Hashtag's front three appears much diminished.

Gregory soon emulates Smith's hold-up play and sets up Kris Newby. Newby gets away a clean strike that the Hadley keeper does well to save and has the crowd on their feet. At the other end, Newby gets the wrong side of a Hadley forward in the box. The first shot is blocked, before the follow-up is rifled into the bottom corner. Hadley have the lead to the delight of their 12 fans, who show it never takes that many away supporters to create an atmosphere. 'Ee-i-ee-i-oh' and '2-1 to the Hadley boys' are followed up by a charming rendition of 'Another Brick in the Wall', given their nickname of the Bricks.

I can't help thinking it looks much more fun to be a Hadley fan right now. Maybe I should look to be part of a smaller club, as Hashtag's large following is as subdued as an Arsenal crowd. I have no intention of switching allegiance to Hadley though, since they are based in neighbouring Hertfordshire like several teams in the Essex Senior League, so they aren't particularly local.

Ofore turns a defender and his shot-cum-cross hits a defender for a corner. 'C'mon Hadley' to the tune of

'Auld Lang Syne' starts up. There's another appeal for a non-existent foul on Ofore. Hadley are on top and Hashtag are rocking. They get some respite as the ball breaks to Honesty. He gets it out of his feet and makes for the touchline. Honesty swings in an arcing cross and it's met by Joe Gregory with a thumping header. The crowd erupts. The score is all square again at 2-2. It feels like a seismic moment in the nascent title race.

Okay, perhaps I'm getting carried away, but it feels like a turning point. Hashtag's forward line was depleted, and Gregory seems to have gone from gangly schoolboy to wily target man in one move. Hashtag were on the rocks and are back in it – the slight rise in decibel level amongst the home support shows it too. Gregory attacks the next cross with interest, but cannot connect.

Hashtag still look vulnerable at the back and attack appears to be the best form of defence, so they bring on Josh Osude. He takes the game to Hadley. After a couple of touches let him down, he beats his man and gets in a cross. The ball clips the first defender. It takes a deflection off another. It evades the keeper and finds the net. Hashtag have the lead, after a near-instant impact from the substitute. It will go down as an own goal, but Osude made it. Another big cheer from the home crowd.

Even Spencer concedes Hadley have had more chances as the game moves into injury time. Time is moving much slower for Jacko, who bellows 'Big ten' to his defenders. Osude runs at the Hadley defence again, with the ball ricocheting off his knee, before a more graceful stepover and cross, but no one can get on the end of it. Hadley break and Waller-Lassen is fouled; by the Hadley player I saw in the car park, clearly frustrated his team is losing and that his vehicle might get locked in.

Everyone is relieved to see Hashtag run down the clock near the corner flag, apart from the Hadley defenders who grow increasingly frustrated when Gleed acts as a human shield to win a series of corners and free kicks. The challenges bounce off his doorman's physique and he celebrates vociferously when the full-time whistle goes. Hashtag have held on for a battling 3-2 win.

I leave the ground pleased to have seen a good game, and spot a van outside emblazoned with 'Carmichael-Brown solar panels'. It's another tick in favour of Hashtag, since the owners aren't into puppy farming, arms dealing, or some other nefarious activity.

I return to my car with a spring in my step. Hashtag are growing on me. Tonight's result and a recent video about the long-term future of the club are getting me hooked. There is an optimism about the club. They are keen to grow, having taken on a youth development section and hit half a million YouTube subscribers. They're not looking to move to a fan-owned model, but are looking to expand their online following and keep providing all-important content. Ultimately, in order to grow, they need to increase revenue, but it doesn't feel like that's the principal aim. I'm tempted to buy a shirt or a season ticket, but it feels a bit too soon to commit to one club. I feel like I'm in danger of falling for the most upwardly mobile team I come across.

Chapter 9

They're the strongest club in the league. They're propping up all the rest

WORRIED ABOUT becoming some sort of glory hunter and because Hashtag's FA Cup game with Soham is sold out, I decide to check out Wivenhoe Town in the Thurlow Nunn Eastern Counties Division One South. This is the tenth tier of English football and Step 6 in non-league, a tier below the Essex Senior League.

It's the night after Hashtag's shock win on penalties, shown live on the BBC red button. I was glad to catch the action after missing out on tickets, and appreciated a neutral commentator's perspective. There was a sense of satisfaction when familiar players' attributes were acknowledged, along with the cringeworthiness of it being pointed out that some YouTube followers would seriously discuss how these players would fare in the Premier League. There was also mention of the usual debate about whether they were a proper team.

My view on this debate is of course they are a proper team. With other teams merging or going out of business, we need new teams to keep the game healthy. It's unlikely that church groups or factory workers will form new teams, as in the Victorian era. Is a team forming through friends on YouTube really any different from a group of colleagues in a munitions factory forming Arsenal?

That said, there were also plenty of historic non-league teams and community clubs that also needed support for the game to continue to thrive and that's what brought me to Wivenhoe, who have a team formed in 1925. The town itself is on the outskirts of Colchester on the bank of the river Colne, which is always nice to visit for the riverside pubs. I've no time to check them out tonight, as I'm running late and risk getting caught in traffic on the notorious A12. If the team impresses me there are worse places to go to for a game, but I would probably take the train.

Like a lot of nice towns, Wivenhoe isn't exactly a footballing hotbed and the team lie bottom having lost their opening couple of games. They are up against another team from a pleasant town, in the form of Coggeshall United, who haven't made a great start to the season either. Coggeshall supports two teams, with the Olly Murs-backed Coggeshall Town a couple of divisions higher up. I can't find any salacious history of a falling-out between the two Coggeshalls, and United play at Town's ground, so it's hard to tell where any natural affinity should lie. Either way, I'm not about to follow a team in the town where an ex-girlfriend of mine lives.

I imagine following Wivenhoe could be like following the fictional Barnestoneworth in Michael Palin's *Ripping Yarns*. They will be well beaten every week until one day they redeem themselves and I get to trash my house in celebration. I've certainly played in teams where the high of a solitary win in a season beats a long winning streak. The reality is this is my escape from a house already trashed by the kids.

I pay my £6 entry and am more or less given a tour of the facilities by the turnstile operator, who shows me where the toilets, bar and refreshments are located. I take a seat at a picnic bench overlooking the corner flag to flick through the programme, disappointed by the lack of a fifty-fifty draw, but satisfied with the hot dog and hot chocolate combination from the refreshment kiosk.

The programme doesn't reveal any player names I recognise, but I could sponsor one of them for a very reasonable price if I pick a favourite. There might even be some talented footballers in amongst them as manager Gary Monti laments the long-ball approach of opposition teams. Perhaps I've stumbled across a non-league Arsène Wenger, with a collection of diminutive playmakers bullied out of games by more physical and direct sides.

I take my time to pick a spot to watch the game. The main stand is cordoned off so the substitutes can spread themselves out. On the opposite touchline, there are just hoardings with a grass area behind. I discount this option, as I don't fancy being a ball boy for the evening. I like the look of the covered terraces running most of the length of the goal line behind each goal, with a low, whitewashed wall in front. I go to pick a spot and then realise I'm just as likely to play ball boy in the unoccupied space there. In the end, I stay near the picnic tables.

I notice an advert for a local goalkeeping academy, which along with the walking football team mentioned on Wivenhoe's website feels like it might be an omen, but then so does spotting some road cones and a wheelie bin on the terraces. I could either resurrect my playing career or become a one-man band of ultras. There also appears to be a vacancy for club DJ, as they are just playing Kiss FM over the tannoy.

Wivenhoe, nicknamed the Dragons, are in all blue. Coggeshall line up in their golden-brown away kit. There is silence. Kiss FM will not indicate what the silence is for, as they have turned it off. An older fan in front hopes 'they're not going to do the knee thing' in relation to the Black Lives Matter campaign, which makes the silence more awkward. The reason then becomes clear as they dispatch a Coggeshall player to fetch their goalkeeper from the changing rooms. This is the only example I can think of where the referee counting the number of players on the pitch has proven to be necessary.

Wivenhoe kick off and I look forward to what possession-based attacking football Gary Monti has in store. Almost immediately, they send a long ball out wide and someone is offside. Coggeshall's number nine, Hussain Jaffa, soon catches the eye, resembling an even taller version of the already tall former Stoke man, Kenwyne Jones. An older fan gives his seal of approval. 'Personally, I'm in favour of a big lump up front,' he remarks.

The few Wivenhoe fans in attendance congregate behind the goal defended by Wivenhoe keeper George Rae. They must know where the action is going to be. Either that or they want to be near the bar. Neither reason is a ringing endorsement of the Dragons.

Wivenhoe are soon under pressure. A low through ball forces Rae out of his box to deal with the threat. He tries to bring the ball back into his penalty area to pick it up. The visiting forwards close in on him. He picks the ball up just in time. But he's marginally outside his area. The referee sensibly awards only a free kick. Coggeshall fire in the ball and hit the first man and a catastrophe is averted.

Wivenhoe's reprieve is short-lived. Jaffa is in. He sets himself well and strikes his shot cleanly. Rae gets a touch, and the ball hits the bar. It comes back out to a defender facing his own goal. The ball is bouncing. Forwards are charging in. He handles. It's a clear penalty and the referee points to the spot. Jamie Age lines up to take the kick. Rae looks confident. He's doing jumping jacks on the spot. A Wivenhoe youth team gather behind the goal to watch. 'Don't worry about diving,' one of them shouts, as Age doesn't mess about and places it well to the left of Rae, who collapses to his right. The youth team carry on watching the game. On closer inspection, their beards, tattoos and beers in hand suggest they are more likely to be the reserve team.

Coggeshall tails are up. Rae is out of his box to head clear another through ball. The youth team are glad they aren't up against Jaffa, who gets up high to win a header he can't direct. They discuss how they would have to resort to fouling him and recall one of their player's red cards for a studs-up tackle in a finely balanced game with the sort of reverence normally reserved for a screamer into the top corner.

Deep inside the Wivenhoe half, Coggeshall's number ten, Skirmants Bulauka wins the ball back with a slide tackle. A recovering defender holds him up, but he turns him inside-out. Bulauka flicks it past another defender and hits a shot low to the right of Rae. It's 2-0. Rae hasn't done an awful lot wrong, but looks like he could be on the end of a heavy defeat come the end of the night. This divides the youth team on whether it was a good finish, or whether they should have taken Bulauka out.

Jaffa muscles his way past the Coggeshall right-back and gets in a cross. The defence appeal for offside, with the familiar screech of 'Lino!' The linesman calls back 'No he wasn't.' 'He bloody was,' shouts a fan, as if we are in a Mike Leigh-directed pantomime. One of the youth team has seen enough and exits stage left to see his missus. The manager promptly administers him a fine. It's nice to see the entire club getting behind the first team, even if it has to be enforced by sanctions.

I get the impression that I'm the only person in the ground who doesn't play for the club, or have a relative playing for the club.

The game is disjointed. Wivenhoe play another through ball and Jaffa bears down on Rae. They meet at the same time. Rae connects with the ball, but collides with Jaffa and goes down hurt. Bulauka has an empty goal to aim for, but is caught between finishing ruthlessly and stopping for the injury and the chance goes. Rae recovers after treatment and scuffs his goal kick.

The half-time whistle blows and some reserves drift off. A wit in the crowd audibly asks his mate, 'What were you saying about the ref?' as the officials go down the tunnel. The referee smiles. The teams stay in the middle of the pitch in huddles, not keen to trek all the way to the changing rooms, presumably in case they lose another player. Sadly, Monti doesn't dish out a Phil Brown-style rollicking, so it's more Kiss FM for entertainment.

The officials return and the larger of the linesmen checks the nets to see if they haven't disintegrated during the interval and the most vocal member of the youth team, who may be their player-manager, implores: 'Another *big* performance lino!' Their attention then turns to the visiting keeper, Lewis Down, whose distribution comes under scrutiny. 'Not good enough for Coggeshall Town, are you?' and 'lamb shank!' when he tries drop kicks, full volleys and kicking from the ground to varying degrees of success. There's some far-from-accomplished defending on display as a Coggeshall defender clears the ball for a throw with his knee. More jeers from the youth team. Jaffa continues to command their respect as he shrugs off a defender, but can't find an end ball.

Wivenhoe grow into the game and try to work the ball out wide. They don't seem to have enough pace or trickery, so carving out an opening is laboured. The Dragons introduce a couple of subs and one of them sets up a chance, only for it to be blazed over into the car park. Another ball ends up behind the linesman, who gets some grief for not passing it back. 'I can't touch it,' he pleads, which makes you wonder how the authorities have time to come up with such edicts, whilst VAR and handball laws remain such a mess.

No one can seem to get a decisive touch in a goalmouth scramble soon after. Down, already lying prostrate, saves a scuffed shot which just rolls towards his studs, before being cleared. Wivenhoe are on top, but don't look like scoring. Coggeshall look like scoring with every attack, but that's mainly because it's hard to tell whether action at the other end is 30 yards from goal, or three.

'Put it in the box' comes a loud cry from the Coggeshall manager trying to communicate the sort of sophisticated tactics only a manager can. I think I could manage at non-league level by purely bellowing football clichés. Coggeshall are a vocal side, so haven't fallen into the trap of not talking to each other. Their classic 4-4-2 formation with big man, little man forward line is also serving them well. This is no place for sophistication and a Wivenhoe forward is unceremoniously bundled into the wall in front of me.

Wivenhoe take an age to fashion another chance, which ends in a tame shot. Down takes even longer to make a show of gathering the ball, getting back to his feet and then clearing. The youth team optimistically count quickly to six, hoping for a free kick. Wivenhoe win a couple of late corners to keep their hopes alive, but they can't get a shot away, let alone stage an implausible comeback, before the referee blows for full time.

The game hasn't been great, but it did the job of taking my mind off a busy couple of days at work. Wivenhoe were no comedy outfit like Barnstoneworth and kept trying to the bitter end, but came up short. If I lived in the town, I would happily be a regular at their tidy little ground and I hope they can attract enough regulars to continue. For me, there just wasn't that spark and I would continue to check out other clubs.

Chapter 10

Where talent
meets opportunity

ONE OF the few benefits of lockdown is that it forced me to appreciate things closer to home. I found walks and cycle routes in places I often overlooked, and thinking about football I was drawn to several Essex-based teams, instead of those based in London. Heybridge Swifts were one of those teams. I had forgotten all about them even though I had played against their junior teams many years ago. At one point, their men's team was outperforming Chelmsford City, despite having a population 20 times smaller. In the 1990s and 2000s, they were towards the top of the seventh tier and progressing to the first round proper of the FA Cup. Since then, they had fallen to the eighth tier Isthmian League North, two divisions below Chelmsford City and one above Hashtag. They were languishing towards the bottom of the table as well after a handful of games.

I felt a certain sense of unfinished business with Heybridge. After a couple of my junior teams folded,

I was twice asked if I would join them and I'm still kicking myself for not doing so and missing out on a cup win. There might even have been an outside chance I would have been turning out for them tonight as a 40-year-old goalkeeper. The fact I chose instead to play for a team my mates played for, was getting drunk at 15, and failing to impress one girl who was friends with the coach's daughter, suggests my playing days were never destined for such longevity.

I had fond memories of playing at Swifts' Scraley Road ground. I played my first-ever competitive match there in a 1-0 defeat, where our captain, set piece-taker and coincidentally son of the manager, missed a late penalty. Swifts were always a friendly club and weren't considered rivals of the teams I played for. Nor were they rivals with Chelmsford City, so I had a bit of a soft spot for them.

I arrive at the ground, which has been rebranded the Aspen Waite Arena. Arena seems like an optimistic term for a ground with only half a dozen rows of seats in either of the main stands and a car park with puddles the size of lakes after a pre-match downpour. The club motto, 'Where talent meets opportunity', which seemed to be borrowed from an HR consultancy, is prominent.

I dodge the puddles, pay my £10 entry and complete the track and trace sign-in. I don't spot a programme for sale and see no sign of a fifty-fifty draw, which I worry has fallen foul of some sort of coronavirus restriction. I find a seat in the main stand and watch the home side warm up with an intense small-sided game that is low on ball control and high on cutting up the sodden pitch.

Swifts' opponents are Hullbridge Sports, who are taking a much more relaxed approach to their warm-up and well they might, given they sit third in the table going into the match. Hullbridge had only recently been promoted from the Essex Senior League and are only previously known to me as being where the one hill is located on the London to Southend charity bike ride route. All I know now is that they play in yellow.

The PA system is almost nightclub quality and playing the sort of music that members of most football teams would choose, namely thumping dance tunes. This doesn't tempt any fans out of the modern supporters' bar. It also cuts out midway through the teams being read out, so I look them up on Twitter. Swifts have a player by the name of Emmanuel Osei-Owusi and I think I distantly recall him being an Arsenal trainee. Google tells me he's an auditor at a large accounting firm, a Ghanaian politician or a journeyman footballer from the lower leagues who hasn't played for the Gunners.

The game is about to kick off and a Hullbridge defender goes with the unusual battle cry of 'win the first, win the second', which suggests a lack of confidence in his team-mates' first touch. 'Straight in boys' is another more direct instruction from one midfielder. Swifts, playing in black and white stripes, kick off. They send the ball out wide and possession passes back and forth.

Before long, Swifts keeper Jacob Marsden, on loan from Chelmsford City, is called into action, having to clear long. A 40-year-old Coughlan would have been sure to scuff that one. Hullbridge are back in possession either way. Their through ball sees the linesman's flag raised, and it's a free kick. Marsden pumps it long again. I would have feigned injury and let a burly defender take it for me.

There's no hiding for Marsden when he's next called upon. Hullbridge's number 12, George Cocklin, a short, left-footed playmaker, lines up a free kick from the right-hand side near the halfway line. He sends in a high, teasing ball. Marsden punches, which is more sensible than the trademarked Coughlan flap. Swifts break and, swooping forward, they win a corner.

The in-swinging kick is sent towards a flock of players. It's flicked on at the near post and bundled in to a muted cheer. It's 1-0 to the hosts, which seems to take everyone by surprise. About a minute later, there's a slightly louder cheer. From the kick-off Cocklin looks to play a long pass. He's charged down, and Swifts play the ball wide to Ernest Okoh. He bursts forward with pace and gets a shot away. The keeper spills it and they tuck away the rebound for 2-0. Only five minutes on the clock and Swifts are off to a flyer.

Hullbridge threaten with Cocklin's set pieces. The thump of the clearance is met by the smack of ball on head as it's returned. The linesman squelches along the touchline as he shuttles back and forth. Heybridge's frenetic warm-up has turned out to be ideal practice for the match and the cut-up turf forces a misplaced pass from Hullbridge. Osei exchanges passes neatly, but can't break through.

Fouls punctuate. During another stoppage, a Hullbridge defender throws the ball at someone with moderate force. The referee stops play to speak to his linesman. I have time to consider why no one living in a house backing on to the far side of the ground is watching from their bedroom. Is it a disappointing lack of interest in their local team, or are they actually paying to be at the game? The referee calls over a Hullbridge player and produces a red card. Peter Dexter, or Dexter Peter, depending on which Twitter feed I go with, has been sent off.

The Swifts bench loudly appeal after another foul soon after. 'Fucking do your job, ref. Send him off!' is the clearly audible call. With faux will-someone-please-think-of-the-children outrage, the away supporters sat nearby implore the referee to warn whoever it was in the home dugout. I then remember Stuart Nethercott is Swifts' manager and think it surely can't be him. My vague recollection of him is as a timid defender in a powder-puff Spurs defence in the 1990s. Maybe this is what non-league does to a man and maybe I shouldn't consider following a team whose manager has connections with Spurs.

Hullbridge supporters complain about the referee's bias, before a tackle on Swifts' Andy Fennell takes the man and little, if any, ball. No penalty. Hullbridge play the ball wide. 'No cross!' shouts Marsden. It's crossed.

He punches clear. Fennell gives chase like a young Jamie Vardy, or even an old Jamie Vardy. He plays in the even swifter Okoh, who drills a shot straight at the keeper.

Both sides are giving their all. The ball has taken so much of a kicking at this stage that it gives up and is replaced, having gone flat. The replacement ball is accidentally kicked over the roof of the stand, leading to more complaints from the away fans. They might wish more time had been wasted, because out of nowhere Swifts' number 10 lets fly from the edge of the box and curls one into the top corner for 3-0.

Before the half-time whistle blows, Hullbridge have time for further complaint after the linesman leaves the ball when they are keen to get it back in play. I'm shocked their players and fans aren't aware of the FA's important edict that linesmen can't touch the ball. They may be 3-0 down, but there's a sense it's not all over.

There's no time for Hullbridge to pull one back before the break, though. The whistle blows and with it the heavens open. The players jog to the tunnel. Supporters standing on the open terrace move into the main stand. I decide the benefits of a warming half-time hot chocolate are outweighed by getting soaked. I've enjoyed the first 45 minutes. It's been blood-and-thunder stuff, as opposed to the usual thud and blunder. Although there has been some of that as well.

I look forward to seeing Okoh at close quarters in the second half. A quick look online reveals he was an Arsenal trainee. I also find out that Andy Fennell is on loan from Chelmsford City and am surprised he can't get a game for the Clarets, as he's looked lively.

The rain eases off for the start of the second half. Hullbridge players gather in a circle and do a quick synchronised running drill, which will be impressive if that somehow comes in useful at a corner. The pre-planned routine from kick-off is the classic launch-it-to-the-corner-flag one.

Rain drums on the roof of the stand, and Okoh receives the ball near the touchline. He has a sprinter's build and skins the full back for pace, seemingly unaffected by the wet, rutted surface. Okoh puts in a low cross and a defender almost slices it into his own goal, conceding just a corner.

From another corner, Swifts play the ball short to Osei. He goes past a defender and gets to the byline. He looks to have overrun it, but digs out a cross to the back post. Okoh is there to meet it with a header into the empty net for 4-0.

Hullbridge players are shouting at each other, and also at the linesman for no obvious reason. Cocklin gives up on trying to play in one of their forwards and shoots. He finds an adjacent pitch. Increasingly frustrated, he launches into a tackle on Okoh that takes the ball with some force. Both sides are making all sorts of rash sliding tackles in the wet conditions.

A Heybridge tackle is not so well timed and looks like a certain red card. Frustrations boil over and a melee erupts. It's been a few games since I've seen a mass brawl, so it feels like entertainment again. A Hullbridge player cries to the linesman 'If you see it, report it,' in response to some of the shenanigans. Hullbridge supporters are imploring the referee: 'The linesman wants to talk to you.' The linesman doesn't want to talk to the referee. The home fan next to me is emboldened, telling the nearby away fans 'You're 4-0 down, shut up.' 'You shut up!' comes the reply.

There's no real danger of it boiling over between opposition supporters in the stands and there's no red card either. 'Just get on with the game' someone sensibly concludes. Hullbridge do just that and send a free kick towards Marsden's goal. Marsden chooses this moment, when the ball is most resembling a bar of soap, to catch it rather than punch it. The ball squirms away from him and he's lucky just to concede a corner.

Okoh is soon on the ball again. 'Slow him down,' is the call. It makes no difference, as he flicks the ball away from the defender and drives in a low cross-cum-shot. Osei keeps the ball in and squares it to Fennel, who makes it 5-0. Hullbridge are well beaten now.

Yet from the kick-off, they still look to get players forward in numbers. Their supporters also appeal with gusto when a throw-in decision goes against them. It doesn't seem like a decision to get worked up about, but throw-ins seem to do funny things to people. I remember being in the Charlton end when they played Arsenal and one fan was apoplectic whenever Dixon or Winterburn stole a few yards at every throw. He felt they were the biggest cheats in the game. Not Maradona with his handball, or Schumacher flattening Battiston, or any number of divers. The real scourge of the game was this.

Tackles become a little more half-hearted as we near full time. Hullbridge continue to search for a consolation, but the intensity has dropped. There's even a pass backwards to keep possession, and not to someone who will immediately get clattered. Normal service is resumed as a call of 'No foul' is heard and promptly ignored.

The referee blows his whistle for the final time and the game ends 5-0. It's a big win for Swifts, both in terms of scoreline and how it might kick-start their season. Swifts' attacking talent certainly took their opportunities, and the result was harsh on Hullbridge. Would their talent be enough to convince me to take the opportunity to support them, though? I found the match engrossing. It was full of pace and commitment, with a lot of turnovers, fouls and mistakes thrown in. It's hard not to be taken in by a big win and some outstanding individual performances. Going to Arsenal started similarly, so maybe this would be the start of something with Swifts. I certainly liked the look of their Boxing Day derby fixture against local rivals Maldon & Tiptree.

Before I could think of going to other games, myself and most of the rest of the 175 people in attendance needed to get out of the ground after this one. The players' tunnel blocks the only exit and creates a bottleneck that's not ideal in times of social distancing. The players are keen to celebrate with the fans gathered near the tunnel and can be heard shouting as they finally head back to the changing rooms. Eventually, we are allowed through as Hullbridge continue their inquest on the pitch, wondering how they've ended up losing by such a big margin.

It's a short glide home from Swifts' ground after that. I have another team whose fortunes I will follow on social media and one who I plan to see again. Of course, if I were to become a Swifts fan, I would need to find out if they used the collective noun 'scream of Swifts' and make sure I don't prefer their rivals Maldon & Tiptree.

Chapter 11

Oven chip eaters

DESPITE LONGING for Saturday three o'clock kick-offs, I've fallen into the habit of going to midweek games and mapped out a month's worth of fixtures at various places that will avoid interfering too much with family commitments. I extended the invite to several mates, and tonight's game has piqued the interest of my friend Ben.

Ben has spent most of the last six months doing yoga and tending to his allotment, so is glad of a novel form of entertainment. His previous experience of football is limited to a handful of Ipswich Town games, having chosen to support them on the strength of one appearance on *Match of the Day*, which is a dreadful way to choose a team.

Ben is no avid follower of football, but likes the idea of going to Saffron Walden for a game. He asks me what the crowd is like. I say old, not that many of them, and not as middle-class as you might like them to be. He is undeterred, stating that all football fans are 'Basically oven chip eaters'. I need him to explain that one. He elaborates that they're not the dregs of society, but are just a level above that. He doesn't fancy slumming it at a Hashtag game in Pitsea.

We drive to Saffron Walden Town's midweek home game against Enfield FC. The drive is long enough to explain Enfield's storied history in non-league and their more recent strife. They were formed in 1893 as Enfield Spartans. Ben is disappointed they have dropped the Spartans suffix, and I concede I would like to hear their manager yell 'Spartans attack!' Despite that, they have won the Isthmian League on multiple occasions, dumped various league teams out of the FA Cup, and won several prestigious non-league cups.

The rot set in, like it has for so many in non-league, when they sold their Southbury Road ground for redevelopment. At this point, things got rather messy as the club tried to disentangle themselves from a previous owner's businesses. This led to a split around 2001, when supporters formed a new breakaway club, Enfield Town. Enfield FC struggled on, were liquidated, turned down an offer to merge with Enfield Town and reformed as Enfield 1893. The 1893 suffix seems to have disappeared and they are typically referred to as Enfield FC.

At the end of this Ben asks which Enfield we are going to watch, the good one or the bad one. I find it hard to decide who is good or bad in all of this. There's certainly more appeal in the supporter-run Enfield Town, but I can't blame those who tried to keep the original version of the famous old club alive. It's even harder to keep up with the internecine arguments that still rumble on. In terms of performance, we are most definitely seeing the bad one. Enfield Town have risen to the Isthmian Premier Division, while Enfield FC languish towards the bottom of the Essex Senior League, two divisions below.

Saffron Walden for their part haven't got off to a great start to the season and there are rumblings of discontent, with calls on social media to get behind the club and the chairman's statement in the matchday programme saying, 'I know the players are having to deal with so much personally, and when a result goes the wrong way they need our support and not pressure'. He also states, 'I am 100% behind our coaching team and truly believe we can enjoy some great games here at the Lane,' which sounds ominously close to the dreaded vote of confidence. In better news, the roof and ceiling inside the bar area have been waterproofed.

We arrive at the ground and I feel that I'm showing off an attractive example of a non-league stadium, and Ben concedes that it's better than expected. With time to kill before kick-off, we explore the Paul Daw museum, housed in a Portakabin behind the goal. I'm glad to put Ben's history degree to some use, and ask him about his views on the museum. He says, 'A good museum should give a sense of time and tell a story. That was just a collection of old pictures and programmes.' We were both drawn to a black-and-white photo taken from a game in the 1970s. It's a classic spot-the-ball style image of several players jumping for a ball on a muddy pitch. The vintage kits with big collars and what looks like a large crowd of parka-clad fans on the sloping touchline is evocative of a bygone age. It captures something that is missing from modern sport.

After getting drinks from the newly waterproofed bar, we look to take up our seats in the main stand. I pass Walden's manager Jason Maher, who is having an intense conversation with someone on the touchline. I catch his eye and am worried the glare he gives me is his way of saying 'You had better get behind the team.'

When Ben asks if we are supporting Saffron Walden tonight, I feel I should say yes, but something holds me back. I feel like I'm being asked whether I'm an item with a girl I've met a few times. Yes, it's nice to visit them and show them off, but I don't really know them and they're a long way away. I change the subject and note the pitch is looking slimmer. The touchline seems to have been moved in a couple of feet, no doubt to help with the long throw-ins. Ben admires the lipstick-red wooden stand.

We notice that Enfield's nickname is the E's. Ben is tempted to support them just so he can start singing 'Ebeneezer Goode' by the Shamen. He then realises former Norwich striker Jamie Cureton is their player-manager, so decides to support Walden for the night given his Ipswich allegiance. We try to spot Cureton. His is a name we both recognise, but not a face. We wonder if someone in a tracksuit by the touchline could be him, but he has a letter 'N' in the initials on his chest.

Cureton isn't in Enfield's starting line-up. Former Walden player Lewis Francis is, and they read his name out in hushed tones. I miss the rest of their line-up as the fifty-fifty ticket seller comes round. In the Walden team it's only Gavin Cockman and Ross Adams I recognise from previous games. We are then advised to stay in groups of six to comply with the latest restrictions, which, if taken literally, means we need to find four more people to sit with.

Some supporters nearby talk about Arsenal mascot Gunnersaurus being made redundant, with exiled player Mesut Ozil offering to pay his wages, while the teams gather for a minute's applause. We wonder if the applause is for Gunnersaurus, but Walden's chairman confirms it's for the NHS. I know he's the chairman, because he is wearing a hi-viz with 'chairman' printed on the back. Another innovation Premier League clubs might benefit from.

The applause leads into the players geeing each other up with shouts of 'All over', 'Be at it' and 'Get in early'. Cockman just swears, having still not read the signs posted around the ground. Enfield, playing in white and blue, kick off and send a long diagonal ball forward. Walden soon play the ball back to keeper James Bransgrove, who is wearing short sleeves. His kick isn't befitting of someone trying to look like they could play outfield.

Enfield struggle with the slope, and the ball runs away from a couple of players cutting inside. They concede a throw in a dangerous position and I recognise the linesman from a previous game. Once I know what to expect from the officials, then I'll know I'm a true non-league fan. Ben is convinced he is not so much a fan as a curse on any team he watches, with the same powers Eileen Drewery deployed to ensure an Italy v England World Cup qualifier ended 0-0. To add credence to this theory, Enfield miss a sitter and then several balls are cleared out of the ground in quick succession.

Ben soon goes to see what vegetarian options are on offer at the refreshment kiosk. The game doesn't improve while he is away. Enfield send in a cross and they loop a header towards goal. Bransgrove takes no chances and palms it over the bar for a corner. Ben returns with chips, complaining they are out of veggie burgers, and we miss Enfield being awarded a penalty.

Ollie Miles lines up to take the kick. He hits it low and firm to Bransgrove's left. Bransgrove gets a firm hand on the ball. It's diverted round the post and is a great save to keep the score 0-0. Pundits would say that it was a nice height for the keeper, but he made it look easy by guessing right, going early and having strong hands.

Ben is equally sure that Walden's number nine, Ollie Fortune, might also keep the score down. He's chasing the ball gamely, but it eludes him like he's in a bad dream. Ben puts it down to him being too fat and needing to grow a foot taller. 'He needed to set off 20 minutes ago to get on the end of that last ball,' he continues. The game is as bad as he expected it to be.

Enfield have a chance. A player slides to stop the ball rolling downhill over the touchline. He belts it back uphill with all his might. Walden's left-back should cut it out easily, but misses the ball. The visitors are in. Luke Wilson gets back and takes the ball with a perfectly timed sliding tackle. Enfield are restricted to a long shot. Ben informs me it's the sixth ball to have been hit out of the ground.

Walden look to get forward themselves. There's a tangle of players and the referee makes the universally known signal of whisking some eggs in a bowl to explain the award of a free kick to the defending side. Enfield stay on the defensive, as Walden soon have a corner. In a set move I've seen here before, the right-back makes a 50-yard sprint to receive it short. He finds himself in plenty of space and cuts the ball back. There's a foul on a defender. The whistle goes. The ball ends up in the net. Ben and one other person cheer. It remains 0-0.

Enfield appeal for another penalty, but it's turned down. Then their left-back appeals for a foul after evading a late challenge from Fortune. 'Have I got to go down to get the free kick?' he remonstrates with the referee. 'He had a good five minutes to get out of the way of it,' according to Ben. Walden optimistically claim for a handball themselves. Play continues. Wilson is late sliding in for the ball and an Enfield player is left crumpled in a heap. Players surround the referee. 'Go away,' he instructs them. It's going to be a card. The question is what colour? 'What about the handball?' asks Wilson, while his victim still hasn't moved. The referee awards a yellow. There's just enough time for the free kick to be taken before he blows up for half-time.

The Walden players head for the tunnel. Maher complains to the referee about the supposed handball. Stewards don't allow the away team down the tunnel until all the home team have gone down it, much to their confusion. It's not clear if this is some odd form of coronavirus prevention measure, or Crazy Gang-style gamesmanship.

We settle back into our seats for the second half, which in the old stand feels like a comfy spot in a favourite pub, only the wooden benches aren't at all comfortable. Ben suggests they should provide cushions. Rain is coming down and a long clearance from Enfield skids off a head and through to Bransgrove. His clearance bounces over Fortune, who is having no luck bringing it under control.

A Walden winger cuts inside. 'Not to number nine,' pleads Ben. He doesn't so much take heed as fail to find any team-mate. I tell Ben he needs to get behind the team and not be one of these supporters getting on the players' backs. His response is 'shut up Boris Johnson'. There's more positivity from Enfield's own right-winger, who skips past the full-back. He squares the ball to Miles, who shoots from close range. I expect Bransgrove to block, but the net ripples and the ball has somehow gone through his legs to make it 1-0.

Walden look to respond quickly and work the ball out wide. A cross comes in for Fortune. A chance for glory beckons. I predict he's going to score. Ben is prepared to eat his bobble hat if he does. The cross goes past him. Walden keep it in play and cross from the other side. It's about a foot too high for Fortune, so Ben's head stays warm for now.

Enfield play it forward and Wilson cleverly blocks their forward's run, so the ball runs through to Bransgrove, who clears long. It's flicked on to Cockman in the right channel. He's in on the keeper. He skips round him and slots into the empty net to the delight of those behind the goal as he levels it at 1-1.

Fortune shouts at his team-mates, asking them for 'A bit of quality'. He then shows his own lack of quality trying to get the ball under control and Ben asks me to check whether he's the manager's son. The game opens up and Walden's defence comes under more pressure. Enfield scramble the ball clear from a pass back to their keeper and find a winger in behind Walden's advancing full-backs. He trips over the ball. Not to be outdone, Fortune finally controls the ball on his chest and looks like he might play someone in, but loses the ball between his legs. There are more moans, but this time from the bloke a few seats away and not just from Ben.

The attendance of 255 is announced and most are hoping to see a Walden winner. Fortune has a couple of half-chances, but can't direct them towards goal. And then he scores! I don't convince Ben to take a bite of bobble hat, as everyone has seen the flag go up some time ago and it's very much a frustrated tap in, clearly rueing the fact that no presentable chances have come his way.

Every Enfield throw-in continues to be contested keenly. 'Toes and heels' is the call that wouldn't be out of place in a dance studio, but is a none-too-subtle call to tread on opponents rather than to apply some nifty footwork. Nifty footwork seems beyond Fortune tonight. He holds the ball up well, but then his pass is a yard short. He is then offside. The complaints both on and off the pitch rise, but nothing that hints at any real strife in the club. It's not exactly the non-league equivalent of Eboué or Xhaka being booed by their own fans at Arsenal.

Walden are soon focusing their complaints on the referee. A Walden player bursts into the box and is bundled over for a clear penalty. The referee takes the easy way out and gives a free kick just outside the area. After that spell of Walden pressure, Enfield finish the brighter, but Wilson continues to mop up while others are caught upfield. No side can fashion a late chance and the game ends in stalemate.

Ben and I decide to walk the perimeter of the ground on the way out. When we reach the opposite touchline, both teams are in huddles. Maher is animatedly saying something, but we can't make out what, and I make a note to sit near the bench next time. I also note the pitch doesn't just slope from touchline to touchline, it also slopes towards one of the corner flags, which wasn't obvious from other angles or the way teams have attacked.

I'm not sure if I've noticed the camera gantry on top of the main stand before and it may be a new addition, which explains the improved quality of videos from Bloods TV, and it's great to see all these little things that suggest the club isn't just standing still. Their league form is less dynamic and a draw was arguably a fair result.

On the drive back, we ponder what this all means for the club. Is Maher's long tenure at the helm looking less secure? In Ben's view, picking Fortune did him no favours. I share my theory that I could secure a mid-table finish just by using clichés and shouting a lot. I suggest Ben could be my assistant and through his yoga, promoting a vegan diet and fat-shaming the larger lads, we could whip the team into shape should a vacancy arise.

We discuss options for the lone centre-forward role and I surprise myself by recalling the towering Hussain Jaffa, who plays for Coggeshall United in the league below. He would be perfect for getting on the end of Cockman's long throws. I'm not sure if this is just the result of some cursory research, or suggests I have more of an interest in the team. Maybe I'm in danger of becoming a fan of the Bloods without realising it: going to more and more games, so everyone assumes we're an item, all the while continuing to deny it's anything serious.

Chapter 12

Keep it on the island

A WEEK after the jaunt to Saffron Walden, I go on a more serious trip to see Hashtag again. This time I'm taking Phil and I do feel like I'm introducing a new partner to one of my best mates to see what he thinks of her. I'm asking myself whether I would consider myself a Hashtag fan. I'm certainly keen to see them maintain their good start to the season.

Hashtag have played 14 games in little over a month, progressing in the FA Vase and getting through several FA Cup qualifying rounds before losing on penalties to Braintree, three divisions above. They moved top of the league at the weekend, leapfrogging opponents Cockfosters after a narrow win.

Quite a few of Hashtag's recent games have been tight affairs and injuries have racked up. In their last home game, they struggled to overcome bottom club Woodford Town. I didn't expect things to be any easier against tonight's visitors, second-from-bottom Clapton. Clapton appeared to have appointed a new manager and brought in some new signings in recent weeks.

What was most interesting about Clapton was their past. Much like Enfield, this was a famous old club who had suffered an acrimonious split. Clapton were formed in 1877 and were founder members of both the Southern League and Isthmian League. They won the FA Amateur Cup five times and boasted three England internationals, as well as one of the country's first black players in Walter Tull.

In more recent times, the club had struggled, before they gained a following of continental-style left-wing ultras. This increased attendances and revitalised the club. Before long, there was a falling out with the club's owner related to their Old Spotted Dog ground. The fans split and formed a new club, Clapton Community, leaving Clapton to struggle on, albeit a couple of levels higher up the non-league pyramid for now.

The Clapton playing tonight had been evicted from the Old Spotted Dog, with Clapton Community awarded the lease. Whilst Clapton retained the claim to their long history, the soul of the club had moved with the fans. It was a shame this wouldn't be a game with a large away following, but at least I'm spared the decision of who to support.

I have a dilemma after Hashtag started live streaming their home games on Twitch for free. Should I attend in person, or stay at home and watch the game on my phone? Being an armchair fan was entirely in keeping with Hashtag's origins, but Phil and

I were keen to get out, not least since 'Thursday club' at the Orange Tree pub was on hold due to increased coronavirus restrictions.

We arrive at the ground well before kick-off, so early in fact, there is no one on the gate to pay for entry. Phil checks out the bar, which was a pre-condition of him coming. He returns with a beer, but is told we can't sit inside. The only thing for it is to walk through an empty gate without paying and find a seat in the strand while various youth teams finish their training sessions.

We feel bad about not paying when we are keen to support smaller clubs in whatever way we can. Phil suggests his beer is paying towards it. I point out he is getting a beer for that and whatever profit made by the bar isn't likely to go to Hashtag as tenants at the ground. We consider going back to pay later, but with coronavirus knocking around should we really be encountering more people than necessary? I suggest I might buy one of Hashtag's shirts. There must surely be a fair bit of profit built into those for the club. Phil reacts as if I've told him I'm about to propose to a girl I've just met. 'When would you wear a football shirt? You're not 14 years old,' is his sage advice.

After describing one player as having 'the touch of a trampoline' during the warm-up, he says, 'It's probably free to get in, but you have to pay to get out.' We commit to doing just that and Phil runs through the other classic sayings his dad would come out with when taking him to watch Leyton Orient. We added

'Winners!' and 'Keep the ball on the island' to our lower league buzzword bingo cards.

The players come out for kick-off in dribs and drabs. Phil isn't impressed by their commitment. I point out former Orient player and Hashtag coach Joe Keith to see if that stirs him. He can't recall him from the many players that came and went during the 90s. He is impressed that Clapton form a huddle and all shout 'Clapton' at the end before running to their positions. Their left-back is in front of us and resembles comedian Ross Noble.

Other famous faces surround us. Several members of the Hashtag team who are out injured are sitting in front of us and half of the women's team are next to us. Phil doesn't like their choice of perfume. He toys with getting a burger with extra onions to mask the smell with something he's more accustomed to at a football ground.

Given the number of players out injured, Hashtag can't deploy their usual 4-3-3 with pace on both flanks, which has made them such a threat. Instead, they go for what can either be described as a 4-4-2 with Joe Gregory and George Smith as a front pair, or more of a lopsided 4-3-3 with Josh Osude pushing into an advanced right forward role. The post-match video reveals it was in fact 3-5-2, with Osude operating as a wing-back.

The formation is irrelevant as both sides frequently misplace passes. Phil isn't impressed, but he notes that Samraj Gill looks tidy on the ball and Osude is lively. Injured goalkeeper Jacko is willing Osude on from the sidelines, and encouraging him to get at a nervy Ross Noble. Noble's relatives are sitting nearby and keep encouraging him. Phil finds his defending amusing and is even more delighted to hear the shout of 'Winners' from the pitch. He doesn't see many winners in the visiting team. 'These are shocking,' is his verdict on Clapton. 'And why is their left-back wearing a number two shirt?' he asks.

Play ebbs and flows. Hashtag look the more capable side, but are slack in possession. Smith and Gregory aren't clicking up front. Clapton look to threaten on the counter. 'That's a goal!' shrieks a member of the women's team, as a curling shot just misses. The feeling grows that Clapton could perform a smash and grab. A Clapton forward takes the ball round Pitman in Hashtag's goal. The crowd gasps. He's taken it too wide. He keeps the ball in play, but can only find a team-mate in an offside position.

I'm taken back to watching Arsenal labouring against teams like Wigan in a midweek winter game. I've gone expecting a hatful of goals. Instead, I'm seeing Chris Kirkland taking an eternity over goal kicks, with the dreaded feeling that they will snatch a late winner to the delight of their mini-bus load of fans. One of the women's team is even doing a passable impression of the Highbury screamer every time Clapton come close.

Nerves are frayed as Tim Pitman is called on to make a smart save down to his left. Jacko has gone to the tea bar, so I don't get to see how much encouragement he has for his replacement. When he returns, he screams at a team-mate to 'Finish it'. Phil is incredulous, as the ball is fully 30 yards from goal and there's no obvious chance. It's a typical bit of blind optimism from a keeper willing the ball in from any improbable situation. Hashtag don't get much nearer to the opposition goal before the half-time whistle blows.

Phil and I make our way to 'Bower's Burgers' in the corner of the ground for half-time refreshments, where I get a hot chocolate and Phil decides a Bowers & Pitsea scarf is no substitute for a beer, which isn't available. We do a lap of the pitch and Phil is particularly taken by the old stand behind the goal. It's a claustrophobic wooden shed running the length of the touchline. There's just enough room to pack in fans three or four deep. Phil imagines the sort of racket that could be made and spots a couple of broken floorboards, suggesting there's been a few wild celebrations. He christens it Broken Floorboard End and insists they should put that on a sign in a sizeable gap between the roof panels.

We make our way to the opposite end, which Hashtag will shoot towards and where we expect the action to be. We take up a position near the Hashtag superfans and are immediately under threat from any wayward shooting from the pitch and the kickabout a few fans are having. Normally, I would be worried about my drink getting knocked over, but it's terrible and wouldn't be any real loss.

Most of my time spent watching Arsenal was from behind the goal at the Clock End, so this feels like a big step in finding a similar spot at Hashtag. There's a bit more atmosphere and I'm more immersed in the game. I have far less sense of the overall pattern of play, but I feel more in tune with how Hashtag are building their attacks, probing from side to side. There's a sense of expectation as the ball gets nearer to the goal. Knowing how as a goalkeeper with a similar view I felt the threat of anything entering my half.

What I wouldn't want to see was one of my defenders have a pass intercepted. This happens to Ross Noble and Hashtag spring forward. Osude gets on the ball and plays it across to Gregory. He sweeps it into the corner of the net directly in front of us. The superfans celebrate as the deadlock has been broken.

Phil tests the acoustics of the small covered terrace and gives it a good bang. I suggest he could appoint himself as top boy of a Hashtag firm, given the age of most of the other fans. He mulls it over for a second before going back to his favourite activity, heckling Ross Noble. 'Your next job could be in cyber,' he says, referencing the recent government advert in which they advise a ballerina to retrain.

If there's a feeling of anticipation as attacks come towards us, there's an equal sense of helplessness when Clapton attack at the other end. The lack of perspective means everything looks dangerous. I have a flashback to the mix-up between Wojciech Szczęsny and Laurent Koscielny that cost Arsenal the League Cup, as a mix-up at the back looks like it might lead to an own goal, but Hashtag get away with conceding a corner. Soon after, Clapton appeal for a penalty. I've no idea what for.

Luckily, the referee, employing the quirky signalling usually associated with a cricket umpire, indicates 'play on' with an impression of an aeroplane.

The referee gives Hashtag a free kick in a more orthodox manner. Gill stands over the ball in a wide position. His cross is headed away. A Hashtag player puts it back in the box. Gregory has time to take a touch. He prods the ball past the Clapton keeper with the poise of a young Alan Smith. 2-0 to the YouTube team, as the song from the four superfans goes.

Hashtag look to add to their lead by playing in Osude. Clapton are doubling up on him and one through ball is skewed out of the ground. 'Keep it on the island' is the cry, albeit from Phil. A light rain comes down and Phil feels like he's at a proper non-league game now.

Gregory is looking for his third. He tries to control a ball in the box with his chest. It won't come down for him. 'Header! Header! What's wrong with your head!' is the frustrated call from a nearby fan in a West Ham top. The superfans try to help Gregory out by trying to create an incident similar to the Sunderland beach ball goal. Either that or someone has just kicked a ball on to the pitch by accident. The Clapton keeper isn't amused and doesn't return it.

Hashtag bring on reserve-team manager Kiernan Hughes-Mason as a substitute. I struggle to imagine an injury crisis forcing Arsenal to bring on a fifty-something Steve Bould on the left wing. Kiers takes up his position, but it's another double-barrelled player pulling the strings in the form of Waller-Lassen. He flicks on for Gregory, but he can't get his hat-trick. Waller-Lassen then plays in Kiers. Kiers finds Sam Byles on the overlap. Byles' cross is cut out. It falls to Kiers on the corner of the box. He curls the shot right-footed. It goes around the defender and nestles in the bottom corner of the net in front of us. It's an exquisite finish for 3-0. The keeper had no chance with a Thierry Henry-like effort.

There's something especially satisfying about seeing it from our angle behind the goal. We don't join in the moderately wild celebrations, but it caps the night perfectly. The full-time whistle blows soon after, and we head for the exit. We hope to find someone on the gate to pay on the way out and we're more than happy to do so after the second half performance. There is no one on the gate and everyone seems to leave by another exit. I then realise the main car park was closed on my previous visit, so we had come in the wrong way. I owe Hashtag one, but I will be back again and make a note to pay them.

I ask Phil what he thinks. The levels of fitness and moments of accomplished play pleasantly surprised him. As someone used to watching Leyton Orient, I think he expected several levels below to be like watching the Dog and Duck reserves playing with a hangover. There's some satisfaction to be had in Phil giving Hashtag his seal of approval, but we didn't get caught up in the goal celebrations or start any singing on the terrace. If I ever get to achieve my minor ambition of starting up the

'Bing Bong Song' from Peppa Pig at a game, then I'll know for sure that I've found my team.

It has been an evening well spent. It was certainly more fulfilling seeing a match live rather than on livestream. With lots of clubs turning to online pay-per-view streaming to overcome crowd restrictions, there has been outrage at the Premier League looking to cash in. Others in the National League have had to resort to this model to make ends meet. Chelmsford City invested in automatic cameras to film their home games, but suffered the misfortune of the cameras being distracted by the glare of the sun, ball boys with spare balls positioned on the running track and a bald linesman.

Further down the pyramid, I noticed clubs like Clapton Community livestreamed their games for free. I was tempted to watch, but was put off by Clapton's camera work resembling something from a turn of the century newsreel. I did tune in to Hashtag's next home game against Hoddesdon, but the downside of being at home meant I got drawn into a prolonged bedtime routine and only caught the last five minutes. As it turned out, that was enough for me to see a stoppage-time winner, which suggested only another lockdown would stop Hashtag being promoted and maybe supporting them was meant to be.

Chapter 13

We can see you sneaking in

IT'S THE Jammers versus the Dockers in a top-of-the-table clash. We're talking Isthmian League North, not a battle between rival skiffle bands and their teddy boy followers. The Jammers are Maldon & Tiptree, formed via a merger in 2010. It was Tiptree United under chairman Ed Garty who took over Maldon Town and their ground, but kept a jam-based nickname in reference to Tiptree's famous preserves. Maldon has its own culinary claim to fame with its sea salt. I can't help but think during the merger someone must have suggested the 'Salty Jammers' as a compromise before a committee decided that would leave an unpleasant taste in the mouth.

I'm in Maldon with Ben, who, like many people, is seduced by the picture-postcard image of its riverfront, with Thames barges docked at the quay and a church spire dominating the skyline. It is indeed a nice place to visit, with two brewery taps, an annual mud race across the gloopy riverbed at low tide, and a weekly parkrun that's less busy than my usual one in Chelmsford. Based on the somewhat flimsy logic that I'll often choose Maldon parkrun over Chelmsford parkrun, I'm here to consider whether I should choose their football team as well.

Chelmsford City did ground-share with Maldon for a while and despite some tales of acrimony, it wouldn't count as a rivalry in the same way Billericay or Braintree would. Maldon have consistently been further down the non-league pyramid and came across as a nice local club. There was a family connection, too. Now you might expect that would be a grandparent who played there for 40 years, before taking on the part-time role of first-team manager/kit man/treasurer/programme seller/tea lady/life president. In my case, it was something far more obscure. My brother made a solitary guest appearance in goal for Tiptree United's reserves. Most people might embellish such a tenuous claim to fame by saying they suffered a career-ending injury saving a last-minute penalty. My brother was instead just a little evasive about quite how many he conceded and how much abuse he got from the crowd.

Not having a Coughlan in goal had helped Maldon & Tiptree rise towards the top of their division. This was a club on the up. Last season they dumped Leyton Orient out of the cup and were 13 points clear in the league, with games in hand, before the season was declared null and void. This was too much for Garty, who stepped down as chairman in the wake of the way that decision was handled. Several key players moved to Wealdstone, a couple of leagues above. It was a testament to manager Wayne Brown that the Jammers were unbeaten this season and once again through to the first round of the FA Cup.

Tonight, they were facing the Dockers from Tilbury. I'm not sure how many of their first XI worked on the docks, but a few of them looked like they could. I was familiar with Tilbury's home ground, having seen Hashtag play there in the previous season, but I knew nothing about their team. The free online programme didn't reveal any familiar faces, but did show they were top, albeit having played several games more than their hosts.

After struggling to find somewhere to park, which is more a reflection on the size of the car park than the crowd, Ben and I pay a tenner each and go through the turnstiles. We come out near a corner flag in the Wallace Binder Ground. In my mind, this is a brand-new ground, as I remember playing against one of Maldon Town's youth teams at both their old ground and this one. I'm surprised to discover it is in fact just over 25 years old.

We walk round the perimeter in search of a vantage point. The layout on the near touchline is odd, with a small seated stand to one side of the dugout and low red-brick buildings containing the dugouts, tunnel and some toilets, but no seating. I feel like we're lost inside a newly built bus station.

We pass behind the goal, where there's a row of tall conifers that show the ground's age. I think I can spot the junior pitches behind them. There were no conifers when I played, and an icy wind off the river Blackwater whipped across the open fields. I recall one game where I couldn't clear the ball further than my penalty area in one half and then in the second half, I launched everything into the opposition box and caused chaos. An old history teacher, who taught Ben and me, was furious. He was berating his son, in the Maldon defence, with the sort of profanity that you might expect from contemporary critics of Catherine the Great.

We pass along the far touchline and see Wayne Brown put his defence through their paces. He is belting a ball at them from 40 yards and expecting them to head clear, which is presumably good preparation for this level of football. We take up our seats in the small stand, which has open sides, giving us an unobstructed view and allowing the wind an unobstructed route to us. I feel like we are a long way away from the other stands. The handful of families and people in Spurs hats sat nearby don't look like they will generate much atmosphere either.

The teams soon emerge from the tunnel/bus station. Tilbury are in a red and white chessboard-pattern shirt, normally associated with Croatia. Their number 14 even has a passing resemblance to Luka Modric, although their number nine, Brian Moses, is more the build of former Birmingham forward Kevin Francis. The Jammers are in red and blue stripes with no sponsor's logo, reminiscent of Barcelona.

Maldon kick off and launch it out wide to their own sizeable number nine, Shomari Barnwell. There's always an expectation that a big lad will cause problems, probably stemming from junior football when a bearded ringer, often arriving in his own car, would boss the game for our opposition. The cross that comes in could do with someone tall on the end, as their effort can't be directed on target. The excitement prompts the home fans to bang on the hoardings, so the atmosphere is already better than expected.

After Moses fails to part the Maldon defence, the home side release Barnwell. He pulls it back for a chance, but the Jammers can't squeeze in a shot and Tilbury keep a lid on things. Barnwell is played in again, this time down the right channel. He shrugs off a defender. Face to face with the keeper, he shapes to curl one in left-footed. He shifts the ball to his right and puts the keeper on the floor, before coolly walking the ball into the net. It's a classy finish to make it 1-0.

Barnwell's opposite number is keen to bring Tilbury right back into it and gets a good flick on into space for a team-mate to get in a first-time shot. The Jammers' keeper back-pedals and tips it over. A kid nearby isn't fooled into thinking the save was difficult in the way commentators always seem to heap praise on the routine. 'Our team's keeper could have saved that,' he says. His dad points out he would have been too short to reach it.

Moses looks to intercept a pass back to Maldon's keeper, who slices, but gets them out of a jam. The ball ends up on the sodden grass bank next to our stand. A steward complains that he should have brought his wellies as he goes to retrieve it. Barnwell is much keener to get on the ball. He brings it under control out on the right flank and sweeps it into the path of a midfielder who sends the keeper the wrong way to make it 2-0. Ben decides he has found the team he is now going to support, having enjoyed the opening 20 minutes more than anything he's witnessed at a few dozen Ipswich games.

The Jammers spread the ball around with confidence. Some fans try to get in for free and the home crowd sings 'We can see you sneaking in'. Pre-match heading practice pays off as a corner is cleared emphatically from inside the six-yard box. A fan calls Modric a 'fucking clown' for going down too easily. Maldon find themselves in a sticky spot as Tilbury try to get a cross in from the right. Eventually, a forward works the ball on to his left foot. He shoots. It takes a deflection. The net bulges. A relatively sizeable away following cheer. The deficit is reduced to 2-1.

The Jammers look to restore their lead as Barnwell releases a midfield runner. He takes an early shot low to the keeper's left. The goalie gets a firm hand on it and the ball is cleared. Maldon soon have another chance as a cross is dug out from the byline. It's flicked on. The Jammers' number 11 controls with his chest and lets it roll across him on to his right foot. He hits it cleanly through a crowd and makes it 3-1. As the Maldon players run off to celebrate, Tilbury's goalkeeper runs after the linesman to berate him as if possessed by the spirit of Peter Schmeichel. 'You're not singing any more' is the cry from the home fans. The referee gives the

Tilbury keeper a similar word of advice.

Tilbury are still looking to get forward and a neat flick round the corner puts in Moses. He smashes a left-footed shot from a tight angle. It crashes off the underside of the bar. Ben and I concur that both number nines have good feet for big men and tick that cliché off. Another one soon follows as supporters nearby are shouting 'He doesn't want it' when a Tilbury player is under pressure and is forced to pass back to his own keeper.

The Dockers are up for a scrap though and start a wrestling match, which the referee ignores. This prompts the home fans to sing 'Top of the league? You're having a laugh'. A lone child's voice can then be heard yelping 'Tilbury are crap. And so is their goalie.' There's a delightful blend of skill and niggle, with more atmosphere than I expected. Yet I'm not feeling the sort of instant affection for the Jammers the way I did for their neighbours, Heybridge. In an action-packed first half there's still time for a Tilbury shot to ping back off the post, a foul that leaves a player in a heap long after the ball has gone, and for Peter Schmeichel's love child to have another rant at someone.

Forty-five minutes is enough for Ben to decide he wants to become a Maldon & Tiptree ultra. I ask if he will take his top off and paint himself red and blue. He's up for it, despite having complained about the cold for most of the half whilst wearing several more layers than I had thought to. The Jammers have been impressive and I've enjoyed the football, even if I haven't found a team I want to support with Newcastle United levels of devotion and nudity. I'm rooting for them tonight, mainly in response to not caring for Tilbury much.

Barnwell enters the field for the second half with what appears to be a tampon up his nose. I didn't see an incident to cause the bloody nose, but my money would be on Tilbury's number 18, Darren Philips, being involved. Philips looks like he could be Vinny Jones' scarier older brother, only he's actually much younger. He's one of the Tilbury team who could put a shift in down the docks and then kick a few forwards in the air for fun afterwards. He's soon given a lecture by the referee at a corner.

The second half begins sluggishly, so Ben goes to the refreshment kiosk on the other side of the ground. This time all he misses is the bloke behind say 'Dry your eyes 14' after another Modric dive and 'Don't be a twat 17' after he complains about the time needed for a free kick to be taken, even though the referee hasn't blown his whistle.

Modric's theatrics are rewarded with a free kick. The Jammers' keeper lines up a wall and the Tilbury fans try to drown out his instructions. The shot doesn't trouble the goal, but I'm worried Ben might walk past with my hot chocolate. He appears from the other direction with a warming hot chocolate for me and the go-to veggie option of chips for himself. The hot chocolate is still scalding despite the distance from the kiosk.

Tilbury's hot-headed keeper politely asks the referee if he understands what's a foul and what's not a foul and asks him if he wouldn't mind doing his job. Only without the politeness. A fan behind offers his help. 'Ref, he's abusing you,' he calls out, sounding like he's keener to offer counselling rather than see a booking. At this point, I feel confident enough to predict another 22-man brawl.

Barnwell is booked, albeit for inadvertently blocking a free kick as he ambles back into position. Another free kick goes Tilbury's way, but the Jammers' number 10 carries on and is soon on the end of a jarring tackle. The Tilbury players are incensed and wade in, led by their keeper, which prompts a few Maldon players to respond. It's not even a case of handbags; everyone just about keeps their composure. The Tilbury keeper is finally booked and so is a random Maldon player. My prediction of a brawl doesn't quite come to fruition.

There might be more action in the car park afterwards. As the ball bounces out of play in front of us, a fan cheekily flicks it away from the onrushing Philips, who wants to collect it quickly. 'See you after the game,' is his menacing reply. This amuses the crowd, apart from perhaps the bloke he's just threatened.

Philips almost has even more cause to be annoyed as a glorious chance presents itself to Maldon's Alfie Mason, who has ghosted in at the far post. He slashes his effort into the conifers. Ben complains that he's more Billy Bunter than Billy Bremner and seems to have found someone to abuse for the second game running. It surprised other supporters as he usually plays as a forward apparently, which explains some of his defending. Mason shows his ability going forward as he bursts into some space on the left and lets fly with a shot from the outside of his boot. It cannons off the crossbar and into the air. It would have been some goal and Ben can't believe how good his new-found team is turning out to be.

The Jammers continue trying to catch Tilbury on the break as they send players forward, leaving space at the back. Neither side can create a clear-cut chance in the closing minutes and Ben ruminates on his own attempts at making jam. Blackberry concrete and the final whistle are the eventual conclusions.

Despite the match petering out towards the end, it's been a decent game of football, witnessed by a crowd of 286. We troop past the away supporters who stay to applaud their team off. Ben is a convert and resists the temptation to goad the Tilbury fans. Maldon were impressive, but I wasn't necessarily inclined to take things further.

I would happily come and watch the Jammers again though. It reminded me of some Arsenal old boys who would watch the Gunners at home one week and Spurs the next. Unthinkable these days, not to mention prohibitively expensive. At this level, I might see myself watching Heybridge one week and Maldon the next.

My slight preference was for Heybridge, but I would put this to the test when they meet later in the season. To whet my appetite, I found video highlights of Heybridge's play-off final win on penalties over Maldon a couple of seasons ago, which rather oddly didn't result in Heybridge being promoted. It felt like both sides had legitimate claims to belonging in the next level up and I expected the derby matches to be keenly contested.

Chapter 14

Take me home, country road

HEYBRIDGE AND Maldon & Tiptree might not be in the Isthmian Premier Division, but I decide to make Step 3 my next port of call. I'm at the Queen Elizabeth II Stadium to watch Enfield Town v Brightlingsea Regent. This is the seventh tier of English football and the highest level allowing in fans. It's also my last chance to see a game before the second national lockdown.

I'm interested in both sides and feel like I'm auditioning both clubs in a football version of speed dating. Dressed in white and blue are Enfield Town, the first fan-owned club in the country and, in Ben's view, the good Enfield team. In a red-and-black-striped number are Brightlingsea Regent, who sound like the sort of nice old cinema I might like to visit, and are based on the Essex coast.

Being fan-owned gives Town the same appeal as a micropub or a CAMRA pub of the year; worth checking out, even if it's in a rough part of town. I'm not sure how rough Enfield is, as I've only seen the dismal bit of the A10 I've driven in on. Either way, I'm looking forward to the match.

I've seen a few videos of Town online and expect a lively atmosphere. That is despite their ground being an athletics stadium. Said stadium does have a wonderful curved art deco grandstand, which contains a café at one end with views over the pitch. The café isn't open because of current restrictions, but having been taken in by Highbury's art deco stands, I'm liking the look of the place.

On the downside is the fact this is Spurs territory, and Spurs fans are being encouraged to watch Town and nearby Wingate & Finchley by their supporters' club. I check to see if Arsenal's supporters' club is doing something similar and find one of them backing the Dial Square protest club. I decide not to let this sway me.

Regent sound like they would be a grand old club, but it turns out the name came about following a recent merger. More surprising is that a team in a small town between Colchester and Clacton-on-Sea should be doing so well. They're not well-placed in the league, but are still a few divisions above Wivenhoe, who are based in a similar location. If anything, Brightlingsea is more remote, being further out and not on a train line, so I've never been. I'm vaguely aware it has a seafront of sorts and some beach huts.

Regent are relatively local to me and I work out my house must be equidistant between both clubs. I'm as near to a neutral as it's possible to be, but find it hard not to be drawn to the team I know more about, am at the home ground for and, let's be honest, are doing much better in the league.

I've had to navigate Enfield's website to buy my ticket online for £10. I've paid a further £4 to upgrade to a seat in the grandstand, given there's a chance of rain. I make my way to my seat like a rank amateur who has never been to a game before, needing the help of more than one steward to find my way up into the stand. When I arrive, my name is on the list and I look to choose a seat. Most have name plaques on them and I can't tell if they're memorials or reserved for people. Several other seats are taped off to help with social distancing, but handily the perfect seat right on the halfway line is free.

The elevated view at the front of the stand makes up for the distance from the pitch created by the running track and long-jump pits. While the café is closed, this area is being used as an impromptu bar, so it has a feel of the paddock area at the horse racing. I feel like I'm in an exclusive seat and wonder if I'm going to be wowed like the German officer in *Escape to Victory* who gets up and applauds Pelé's bicycle kick.

I watch the teams come out and play my favourite game of lookalike-spotting and see if any of the players resemble more famous ones. From this distance Brightlingsea's number seven resembles Scott Parker, with shorts pulled up and shirt tucked in meticulously. His opposite number, Sam Youngs, bears an even more tenuous resemblance to Dimitar Berbatov, with slightly floppy hair and a languid demeanour.

Enfield fans are spread out behind the goal. There's a cry of 'C'mon Towners', but it's more subdued than I expected. Town kick off and send a ball wide to Berbatov on the near touchline. It's intercepted by the full-back, who goes on a jinking run, which may only appear jinking as he disappears from view behind both subs' benches. He cuts inside and is tripped.

The Town fans get going with the help of a drum and some banging on the stands. The non-league ultras' staple of 'Everywhere we go' with 'ETFC' appended starts up, and then a rising call of 'Towners, Towners' when they get a set piece. A cross comes in from Town's right-back and evades live-wire number 10, Neville Nzembela, who looks to carry on where he left off from an 8-1 cup win at the weekend. Lyle Della Verde, with socks rolled down like Steve Claridge, is next to threaten, skipping past a couple of challenges before sending his shot wide. Percy Kiangebeni drives forward from Town's midfield.

Regent offer little going forward and are one of those teams where it's not apparent what their game plan is. They have been tidy in possession, but haven't committed many players forward, or looked secure at the back. They send a hopeful ball forward to Lewis Byrne-Hewitt. It looks offside, but no one appeals. No one expects much to happen. Byrne-Hewitt cuts inside on to his left foot and hits a low drive into the bottom corner. It's 1-0 against the run of play. Also out of the blue is an announcement for the golden goal time of 15 minutes, when I had seen no tickets for sale.

The six Regent supporters celebrate and the Town fans respond by drumming again. On the pitch, Town's right-back floats in a cross. There's a needless push on a forward who will not reach it. A few claims go up for a penalty. It would be soft, but as they say, 'I've seen them given,' usually accompanied by uproar for the penalty being too soft.

Town's keeper, Nathan MacDonald, launches a kick long towards Berbatov, who wins the header. It falls to the burly number nine, Billy Bricknell, who keeps the ball in play and pulls it back. Someone drags their shot, which falls kindly for Nzembela to sweep it home from close range for the equaliser. Regent's lead was short-lived, and Town celebrate.

After the restart, Berbatov has a couple of delicate touches. I can't tell whether he is calm under pressure and making space for himself or if I'm just imagining he has the quality of his near-lookalike. I decide against Googling a close-up picture, so not to ruin the effect. He twists and turns before digging out a cross. Kiangebeni makes a late run. He is in time to connect and smashes the ball into the roof of the net. Town have the lead.

It's tempting to compare Town to a 90s Manchester United, with their steady supply of crosses, but that would be over-selling them. Something else not being over-sold are fifty-fifty tickets. After I expected someone to come round selling them, I hear the winning numbers read out and wonder how many other prize draws I will miss.

Up goes the shout of 'winners' from MacDonald, which I now hear at every game since Phil pointed it out. Something I haven't heard at many, if any, games is the song 'Take me home country roads' by John Denver, but thanks to the Town fans I have now. Regent are less inventive, keeping the ball well in non-threatening areas of the pitch and then lacking ideas to break through the Town midfield.

Berbatov and Kiangebeni bring the ball forward with a series of neat one-twos, before sending it wide to Della Verde. His low cross is cleared. There are some hopeful claims for a penalty from those in the main stand, but before I mark them down as typical main stand moaners, they consider whether they will volunteer as a steward. There's plenty of pride and community spirit running through the club. Although some deliberation is needed when they realise they need to arrive 90 minutes before kick-off. It's an important role with coronavirus restrictions to enforce and idiots to direct to their seats.

I leave my seat at half-time to get a burger from the Food Lovers Delight catering van. I suspect they are over-selling themselves, but my primary concern is whether they accept cards, after I realise that I only have £1.70 in change on me. Most people in front are paying with cash, which I've barely seen since March. I'm equally surprised to hear a group of lads ask each other what a fifty-fifty draw is. Town really need to do more to promote this classic non-league tradition.

I continue to shuffle towards the front of the queue as the start of the second half approaches. I'm relieved to spot the card machine and I order a burger, hot chocolate and a chocolate bar. There's not much I can say about these delights. It's notable that food critics seldom come to football grounds to review them. The burger does the job and the hot chocolate actually tastes of chocolate, which is practically Michelin-star-worthy in the world of football catering.

The half kicks off and Town are soon on the front foot again. Nzembela flicks it past a defender before Regent clatter him. The ref waves play on and they cross the ball to Bricknell, who looks like his half-time might have involved a couple of burgers as well. He can't finish the chance. Pinball ensues before it breaks to Della Verde. He relishes the opportunity of a shot at goal, but slices it over.

Soon after, another ball is sent towards the 200m start line on the running track, which requires a new ball, since there aren't any poor ball boys positioned out there. Kiangebeni could probably cover it, as he's just about everywhere else on the pitch and has looked good alongside Ryan Blackman in the middle. The Enfield centre-halves may also have been standing there in admiration, as they get in each other's way and concede a corner out of nowhere. Regent swing it into the mixer. Charlie Durling gets up highest and heads it into the net unopposed. It's level again at 2-2.

The home fans in the main stand shake their heads in disbelief. The hard core at the other end continue singing 'Everywhere we go' to the accompaniment of the drum. It's only then I realise this has been going on all half and will seep into my subconscious and I'll hum it for the next week. They mix things up a bit with a rendition of 'Towners till we die', and versions of songs ranging from some Sex Pistols to 'Yankee Doodle Dandy'. Bricknell has a less extensive repertoire and continues to labour against the defence. He looks for a foul, which isn't given.

Town do have a Cockman-style long throw in their armoury, which is the non-league version of a Rory Delap throw. Lee Chappell sends it towards the edge of the six-yard box. Regent get a head on it, but it isn't cleared far. Della Verde runs on to it and lashes it into the top of the net in a way only someone I've made notes questioning their end product can.

There are a few niggly fouls before a full-frontal assault on my ears, when the home fans sing a song normally associated with Spurs. Fortunately, Town's singing practice makes their rendition of 'When the Town go marching in' more tuneful than Spurs manage, with any regular Spurs fans presumably drowned out. It's also not the drawn-out version, unlike Bricknell's attempts to get past a defender.

Regent burst into life with a quick interchange of passes. Byrne-Hewitt is forced to check his run and play it sideways. He gets the ball back and curls one on to the underside of the terrace roof below a sign for a property agent. Even the most deceitful property agent would struggle to convince me that Regent still deserved to be in this contest.

Town continue to create chances, which I barely notice as the drumming has left me in something of a trancelike state. Then it stops, but only to start up a different song with lots of la la la la lahs. The game itself stops for a substitution. Della Verde comes off for Town, replaced by a large lad who will be useful attacking the long throws. A young fan nearby shouts 'Well done Della Verde' and the player claps back, much to his delight. He is less supportive when Bricknell is awarded 'man of the match'. Nzembela has been more impressive, but his dad points out that he can't win it every week. I wasn't inclined to agree after I was once overlooked for the same award in favour of someone whose only contribution was to turn up when it was raining for once.

Regent win a free kick late on and their goalkeeper comes up for it. The cross comes in low; the ball is flicked up to a Regent player on the edge of the box. He bursts forward to meet it and is pulled down. He gets a shot away. It's blocked. The referee blows his whistle. It's a penalty surely and a chance for Regent to nick an equaliser. The ref signals for a free kick on the edge of the box. The Regent players are incensed. It's hard to know whether to feel sorry for them not getting a penalty, or glad they won't come away with an undeserved point.

There's still a chance from the free kick. Scott Parker lines it up. A Town player lies down behind the wall. Parker curls a low shot around the wall. The Regent fans are up cheering. MacDonald goes down to his left. He gets a palm on it. He does just enough to turn it round the post after being a spectator for most of the match. It's the last touch of the game, as the referee blows for full time.

Three hundred and thirty-one people have been entertained in a 3-2 home win. They can also buy chocolate that is going out of date from the club shop for 50p. Luckily, I have £1.70 in change, so that's souvenirs to take home for the kids sorted and a treat for me. I don't think I'll be going home with a new team to support, though. I've enjoyed the atmosphere and there's a lot to like about Town, but they're not for me. I'm more than happy to come again and show my support by paying for a ticket if they're up against another team I might be interested in. As for Regent, they offered little, a bit like a not-at-all-talkative date. Maybe they would be better in their home surroundings, open up a bit more and give me more to go on.

For now, we head into the second national lockdown and plans to see any games are on hold. Once again, I have to cancel plans to see Saffron Walden Town host Hashtag United, but this time I expect the season to resume. It's far from clear whether the season will conclude and there don't seem to be any plans to resolve a mostly completed campaign through points per game, splitting leagues regionally, or playing each other only once.

Another null and void season remains a possibility, but for now it's been good to be regularly attending games again and a month off now should lead to some more midweek fixtures I can attend when matches are rearranged. Quite how this will affect the players and clubs is less clear.

Chapter 15

Box 'em in

NESTLED IN between the second national lockdown and a likely move into Tier 3 restrictions and another pause in the season, I fit in a visit to Catons Lane, when Saffron Walden host Ilford. It's a Saturday three o'clock kick-off and I've genuinely looked forward to the game all week.

I invite my dad along, as it's a chance to meet up halfway between where we live. In many respects, it's like a nice rural pub to meet up for Sunday lunch. Only much colder and with worse food on offer. It's not a case of introducing a new partner to my parents, it's more like a convenient meeting place with a nice homely feel.

Walden have continued to do the place up, with a new can bar running from a shed to take the pressure off serving beer from the door to the clubhouse. Walden's chairman, Stuart Vant, was keen to show off the facilities on social media and drum up some more support for the club. I appreciated the effort they were making and was glad to come along and support them with money at the gate, even if my dad insisted on paying.

After passing through the turnstiles, I am pleasantly surprised to get a friendly hello from Vant, which I don't recall happening at many league grounds. The personal touch you get at this level really helps you warm to a club. To warm me further, I get a hot chocolate and suggest we sit in the ground's equivalent of the snug bar in the main stand. At this point, you might expect some sort of profound father–son bonding. Since neither of us are like that, we discuss the intricacies of the non-league pyramid system and chuckle when we see Ollie Fortune hit on the backside with a stray ball during the warm-up.

Once we have worked out where these teams are in relation to my dad's local team, St Neots, we talk about Ilford. They follow the pattern of seemingly every other team at this level of having had some fame before the war, sold their ground as support for the amateur game dwindled, failed to find a new ground, and then ended up involved in various mergers and splits.

In Ilford's case, they could boast two FA Amateur Cup wins at Wembley, having played prestigious friendlies against Barcelona and Ajax, and attracting five-figure crowds during the 1920s. The attendance for their home game earlier in the season against Walden was 85. This was at the Cricklefield Stadium, having sold their Lynn Road ground in the 1970s. They didn't find an immediate replacement after what is described in various places as a 'mysterious tax bill'.

At this point, Ilford became caught up in the various mergers and de-mergers involving teams from Leyton and Walthamstow, which eventually resulted in Dagenham & Redbridge coming into existence. Ilford was reformed in 1987, but doesn't seem to have the same supporter-led credentials as Enfield Town, or at least they don't play on them. I'm intrigued. Ilford's website doesn't give much away either, so maybe I could have my head turned by another club.

Ilford come out in blue and white hooped shirts, looking like a QPR team. Walden line up with Luke Wilson marshalling their defence, but no Gavin Cockman. Soon after kick-off Wilson urges his team-mates to 'Go early on the throw, there's no long throw today.' In a reversal of roles I break the news to my dad that we won't be seeing one of Walden's main attacking threats, although I don't think he's as upset as I would have been if he'd told me Ian Wright wasn't playing.

Come to think of it, we hadn't been to many games together since those early Arsenal games. There had just been a couple of dire England friendlies and a match at St Neots Town, where the prime entertainment was seeing if a stray clearance would land on the east coast main line. It didn't bode well.

Today's match doesn't get off to a promising start. Ilford's number nine, Oladele Sotoyinbo, has a couple of nice touches before giving the ball away. Wilson calling for the ball seems to scare off one of the other forwards. Sotoyinbo gets on the ball again and spots Bransgrove off his line. He goes for the lob, but it's well wide. You could see what he was trying to do and so could Jason Maher, who is fuming on the touchline.

Ilford look bright going forward, but Walden are firm in the tackle. Ilford's pacey number seven, Mo Kargbo, goes down under a challenge and has the ball belted into him from point-blank range. Play continues until Walden eventually win a corner. The referee goes to check on Kargbo, which feels like a PE teacher leaving everyone else to settle scores while his back is turned.

Walden can't make anything of the corner and it's Ilford who present them with a chance soon after. A back pass to the keeper bounces up off his knees and Walden's Ross Kochan is on to it. I can't quite decide which bald footballer from the 90s he looks like and Kochan can't quite get there before the keeper recovers. It's another foul and a harsh booking for Kochan, as the ball was there to be contested.

Another contest is going on next to the pitch with a game of panna, where kids are trying to nutmeg each other. It seems to have caught the linesman's attention, who isn't happy that a ball has strayed on to the field. Maybe he is just as perplexed as I am why something that might draw an ironic cheer during a game has become so popular.

Some kids return to the stand to watch as Walden get away a scuffed shot from a corner. The keeper saves with his feet and Ilford break forward. A Walden player is shoved over, as he tries to block the keeper's clearance. The kids are worried they will be thrown out of the family stand if they swear. Me and my dad are unlikely to be offended. Soon enough we hear Wilson tell the ref to 'Get a fucking hold of it.'

We approach half-time and Wilson has some time on the ball. He composes himself and sends it long into the right-hand channel to the new forward, Balde. The tannoy announcer and team sheet didn't seem to agree on his first name, but what is clear is that he has the beating of the full-back. The defender does well to force him wide. Balde still gets his shot away and beats the keeper from a tight angle to make it 1-0. He celebrates with a knee slide and shows Maher has a much better knowledge of non-league forwards than I do.

It's good to see a moment of quality in what many might see as unrefined football. We have enjoyed some of the full-bodied tackling on display. There are crunching ones in midfield that swing the attacking momentum, over-excitable slide tackles making the most of the muddy pitch, and ones where players steam in for both man and ball. There has been a gladiatorial quality about the contest.

It soon looks like they have fed Bransgrove to the lions with a pass back. Sotoyinbo clashes with him as he clears. Bransgrove stays down. He appears to be holding his ribs before getting to his feet and hobbling back to his goal. He signals to the bench he is okay to continue. Maher is keen for the referee to deliver some sort of punishment.

There's time for a few more fouls before half-time. Both teams stay out on the pitch for their team talks. It's not clear whether this is a show of strength in the cold, or gives the managers more time to discuss whatever tactical plans weren't being followed in the first half.

We move stands for the second half for a bit more atmosphere and so my dad is nearer to the exit to catch his bus home. I expect most of the shouting to be coming from the dugouts, so we move to the stand on the far side and not behind the goal Walden are attacking. We find seats practically on the Ilford bench, a row behind the substitutes. We could pass as backroom staff if we didn't look like two old men worried about catching a chill. The chief concern amongst the Ilford staff is making sure they account for all their practice balls, which, given the cost of a Mitre and the fine margins of the game's finances at this level, is understandable.

My vantage point helps me think tactically and I notice an important development since the recent introduction of one-man kic-offs. A dummy kick will often draw out a player keen to charge down the all-important long ball to the corner. When the referee forces the player to retreat, they can kick off and send the ball to the corner and 'box 'em in' from the defending team's throw.

What my new seat doesn't allow me to see is Ilford hitting the post, as there is a pillar in the way. One sub complains they must be the unluckiest team in the league. Bransgrove is clearly struggling with his injury and the Ilford manager instructs his team to 'put the big man on him' at a free kick to try to change their luck.

The set piece comes to nothing and Bransgrove goes down. The referee goes to check on him, but won't let the Walden physio on. I feel like I've stepped into The Impossible Job, the Graham Taylor documentary, as Maher berates the linesman. It's a moment of high drama. The sub keeper gets ready. He appears to be an outfield player, who doesn't have his own gloves. The programme confirms it.

Maher takes Bransgrove's word that he is okay to continue. Wilson insists Maher makes the substitution. It's not exactly Kepa in the League Cup Final, but would be the sort of thing the media might make a big deal of at a higher level. There is a clear determination to hold on to their lead, mixed with the fear it might slip away. Ilford spring the offside trap, but the shot is straight at Bransgrove. His reaction forces the substitution. Billy Jones comes on and has to borrow Bransgrove's gloves.

Ilford sense an opportunity, but their management team check to see if Bransgrove is okay when he trudges past them. Ilford are forced into making a change themselves, when the lively Kargbo seems to have pulled something. The replacement hurriedly puts some shorts on and gives his earrings to the assistant manager, who looks at them in utter disbelief.

Jones's first touch is to receive a through ball and do some keepy-uppies. 'Stop fucking about' is Maher's response. He is equally unimpressed with Wilson and tells him, 'Stop playing offsides against the fastest players in the league.' An argument ensues between the two loudest people in the ground, as Wilson dismisses Maher with 'Jase, calm down. We're fine.'

Maher makes a tactical change and brings on a left-back, with the instructions to 'Stay at home' and 'Don't play any of Wilson's stupid offsides.' Ilford make their own tactical changes, with detailed instructions that seem to involve a lot of 'two players here, two players there'. The upshot is a 4-2-4 formation and a sub who looks to take a long throw. It's cleared, but Maher wasn't happy about a defender's positioning.

Walden feel like a team with ten men trying to hang on to their lead. The slope seems to be a more noticeable hindrance than usual on a pudding of a pitch. Maher implores Jones to kick for distance and sends one of their taller forwards back to defend every corner, despite Wilson insisting they don't need any help. An opening presents itself to Ilford, and they hit a curling shot from outside of the box. Jones flies to his left and palms it clear. 'I told you he was decent,' says one sub, sounding resigned to defeat.

Walden finally break. A through ball plays in Balde. He flicks it inside the last defender and hits his shot firmly. The keeper is there to smother it. Maher is unhappy Balde seemed to hesitate, expecting the flag to go up. Balde's head goes down and Maher is quick to tell him, 'Don't worry about it, another chance will come.' It feels like a costly miss and the tension mounts. Wilson is calmly organising the defence, winning headers and last-ditch tackles. Maher is on edge. 'Jase, don't worry, they're knackered,' Wilson reassures him.

Late in the game, Wilson wins another header. The ball falls to Ilford's number 14, who lashes a volley from outside the box. Jones doesn't move. The net ripples and Ilford's pressure pays off. They have a late equaliser and celebrate as wildly as a subs' bench and three travelling fans can manage.

Walden try to muster a chance in the closing minutes, but can't create an opening. Ilford cannot counter and the game ends in a hard-fought draw. It's disappointing for Walden to lose a lead late on, but a fair result. I've grown rather fond of this Ilford side and make a note to check out one of their home games.

I'm surprised to find the attendance was only 233. There was a far greater sense of scale sat so close to the dugouts. The passion from the benches was no less than you would see at a much higher level. I don't have a chance to discuss the game with my dad afterwards, as he has his bus to catch. Although I suspect I wouldn't have said much more than 'It was alright'. I thoroughly enjoyed the game. There's something special about a chilly Saturday afternoon; the floodlights switched on to help the weak winter sun, a heavy pitch and two committed teams. They are all the ingredients television journalists, dispatched to report on a potential giant-killing in the cup, try to convey. It's a cliché, but football is all about clichés and there's something comforting about that timeless quality.

I'm glad to enact the tradition of father and son going to a game together, even if it's just to have someone there to ask, 'Was that really offside?' I am keen to take my own kids to see some non-league football. My youngest wouldn't be able to sit through the warm-up, but Ruby had shown some passing interest.

The next day I plan to take Ruby to see Hashtag Women's team play Cambridge City at Canvey Island's ground. Waking up to a wet and windy day, with Ruby coming down to breakfast in a princess dress, was an inauspicious start. In the end, she decided not to go, and I wasn't about to force her. The game would have been an ideal introduction, with Hashtag scoring in the first minute and racing into a 5-0 lead by half-time. The conditions were described as 'bracing' and no amount of warm clothing, hot chocolate and sweets would have helped overcome that trauma.

I'm eager to get to another game and decide to go back to Saffron Walden for their fixture against Hashtag on the Tuesday. The announcer at the Ilford game had been full of warnings to get there early, as capacity was limited to 300. I didn't want to drive all that way and be turned away, so I hurry to the ground after work and get there over an hour before kick-off. I find it strange that the floodlights aren't on and realise in my rush to get there early; I haven't checked to see if the game is actually going ahead. I check now, and there is the announcement, made at midday, calling the game off due to coronavirus-related reasons.

I knew there would be some other games nearby, but they had also been called off. I then spot that Maldon & Tiptree are at home in the FA Trophy. It would involve driving over an hour back the way I had come. I was tempted, as I expected a good game. I had just enough time to make it. Instead, I went to find a burger for dinner, after banking on getting one at the ground. It was at this point I realised I could rule the Jammers out of the running to be my new team. Unperturbed, they knocked out Bognor Regis, from a division above, courtesy of a last-minute winner.

After that, Tier 3 came into force, which soon became Tier 4, and football was off the menu. Once again, my plans to see Walden vs Hashtag had been scuppered, so I donated what I would have spent to their chairman's couch to 5k fundraising campaign. The Clapton Community game I had my eyes on the following week was also off, so I donated to their campaign to fund repairs to their clubhouse.

I was keen to follow the fortunes of these clubs I had gotten to know a little about and help them where I could. One struggler where my support would not make a difference was Arsenal, who once again found themselves languishing in the league table, with questions being asked of the manager.

The unthinkable prospect of relegation felt like a genuine concern. I dreaded to think how it would have affected me if I hadn't drifted away. It highlighted the madness of investing so much of your identity in something you can't influence. While hoping for an upturn in results, the thought crossed my mind that if they plummeted through the leagues, then I might get more involved in the club.

Going from Wembley to crowds of 85 at home to Saffron Walden seemed far-fetched in Arsenal's case, and I was more worried about how some of the current non-league clubs would fare. When Tier 4 became another national lockdown, it became increasingly apparent that they would once again curtail the season.

The Hashtag season ticket I invested in before Christmas would go unused. It was already a pretty poor investment, given it cost more than the total cost of each remaining home game, but I was keen to show my support and pay them back for mine and Phil's free entry to the Clapton match. Hashtag's Spencer Owen had more reason to be concerned about his investment, as it looked like another season would be null and void.

I once again felt sorry for teams like Hashtag and Maldon & Tiptree, who had been flying high. Like Spencer, I was annoyed that the FA hadn't planned for the entirely predictable scenario of another lockdown. He was keen to see last season's results reinstated and combined with this season's results.

Several months later and the news is confirmed that the season will once again be abandoned. I'm less frustrated this time round. It's been on the cards for a while. Far fewer games had been completed, and the FA tease the prospect of a long overdue restructure. I hope teams will be rewarded this way and look forward to the new season, albeit not as much as I look forward to the end of home schooling.

Lockdown drags on and there's little to get excited about on club Twitter feeds. In the same way no one has any appetite for online quizzes this time round; it seems those running the accounts are equally despondent. In among the occasional birthday wishes for a player, I notice Saffron Walden advertise for a goalkeeping coach and club secretary. I didn't have the qualifications to kick balls at a goalkeeper, or the inclination to be the person responsible for player registrations and the inevitable points deduction when it all goes wrong. I let the opportunities pass.

Grassroots football starts up soon after lockdown ends. I cycle past a Sunday League game and the thought crosses my mind that I could watch games at this level. Hans van der Meer's videos show there can be a real beauty in this form of the game and there are groundhoppers who will talk enthusiastically about it on various forums. I can't summon up the same enthusiasm. That level doesn't have the same appeal as watching a team in the pyramid in the hope they will move up, or go on a cup run.

At the top of that pyramid, I'm equally turned off by the behaviour of the big clubs and their short-lived European Super League proposal. The day after Arsenal snatch a draw at home to relegation-threatened Fulham, they announce themselves as one of 12 founder members of this new league. Looking to join based on wealth rather than on sporting merit, with no threat of relegation, is ideal for absentee owner Stan Kroenke. Money would roll in regardless of on-field performance, which had become increasingly mediocre on his watch. Universal outrage at the proposal sank it barely 48 hours after they announced it.

I wasn't surprised that Arsenal and others would chase the untold riches the breakaway league promised, but I was shocked about how it all unfolded. It was another example of how the game is corrupted by greed. Many fans vowed to turn towards non-league football. Others were optimistic the episode would herald an era of community ownership, taking over from distant venture capitalist owners.

The 'Kroenke out' movement gained some momentum, but I wasn't inclined to get involved and help Arsenal move towards some form of fan ownership that I had seen work so well at lower tiers. The game at the top level seemed just too rotten. Commercial interests would abound in one form or another. It felt like there was more camaraderie amongst non-league clubs, who were in it for the love of the game and some hard-fought competition.

I didn't need to see the best teams in Europe (and Spurs) play each other every week. I could enjoy football with two committed sides, a ramshackle ground and a fifty-fifty draw every other week. The prospect of this felt much closer when the FA announced its restructure at Steps 3 to 6. Teams were moved to create a more streamlined pyramid, with some moved sideways for geographical reasons and 107 teams rewarded for their efforts over two curtailed seasons and being elevated to a higher level.

One of those teams who were elevated were Hashtag. Sat in my office I saw the YouTube notification come through: 'Are we promoted? Livestream'. I hurried to click on the link and catch Spencer Owen doing some impromptu karaoke and various 'Up the Tags' comments. I wasn't sure this was sufficient confirmation. The ever-reliable Twitter feed of Ollie Bayless had full confirmation of all the moves.

I was delighted. It wasn't seeing the team win a dramatic title decider with some sort of Aguero moment, but it was a deserved promotion and not an underhand administrative elevation. Hashtag had racked up 96 points in 38 league games over two shortened campaigns and I was pleased for the team. I felt the need to text friends and family to share the good news, but stopped short of cracking open the champagne, as I had in a pub watching Arsenal clinch the league at White Hart Lane nearly 20 years before.

I look at the teams Hashtag would face in the Isthmian League North next season and see the familiar names of Heybridge Swifts and Maldon & Tiptree. There weren't any moves up from this level to the Isthmian Premier, so the Jammers would once again miss out on promotion, despite their incredible record. This will be a much tougher league for Hashtag. After half-expecting them to race through the leagues like AFC Wimbledon, or Salford, I realise this would be a proper test. I could take nothing for granted, and I could not wait to see it unfold.

Would the Gulag at Chelmsford leave me feeling cold, and not just in the meteorological sense? Don't be fooled by the blue sky, it's always freezing there.

Lucky not to be stuck behind Hashtag United's thousands of subscribers, at Chadfields' turnstiles, where they groundshared with Tilbury.

It was only after taking a photo of the corner flag at every ground, I realised they are generally used to accompany an article about a serious issue in the game. Would this denote my feelings towards Saffron Walden Town would get serious?

An historic feature from Ilford's old Lynn Road ground almost makes up for the running track at Cricklefield.

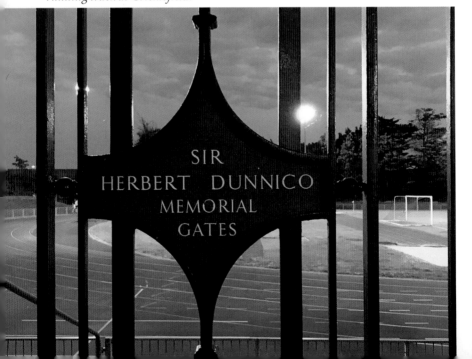

A fourth official's view of the technical area at Clapton Community's Stray Dog ground. If they had fourth officials at that level.

I like bikes, I like non-league dogs and I like an atmosphere, so presumably I would like Clapton Community?

A spot just behind the goal at Hashtag's groundshare with Bowers & Pitsea, where I would be caught on camera celebrating a goal. Had I found the equivalent of my old seat in the Clock End?

Getting arty at Saffron Walden's Catons Lane, trying to capture the feel of the wooden benches in the cow shed style main stand. One of my favourite grounds, but would they become my favourite team?

Clapton Community playing on the main pitch at Wadham Lodge, and a beginner level spot the ball photo.

Clapton Community v AVA. Fading light, drizzle, huddled on the terrace, beer in hand, what's not to love?

Always in danger of inadvertently becoming YouTube content at Hashtag United.

All the family, and Snowy the giant cuddly rabbit, enjoying the beach hut at the Dripping Pan, Lewes.

Chapter 16

You're too easy to mark

MY FIRST game back after nine months isn't to be Hashtag, though. After retaining some fond memories of my trip to see Walden vs Ilford, I seek out an Ilford home game. I miss their opening match of the season, a 3-1 loss to Stansted FC, nicknamed the Airportmen. This denies me the opportunity to use lots of aeroplane puns. I imagine one team getting off to a flyer, some turbulence, and a defence demonstrating excellent air traffic control. Taxiing down a runway would have been harder to shoehorn in, and that sort of rapid progress doesn't describe driving down the A12 on a Wednesday evening to get to Ilford's ground.

I find myself in traffic going to the Foxes' game against FC Clacton. Not to be confused with Clapton, the visitors are from the Essex coastal town, notable for being a bank holiday battleground for rival mods and rockers in the sixties, as well as the constituency for UKIP's only ever elected MP. One car I did spot was full of Clacton fans, with a scarf in the back window.

Seeing cars full of a different team's supporters always used to liven up a motorway journey, and this was no different.

There is a queue for the one turnstile into the ground, as my arrival coincides with what must be the entire away following, namely the carload of Clacton fans I saw on the A12. The card machine isn't working either. I pay £7 in cash and another £2 for the programme and enter at the corner of the ground by the modern clubhouse.

Cricklefield Stadium is an athletics ground dating back to the 1920s and used by several teams in the area. It's been Ilford's home since the early 1990s. The track is only six lanes wide and terracing runs most of the way round the perimeter, so it feels less cold and clinical as a football venue than many athletics grounds. Someone has added a few blue and white balloons to the railings and flags of what I presume are the players' nationalities. I recognise all bar one African and one Caribbean country, which would appal my younger self as much as my current lack of top-flight football knowledge would. I clearly didn't watch enough of the Olympics.

I find a seat in row seven at the back of the main stand, near the halfway line. The Clacton fans set up on the covered terrace opposite, with a large England flag. It's a bright sunny evening, perfect barbeque weather in fact. Although a sign does expressly forbid the use of barbecues in the ground, which I'm sure would otherwise be a common occurrence.

I read up on Clacton, who made a lateral move into the Essex Senior League as part of the pyramid restructuring in the off-season. They are another team who lost their old ground, the Old Road ground, in the 1980s. The council sold the land to developers as shopping became more popular and attendances dwindled for football and greyhound racing, which also took place on the site. The Seasiders moved to another ground in town soon after, but have been up and down since, with the club re-forming in 2007.

The teams come out on to the pitch. Ilford are in a new blue and white Hummel strip, which looks sharp. Clacton are in an away kit that could pass for a Watford strip that's got too much black on it. There's a very muted acknowledgement of the teams when they come out to silence from the tannoy. The teams go into huddles before the referee calls them to the centre circle for a minute's applause. Someone asks if this is still for the NHS and no one knows, so the crowd claps less enthusiastically than the teams.

After the toss, Ilford decide to swap ends and play with the wind at their backs in the first half. Ilford's photographer complains his camera is now at the wrong end of the ground and takes some time crossing the pitch. The first action sees Ilford look to get Tigana Quebe in down the left wing. He attacks the full-back and cuts inside, but his shot hops, skips and jumps over the long-jump pit to the right of the goal. Quebe has the measure of the full-back and crosses to Dimi Christou. The Ilford number 10 clearly fancies himself as a Jack

Grealish-type playmaker, with socks beneath his calves, but opts for a half-volley rather than a dive, and it's blocked.

Clacton's number nine, Mekhi McKenzie, barges his way through the Ilford defence and wins a corner. A chant of 'Sea, sea, seasiders' goes up from the opposite stand. Finlay Shorten in the Clacton goal instructs his team: 'Don't be easy to mark.' Outfield players never seem to take kindly to a goalkeeper's offer of attacking advice and to prove the point they allow Ilford to clear with ease.

Clacton's assistant manager Kevin Coyle tries to dictate the play from midfield. He looks to play in McKenzie whenever he can, but has the gait of a much older man whose legs have taken a pounding over the years, and needs an extra touch before playing it safe. That's before he is caught by a late boot and is then really struggling to move. McKenzie is also clattered, allowing Christou to break. The referee keeps the game flowing, but the Ilford forwards don't, as one of them treads on the ball trying to manoeuvre it.

Another Clacton corner sees Shorten instruct his forwards to 'Lose your man' and 'Don't be easy to mark.' Ilford clear again and the ball makes its way back to Shorten, who fluffs his kick. It rolls behind him, but the hosts aren't quick enough to react, so the keeper's blushes are spared. Shorten is quieter at the next corner. Clacton swing the ball into a crowded near-post area, which Ilford do well to clear. On the break, the Foxes scamper away, but when someone trips over the ball, the move breaks down. The game goes back and forth in what is often described as being like a game of basketball. The key difference is that most moves in basketball lead to a change in score. There's more jeopardy here as most moves break down, but it only requires a good or bad touch either way to get a crucial goal.

As the setting sun creates a golden glow on the conifers running along the far terrace, it's Clacton's giant forward in a golden yellow shirt, McKenzie, in a mismatch with the Ilford full-back. Again, a covering defender does enough to hold up play. The ball comes back for a deep cross to the far post. The shot is blocked, and Ilford soon shuttle the ball out to Quebe. He's pulled back. The referee rightly plays an advantage. Nothing comes of it and the home dugout are furious when there is no punishment. The Ilford photographer is even more incensed and makes his thoughts known to the referee when he blows for half-time soon after. Ilford manager Adam Peek has to remind him he's not on the bench so shouldn't be on the pitch remonstrating, which is clearly his job.

I join the queue for the refreshment kiosk, which has backed up because they've run out of change. Luckily, the photographer is on hand to provide some. While I'm waiting, I notice inside the clubhouse is a shop selling sweets and balloons. Sadly, there aren't any of the sweets I liked to get from the 'Two bags of sweeets for a paaarnd' man at Arsenal. I stay in the queue and get a good look at the Sir Herbert Dunnico memorial gates from the old Lynn Road ground. I then make the less fancy purchase of a Snickers and a liquid that is the colour, if not the taste, of hot chocolate.

There are grumbles about the foul not being given before half-time and about how the wind has led to passes being over-hit, but most of the crowd seem happy to be just taking in a game. I pause on returning to my seat to take in the view from the terrace. The floodlights are on, throwing a warm orange glow across the pitch. These aren't the sharp bright white lights you get at a modern stadium and have more in common with one of my old junior team's training sessions, which relied on using manager Terry's Cortina headlights on full beam. Shooting one way, everything was in shadow, and facing the other you were blinded. Here at least feels like being in front of a nice, warm fire.

Ilford look to dazzle Clacton by bringing on the pacey Mo Kargbo to get at the Seasiders' defence on the break. Indeed, one burst elicits an actual whoop from someone in the crowd. Clacton cut a cross out, and Ilford have a rasping shot blocked and another low drive saved by keeper and post. Soon after, Quebe has another effort into the side netting, which would have prompted an erroneous cheer had there been more fans in attendance for some to think it had gone in.

Despite the Ilford chances, Clacton are in the ascendency, and someone takes a pot shot from near halfway. Josh Blackburn in the Ilford goal back-pedals. He attempts to pluck the ball out of the air. He drops it. The ball stays the right side of the goal line and no one can follow up. There is a sense the game is drifting away from Ilford. Passes are misplaced and chances aren't taken. Clacton have a good shout for a penalty, which is waved away, and soon after they are awarded a free kick on the edge of the box for a similar challenge. A bloke nearby takes his phone out to film it. The shot goes innocuously wide. A corner is given. The camera has been put away and misses the ball going directly into the goal. The referee disallows it and a replay would have been useful to see why.

Ilford have their own chance from a direct free kick in a central position, close to the D. There's a deliberate run-up and it's hit at the sort of height a pole-vaulter would be happy with. I suspect the game might well end goalless. The Clacton keeper intercepts another hopeful ball forward. He hits it long. The ball bounces between Blackburn and McKenzie at the edge of the Ilford area. The players go up together. McKenzie gets there first and heads past Blackburn into the empty net.

It's 1-0 to the visitors and everyone is keen to ask the referee how long remains. There's under ten minutes and the Clacton manager, Mark Nicholls, now on as a sub, is instructing his players to play it in behind the defence for the next five minutes. Clacton soon have a free kick to defend. Nicholls is trying to keep a high line. Ilford swing the kick in. A blue and white head is on the end of it to send the ball back across the goal. It hasn't got enough on it, but is bundled in, only for the linesman's flag to go up. Ilford are denied again when nothing is given for a shirt pull in the area soon after. The Ilford bench are on their knees in frustration, pleading with the football gods. The players take out their own frustration with a couple of knee-high tackles. Clacton run down the clock and take the points.

The A12 is quieter on the drive home and I'm in a better mood than if Arsenal had been edged out in a close game. In fact, the result sees me even more sympathetic towards Ilford. There's a lot to like about them, but I'm intrigued what the future holds. They have their own ground and a small band of faithful supporters, but they are some way from where they once were, and it doesn't seem all that likely they will return anytime soon. It's not clear if that will be enough to bring in new fans, with most of the younger supporters seemingly there for their mates in the team. I expect to follow their results in the manner of someone Facebook-stalking an unsuitable ex in the hope things turn out okay for them. Only turning up at Ilford's door again would be less weird.

Chapter 17

Only here for the buffet

I FIND myself with some spare evenings and I'm still excited enough about the new season, despite Arsenal's opening day defeat at Brentford, to look up some local fixtures. Perhaps tellingly, I went for a bike ride instead of watching Hashtag's match on the Sunday, before heading to Saffron Walden on the Tuesday.

I pick up my friend Vicki on the way to the ground. Vicki works for the Football Supporters' Association and wants to check in with Walden as one of their affiliate members. The FSA represents fans, pushing for better fan engagement and advocating supporter ownership of clubs. Vicki helps run the members' network, so supporter-run clubs can help each other out. Vicki tells me that our names are on the gate and they might invite us into the boardroom. We pay our £7 entry anyway, as we are there to support the club and not get a freebie.

Vicki is keen to introduce herself to chairman Stuart Vant, and we find him by the clubhouse. Vicki explains what the FSA does and is keen to involve Walden more in the network. Stuart tells us he only took over as chair about seven months before Covid struck. Before that, the club was apparently in danger of going into administration, and he used his business experience to turn things around. Stuart is a bundle of energy and despite delegating a lot of tasks to the committee he is still found taking beer deliveries in the morning. He mentions the £3 a pint offers on tonight, and will work long after the game as his courier company does business in the US and Asia. Before he dashes off to make stadium announcements, Stuart tells us about plans for the ground and the new sprinkler system installed on the pitch. He's quick to ask if there's any money to be had from the FSA, but is equally quick to check we're okay and says we're welcome to use the President's Suite.

Stuart announces the teams as we settle into seats in the main stand. Walden are in their usual red and black and I recognise a few names from my last visit. St Margaretsbury are the opponents in their change strip of yellow, with some sort of black detail, which again could be a bad Watford kit. They hail from the same county, being based in Hertfordshire. Walden create a couple of early openings before a Bury defender implores his team-mates to settle down.

A goal would settle them down and Bury attempt a potshot, which pleasingly ricochets off the barrier behind the goal and back into keeper's hands to take the goal kick. Stuart clearly isn't concerned he will have a goal to announce and walks round the ground checking everyone's alright. He's followed by a volunteer asking if anyone has lost their programme. I'm hoping the fifty-fifty ticket seller will be along next.

Bury's number nine, Roddy Lemba, stands out as a player to watch from the opposition, as he has the physique of Adebayo Akinfenwa. Vicki points out that a player that size getting in the team must offer something. He battles for the ball and is barged over. The only chastisement from the home crowd is a bloke saying 'Get up number nine'. Bury argue about the award of a free kick and another one Walden are awarded soon afterwards. They send a deep cross into the box, it's headed back across goal and bounces in off Michael Toner. I strain to see round the side of the stand to check whether the linesman's flag is up. It's not and Walden have the lead.

Walden continue to play on the front foot and win a corner. They line up for a pre-planned routine, but Bury clear. They make no headway in bringing the ball forward and Walden regain possession in their own half and switch the play uphill to the left flank. The low cross is scuffed behind Charlie Smith, but he reaches to control it, spins, and gets a shot away across the keeper. It bounces off the far post and into the net with a gentle ripple. 2-0 to Walden.

The tempting smell of £3 pints of San Miguel wafts across the stand, but sadly, I'm driving. Walden have the scent for goals, although Gavin Cockman is too easily lured into a long-range effort which drifts towards a shed in the corner of the ground that doesn't quite need someone to get in a car to fetch.

Equally wayward is a tackle soon after from Matt Hurley. He catches a Bury player late. The visitors are up in arms and surround the referee, urging him to give a red card. James Solkhon is quick to come over and tell the ref, 'That's embarrassing what they're doing there,' before repeating the same to several Bury players. He expects the referee not to be fooled by the orchestrated appeal, or the crunch of foot on shinpad. The tackle wasn't high or studs up. It should be a booking and left at that.

To everyone's surprise, Hurley is given his marching orders, and he heads down the tunnel. The home fans become animated and let the referee know what they think about the decision. A group in front try to get the linesman's opinion. He is unmoved and uses the break to have a vape on an e-cigarette. After the injured player is treated, someone in front asks the physio if he's alright. 'He's okay,' comes the reply to what seems like genuine concern. She is less impressed with the 'Does he want me to kiss him better?' follow up.

Bury try to make their advantage count just before the break and pin Walden back in their own half. 'Let's get out!' comes the rallying cry from the Walden defence when the move breaks down. Two players leave their feet in when going for a fifty-fifty, but things don't spill over. My fifty-fifty tickets have been bought and stowed. Walden make it to half-time safely themselves.

I ask Vicki if we should take advantage of the offer to spend half-time in the President's Suite. Never knowingly one to miss a buffet, she is unequivocal in her response.

We walk in and all the talk is about the sending off. No one thinks it was a red, mainly because the Bury committee isn't in attendance. Someone asks whether that is something they can be fined for, but someone else says they just need to attend the game. Stuart invites us to tuck into the generous spread. Manager Jason Maher is likely to be in a less generous mood towards the referee and a committee member speculates that he probably has him up against a wall by now. Another member jokes the ref is probably boasting to the rest of the Inbetweeners about sending Hurley off. I pretend not to have noticed the similarity to the character Jay and that I'm above that sort of thing. One wag suggests the sprinklers were to blame for the late challenge.

There's more than enough sandwiches and cakes to go around and they will put the leftovers out for the fans afterwards. Karen, the club secretary, suggests the Bury committee might expect the buffet to be laid on after the game, which is more traditional. Talk turns to the post-match chicken casserole dinner for the team. The ref has already made his apologies and they need the chap running the refreshment kiosk to get the food on straight after half-time for it to be ready. Fiona, the social media manager, comes in and complains that the website provider still hasn't updated the fixtures page. The takings for the fifty-fifty draw are being counted out and there's £153 in the prize pot. Before we know it, the second half is nearly upon us. After one final check to make sure we're okay, Stuart leaves to make some announcements over the tannoy.

We find somewhere to watch the second half from the far stand behind the dugouts. We can see Maher prowling around the technical area. He isn't pleased when the Walden keeper misjudges a back pass and slices his kick. The defence back-pedal and block a goal-bound attempt, and then snuff out the follow-up.

Maher is abundantly clear in how he wants his forwards and midfielders to restrict the space for Bury to build any attacks and cajoles his team forward. Bury commit a foul to stop Walden in their tracks. Maher is fuming with the referee. 'You said another foul and they would go in the book.' 'Where?' the ref answers back. 'Over there,' replies a gesticulating Maher, before one of his players says, 'He can't count, he thinks it's a different number player.'

While this is going on, I notice Hurley is standing a few places down from me in a club tracksuit and he is talking to a couple of fans. They commiserate with him on what was never a sending off. Hurley is gutted he will be suspended. He works out what games he will miss and is worried about getting back in the side, having recently joined from Takeley. The fans console him, and he says he will just have to graft to get back in.

A couple of other Walden players' participation ends when they are substituted. More signs of the club's investment are on show as they use an electronic subs' board. Although without a fourth official, Bury are forced to use cards for their subs. The Bury keeper shows some flash footwork, taking the ball past an onrushing forward. He's less impressed with one of his forwards when he fires a shot into an adjacent field. 'Oh, fuck off,' is his response, and that's about as threatening as the visitors get.

Maher issues an instruction to another sub that could also be seen as a threat. 'I want you up to speed, okay?' He's then full of encouragement as his team presses the opposition and keeps them at bay. Cockman is working hard to keep the ball in Bury's own corner, winning headers from defensive throws and chasing down defenders in the channels. He gets on the ball and is audibly clipped in the box, but doesn't go down. Maher appeals for a penalty and takes it personally when it's not given. 'Does he have to go down for it?' The linesman, who is running the gauntlet past Maher on the near touchline, is equally firm in his conviction that it wasn't a penalty.

Vant announces the attendance is 236. 'Bet that's more than you got at Takeley,' says the bloke chatting to Hurley. 'Must be more like 26 there. And half of that is the committee. There for the buffet,' he continues. The conversation turns to Enfield, who seem to have been throwing money about, having brought in James Bransgrove and Luke Wilson from Walden. It's nice to be finding this out on the terrace rather than seeing moves talked about for weeks on Twitter.

Maher doesn't like something he's heard coming from our direction. 'Why don't you shut up?' he insists. It's not clear whether he aimed this at two young girls to our left, me and Vicki chatting about random non-league issues, or at Hurley to our right. Hurley isn't sure

175

either. I move under the cover of the stand to get out of the rain, but with the added advantage of being out of the firing line from Maher. He turns his attention to how quiet the ground is, particularly those behind the goal Walden are shooting towards. As the team continues to hold on, Maher wants the crowd to support them. He scares a few fans behind him to applaud and say well done for a good tackle. Maher then enlists Hurley to get the crowd going. Vicki notes it's a group of senior citizens behind the goal and they don't look like the sort to start a chant.

One person who is fired up is Cockman. He boots a player on the back of the thigh. Cockman apologises and helps the player up in a show of contrition to avoid a booking. He doesn't avoid a rebuke from Maher for helping the player up when he could chase someone else down. Soon after, Cockman slides in late and fouls someone else on the well-sprinkled surface. Once again, he escapes going into the book. His next late slide tackle earns him a yellow card and this time he's adamant that the player jumped over him.

The booking was deserved and so too was the 2-0 win. Bury offered very little and part of me thought a goal for the visitors would make things interesting, which is a worrying sign if I'm going to be a Walden fan. Then again, I felt equally strongly that the red card which stopped it being a totally one-sided contest was the wrong decision.

Either way, I've felt energised by the match. I felt privileged getting a behind-the-scenes peek into the running of the club. And in the second half, I was immersed in the game, watching Maher, and listening in to the football chat between Hurley and a couple of fans. The match was the least interesting of those and it's only at this level that you can have this sort of up-front-and-personal experience of the game.

I was keen to experience more, and try to think of a way I could convince Mrs C that a family trip to watch the FA Cup tie vs Hadley at the weekend was a good idea. Vant reminds the departing crowd about the fixture over the tannoy and I settle on looking up their games against other potential title contenders, hoping to see Walden build on their 100% start.

On the way home, I talk to Vicki about fan-owned clubs and wonder if Walden fit the model of other clubs she has been involved with. It sounded like they had become an affiliate member before Vant became chair and Vicki's colleagues would need to follow up on her visit. I expected Walden to be run as some sort of cooperative, with hundreds of members, but this seemed like more of a traditional board-run club, with a few key people taking on a whole host of jobs to keep things going. There was no questioning the commitment of Vant and his team, but there would always be the worry about what would happen were he to leave. Then again, Vicki could point to examples of strife in other ownership set-ups. It's easy to expect clubs to last forever, but things change, which makes it hard to pick a club on a few viewings.

Chapter 18

Only one F in Fisher

IT'S MY dad's birthday and being a little short of ideas for someone who I point out was born closer to Arsenal being formed than the present day, I offer to take him to a match. I decide against taking him to see Hampton & Richmond in the Conference South after they refused to name their ground after me. I've not yet started making outrageous demands of potential clubs, but I did enter a raffle to have the ground called the Matt Coughlan Beveree Stadium for the season, which if nothing else helped put funds into the club during their centenary year. Instead, I take him to Fisher FC.

Fisher FC were formed in 2009, after the original club, Fisher Athletic, were wound up due to financial difficulties, 101 years after they were founded. The original club was set up by a local headmaster to provide sporting facilities for the underprivileged, and were named after the Catholic saint, John Fisher. I recalled the intriguing name from my *Shoot* magazine's league ladder when Fisher graced the Conference. The club soon went the way of its little cardboard nameplate and disappeared into oblivion.

The current incarnation of Fisher FC is a supporter-owned club and they play at the St Paul's sports ground in Rotherhithe, a stone's throw from their old Surrey Docks ground. The Fish play in the Southern Counties East Premier League, which is the ninth tier of English football, and the same level as the Essex Senior League. A potential advantage of falling for a team in this region is the possibility for some away trips to the Kent coast. Tonight's opponents, Glebe, are from the London suburb of Chislehurst, which is known for its caves and not its beaches. The club was formed in 1995, starting as a single junior team, and disappointingly aren't nicknamed the Cavemen.

I meet my dad in the Mayflower pub near Rotherhithe overground station. Straight away I see the advantage of following a London club, as it didn't take long to get here by rail and since I'm not driving, I can have a drink. I get a pale ale from a local brewery and find a seat on the wooden terrace, with the tide lapping worryingly close beneath our feet. Over dinner and a few pints, my dad tells me about the underground stations he's spent the day going to look at, and about growing up in the area.

We set sail from the pub and take a leisurely walk to the ground. We pass old docks, filled-in docks and flats where Fisher's old ground stood, before reaching St Paul's. It's £8 entry. My dad points out he's entitled to a concession. To make up for this, I feel obliged to enter the prize draw. It's £5 and you have to pick a team from a selection of league clubs. I pick Arsenal to the derision of the ticket seller after their latest humbling defeat.

It's well before kick-off, so we take a stroll round the compact ground. We pass a small stand, an area for spare goalposts and a bike shed before reaching the Pond End. There's a sign saying 'No one stands here, we don't care'. It's just a railing with a high fence behind. We pass behind the goal, dazzled by the setting sun. On the far touchline, the dugouts prevent us from doing a full lap of the ground. I'm tempted to duck under the fence and carry on, but I know ground staff can be funny about what footwear is worn on an artificial pitch. I later spot in the programme that this also counts as entering the field of play and could result in us being ejected.

We return the way we came and spot some local wildlife behind the Pond End, a fox and some wild parakeets. We pass the dressing rooms and quietly shake our heads at the team's choice of music, before reaching the Fisherman's Rest. They're selling cans of Anspach & Hobday, which is brewed nearby, and it would be remiss of me to pass up an opportunity to drink within sight of the pitch. I also can't resist tweeting the club in jest to say I should have been more organised and arranged for my dad to be a mascot on his birthday. The club account replies to say if he's in the ground he can lead the teams out. He's not so keen to get that close to the action and is happy to stay where we are next to the covered terrace with a view towards Canary Wharf.

The teams come out on to the field without my dad. Fisher are in white and black stripes, Glebe in sky blue and white. Fish goalkeeper Tommy Taylor is keen for his side not to commit any fouls early on. 'No foul' is the cry when it wouldn't matter, 'No foul' when there's no one near enough to commit a foul, and 'No foul' when it might be worth someone stopping Glebe on the edge of the box. Luckily, Glebe overrun the ball and the danger passes.

Fisher create a chance early on themselves. There's an 'oooooh' from the crowd as a through ball creates the chance. A Fisher forward prods it past the advancing goalkeeper. Then there's an 'ahhhh' from the crowd as the ball rolls wide. Glebe control possession and look to thread a pass through the defence. The crowd is being kept quiet. A regular walks past and someone tells him, 'You better rally the troops, they're a bit lethargic.' Soon after there are a few songs. 'Come on you Fiiiish' and 'Only one F in Fisher', which hints at a fanbase more accustomed to higher levels of non-league football and creating a bit of atmosphere.

The team responds. Christian Udo is played in and shoots across the keeper. It comes back off the frame of the goal. From where we are standing, me and my dad think it has hit the frame inside the portable goal and has gone in. Play continues and Courtney Swaby tucks it home to make the score 1-0. 'Na na na nananana, Fisher' sings the crowd.

Glebe look for an instant response and soon win a corner. The referee once again shouts 'arms down', which isn't against the rules, but makes his life easier. A near-post in-swinger beats Taylor, who doesn't get his arms near it. Michael Sarpong clears a Glebe header off the line, using the technique Luis Suarez deployed against Ghana, which doesn't involve keeping his arms down. He's sent off and Glebe have a penalty. After a delay and some minor gamesmanship, captain Antoine Douglas steps up to take it. I predict he will send his kick our way, meaning to the keeper's right. Taylor goes left, but Douglas drags his penalty wide and almost literally sends it our way and I wonder if I have some sort of Uri Geller-like powers.

My powers don't extend to getting a Glebe player sent off to even up the numbers. Along with the Fisher bench and several in the covered terrace, I appeal for a red card after a blatant elbow in the face visible from 80 yards away, but not to the referee. He stops play, allows the physio on, tells a few players what's what, then restarts with a drop ball. The Fisher fans take it in their stride and have clearly suffered worse misfortune. They start up a rousing rendition of 'Oh when the Fish go swimming in'.

Glebe look to turn the tide and smash a shot from outside the box. Fisher's number five, Sam Fitzgerald, a disciple of the John Terry school of defending, gets a combination of face and torso in the way of it. Glebe have a couple more chances before the referee blows for half-time, with Fisher's slender advantage intact.

I take in the scenery during the interval. Canary Wharf is lit up against the blackening sky in the distance.

Under the lights, the artificial pitch is glistening. The tight fencing round the edge could fool you into thinking this is a midweek power league, but being stood near Fisher's committed following on the covered terrace and right next to the play has me engrossed. Consuming several pints might also be responsible for a growing fondness towards the club.

Glebe start brightly and hit the crossbar after forcing a mistake from Taylor. Fisher look to counter with Swaby down the left. He gets to the byline and cuts the ball back. A defender slides in to prevent a tap-in. Swaby boots the fence in frustration. From the corner, Fitzgerald attacks the cross. His header is blocked, and it falls to Malaki Coker on the edge of the box. He takes a touch past a defender and strikes it hard and low. The ball takes a deflection and wrong-foots the keeper for 2-0, to the delight of the fans behind the goal.

Some of the older regulars refuse to get too carried away. One predicts they will pull one back, equalise in the last minute, and get a winner in stoppage time. Now most fans are pessimistic about their team's chances, but I suspect Fisher have more justification than most. These words seem prophetic, especially as Glebe have the man advantage and are on top. Sure enough, a few minutes later, a shot from nowhere is too hot for Taylor to handle and they halve the deficit.

They are wrong about the equaliser though. That comes much earlier in the 73rd minute. Fisher cut out a low cross. It falls to a Glebe player, who crashes it onto the bar. The reprieve is short-lived as Glebe turn the ball home for 2-2, to the obvious relief and excitement of the visiting team. I know the goal is in the 73rd minute as me and my dad spend several minutes working out how long is left to hang on, based on what time the second half kicked off. In doing so, we miss an incident over by the dugout. A Fisher player is down and the whole bench is up in protest. Someone has left the digital subs' board upended, so the red and green light illuminates the bench and makes it look like an incident in a nightclub. The referee eventually restores order and issues a yellow. As I did not see the incident and had earlier been wrestling with a jacket caught in the wind, I was doing a passable Arsène Wenger tribute.

Fisher look for a little bit of quality, as the Wenger saying used to go. A throw-in falls to Jack Gibbon, who flicks it over the defender *à la* Gazza vs Scotland. Unfortunately, it then runs away from him and he's shepherded away from goal before the keeper easily picks up a reverse pass. Fisher are then a little ill-disciplined. Swaby can't keep the ball in and flicks it over the fence to delay a throw-in. He's booked.

With time running out, Glebe send a long hopeful ball into the box. Taylor goes up for it with a forward. The forward gets there first and heads into an empty net to make the score 3-2, with around five minutes remaining. We don't have to check the time on this occasion as the Glebe keeper tells his team 'Big five!'. He's also keen to chat to the home fans who've been giving him a bit of stick. One fan dismisses him, saying,

'Don't start chatting to us now you're winning.' A Fisher shot does nothing to silence him, as it's straight at him.

There's a hush for a free kick right at the death. Fisher's giant assistant manager, Luke With, who is on as a sub, stands over the ball. It's going to be the last action of the match. I get my phone out to capture the equaliser on film, which is sure to jinx things more than Uri Geller ever could. Sure enough, the ball flies over the bar and Fisher are consigned to defeat.

On the way out, I see if Arsenal have ended their winless start to the season and secured me the prize draw, but no one is there. I've no way of finding the result and was only asked to provide my first name. It seems like a classic scam, but I forgive them as it's for a good cause and I'm happy to support the club.

Would I become an actual supporter, though? Well, given I'm about to move jobs and will need to go to Canary Wharf, they could be a convenient team to watch. There's more atmosphere than usual at this level, even with an attendance of 131, and I enjoyed getting back into the routine of seeing a game in London and making an evening of it, so I wouldn't rule them out. I ask my dad what he thought of the game and somewhat less sentimentally he says he enjoyed the meal.

Chapter 19

Tons just wanna have fun

I'M BACK in London for my next game. After intending to see Clapton Community for a few years now, I thought it best to get to a game early in the season to avoid any further delay. The Tons' first couple of games have seen 20 goals. They opened with a 2-4 defeat and followed that with an improbable 8-6 win the previous weekend. I'm hoping for goals, but I'm more intrigued by the prospect of finally checking out the club.

Not everyone likes to mix sport and politics and I'm torn between whether I want football to be an escape from politics, and accepting the fact that everything is political. Besides, if I'm turned off by the corporate nature of the Premier League, I should seek something more principled in non-league. Given Clapton's strong anti-fascist stance and support for local charities helping vulnerable groups, they are a club well worth a look.

I'm less inclined to be drawn into the whys and wherefores of Palestine and immigration, which the club is also particularly vocal about. Not wishing to diminish the importance of these social justice issues, I don't want to wade into a partisan debate that I'm far from qualified to talk about. I'm also surprised that Clapton are relatively silent on climate change, given it is the biggest social justice issue of them all. Since most clubs don't go anywhere near these issues, it would be churlish of me to hold that against Clapton. I could always check out Forest Green Rovers, who have excellent environmental credentials, but driving to the Cotswolds for home games would miss the point.

I'm apprehensive about whether I'm essentially walking into a far-left Labour meeting, with everyone trying to outdo each other in their understanding of Marx, and that's before trying to understand any other factions. I hope that I'll find a genuinely warm community-minded club, with a carnival atmosphere on the terrace created by their continental-style ultras. There's no doubt the club is a genuine part of the community, with their hardship fund and fan ownership scheme. They draw fans from different communities in London and there's strong worldwide support helped by an away kit inspired by the colours of the International Brigades and the Spanish Republican flag, which they are playing in today.

I'm joined by my best friend Mark for the trip to Walthamstow, where the Tons are ground-sharing. Mark is partially sighted, having lost his sight in his late teens. He was always a keen footballer and still plays visually impaired football. BT Sport televised the finals of various forms of football for the disabled, and Mark bemoans how the teams for the visually impaired final were chosen after a curtailed season, which meant his team missed out. He goes to games less often these days, with it only being worthwhile if there's a decent atmosphere, or corporate hospitality. We don't expect there to be much of the latter, so we stop at the Collab on Walthamstow High Street for beer and burgers.

Goal updates from Arsenal's inevitable capitulation in the early kick-off at Manchester City punctuate the journey to the ground. Mark, being a Spurs fan, takes great delight in giving me these updates. I'm resigned to the current state they find themselves in. The ground we are going to is part of the Matchday Centres at Wadham Lodge, where Walthamstow also play. Clapton are renting an out-pitch while renovation continues on their Old Spotted Dog ground. There's a banner for 'The Stray Dog' which is the moniker for the grass pitch down an alley next to a series of five-a-side pitches, where their game is.

It's a suggested donation of £3 to enter. We pay £10 on the basis of it being the only note we have between us. I guide Mark away from walking on to the pitch as we walk around a group of fans, almost failing to spot the perimeter fence myself. The main stand is a makeshift affair made of scaffolding and a couple of wooden steps. It has the feel of a warehouse nightclub in Berlin, with stickers and flags adorning the back wall and an eclectic mix of alternative types, traditional non-league fans and more women than you would normally see at a game. We find ourselves a spot on the fence near the dugouts.

The teams warm up in front of us. Today's visitors are Pitshanger Dynamo, from west London, nicknamed the Carrots and playing appropriately in orange. The referee greets his linesman, and he has a slightly hipsterish appearance himself, with a long beard and tied-back ponytail. He seems surprised one linesman has actually made it. The other is wearing trainers. While the Middlesex County Football League Premier Division is the 11th tier of English football, they still conduct their conversation in a way that it can't be overheard or lip-read.

The game kicks off and immediately feels like the lowest level of football I've watched. There's even another game on an adjacent pitch to add to the Sunday league feel. It's certainly no one-man-and-his-dog following though. There's a sizeable crowd and quite a few dogs. Some of the crowd are talking about Arsenal's result. 'You can't sack every manager who loses 5-0 to City or there would be no one left,' is one take on the latest drama surrounding the running of the club. There's not much drama on the pitch, although a couple of the Clapton forward players look handy. The crowd starts up some songs, which are more entertaining.

The Clapton repertoire includes songs occasionally sung by other teams, like a version of Depeche Mode's 'I Just Can't Get Enough', through to more out-there originals, like Prodigy's 'Out Of Space', with the words Forest Gate replacing space. And for those of us who don't know the words, there are ones we can hum along to, including the theme from 'Tetris'. The blocks aren't falling into place for the Tons forwards until a chance falls for Arthur Wright to slot home.

One-nil to Clapton and a rendition of 'Tons Just Wanna Have Fun' starts up. Someone determined to make things no fun for Dynamo is Tons centre-back Dean Bouho, whose no-nonsense clearance nearly takes my head off from point-blank range. East London wouldn't have seemed so wonderful then, as the Clapton version rings out. The standard lyrics are replaced with the more inclusive 'Pies, Mash and Clapton', which also improves the song.

Clapton's assistant manager, Stu Purcell, is trying to improve things on the pitch. His instruction of 'No walking' isn't one I've heard before and tells you something about the level of football. More typical is his berating of the linesman in trainers: 'Fucking hell lino, have you got a broken arm?' 'No, but it can be arranged,' replies a fan. Clapton spring forward. A long ball from Bouho is latched on to by Noah Adejokun, but the keeper turns his shot round the post. There's post of another kind, as I make out the *Postman Pat* theme, with the lyrics of Geoff Ocran's red and white team. Lewis Owiredu cannot deliver a second goal after rounding the keeper and over-running it. He has another chance blocked soon after.

In a lull where players are walking again, I watch the game on the far pitch and see a free kick curled into the top corner. More importantly, I notice people are returning with plastic cups of beer, so it must be possible to buy it somewhere, having not thought to get some from an off-licence before the game. We figure the clubhouse is a good bet and leave to beat the half-time rush.

The clubhouse adjoins the main pitch, where Walthamstow are hosting Sporting Bengal United in the Essex Senior League. We buy our pints and go to sit in the bar overlooking the Walthamstow pitch. Before we reach the window, we're told in no uncertain terms this is the boardroom and we have to leave. There was no notice on the door, and I hadn't clocked the buffet in the corner. Instead, we find a bench on the balcony. From this vantage point, we can see Clapton's pitch through the netting of several five-a-side pitches, and what some grounds would describe as a severely restricted view of the Walthamstow pitch, namely the penalty box at one end.

We watch an informal five-a-side match. The 'skins' team are down to one player in what must have been a feisty encounter, or else he was the only player with a shirt off. He seems to be up against the Zanzibar national team, or five people who all coincidentally had Zanzibar written across their shirts. The standard is even lower than what we had been watching.

The teams come out for the second half and we are tempted to stay in our executive box to watch the match. Pitshanger equalise as we finish our half-time drinks and we decide it's better to get down by the pitch, where there's more atmosphere, and we take a couple of cans from the bar with us. We stand in line with the 18-yard box at the end Clapton are attacking. We can't help but join in singing the 'Tetris' theme. The ball is played into the box and the other Adejokun brother, Josh, restores the Tons' lead. We get carried away in the cheering ourselves. It's an intoxicating atmosphere.

The mood is dampened when Pitshanger are awarded a penalty. Their number five comes up from the back and coolly dispatches it. There's a single loud cheer from the visiting goalkeeper, followed by an ironic cheer from the home crowd and some abuse directed his way. Clapton continue to threaten in wide areas and a low cross from right in front of us is swept in by Noah Adejokun. He seeks out the Pitshanger number five to shush him, obviously not happy with something said after the penalty.

It's 3-2 and the Clapton fans are in jubilant mood. They tease the number five every time he gets on the ball, but he remains composed. The same can't be said for some of the crowd as things spill over into an argument. I can't understand what's being said, because the two canine protagonists are barking at each other. On the pitch, Clapton look to extend their lead, but miss a series of chances. The football feels incidental to the experience. There's a festival vibe. It's hard to tell whether the game picked up, or whether feeling part of the crowd, singing with a beer in hand, was the key factor. Clapton continue to produce chances, but cannot add to the scoresheet, so the game ends 3-2 to the Tons.

After the match there's a sporting chant of 'Well played Dynamo' and fist bumps for the home side. A band of ultras behind the far goal set off red flares. We head to the toilet block in the clubhouse and pass Walthamstow fans coming the other way, leaving their game. It's impossible to tell they have won 5-1, in contrast to the Clapton fans who are celebrating with the team as if they've won the league. We use the facilities and I have to reassure Mark we haven't stumbled into the dressing rooms, as the aroma of Lynx Africa is rather overwhelming.

The attendance was 357. They gave no figure for the number of dogs, but there were quite a few. I'm not sure why bringing dogs to non-league football is a thing, and it's not clear what's in it for them. We had thoroughly enjoyed ourselves, though, and discuss plans to bring some other friends along for a day out. This was by far and away the best atmosphere I had come across in English football. There might have been wilder goal celebrations in bigger crowds, or the odd cup game with an electric atmosphere, but nothing like this for an ordinary league game. I had thought the Fisher fans had been good in midweek, but this was on another level.

My misgivings that this might be like stepping into a 1970s trade union meeting were unfounded. It was just a jovial atmosphere of like-minded people, who were welcoming and without the malice that is evident in some crowds. If clubs known for a far-right following are typified by displays of racism, xenophobia and violence, this wasn't the far-left equivalent. Their politics were on display in the many banners, but there was far more levity on the terrace than you might expect. I may question if I'm sufficiently left-leaning and liberal enough to become a Clapton ultra, but it seemed more fun than the conservative mindset of Arsenal supporters worried about traditional values and financial prudence.

It was a remarkable football-supporting experience and maybe that should be a key factor in deciding who to follow. After all, if players come and go, managers come and go, and at this level grounds come and go, then all that's left is the fans. I tell Mark this would have been a very short book if I'd come here first, but there are other clubs I've grown fond of and he asks who is in the running. I build my fantasy non-league club as one with Clapton's atmosphere, Ilford's history, Saffron Walden's ground, Fisher's location, and Hashtag's online content. If I take Clapton's pre-2018 history and the more conveniently located Old Spotted Dog ground, that might get me closest to that. Logic might go out of the window when deciding. I have already been surprised by how I've built a certain amount of affection for teams like Hashtag. Now was time to put things to the test and watch some of these teams again. I was certainly looking forward to coming back to see Clapton, especially when they return to their Old Spotted Dog ground.

I spend most of the journey home humming the 'Tetris' theme and the next day Mark's wife asks why he's been singing Cyndi Lauper's 'Girls Just Want To

Have Fun'. Our trip has clearly buoyed us. In contrast, the West Ham supporters on our train home were talking about how they wanted to hit some geezer.

Chapter 20

#Devsout

THE FIRST team I put to the test is Hashtag. They are being tested at a higher level in the Isthmian League Division One North. The Tags are looking for their first win of the season at home to Brentwood Town. One thing making it more difficult for me to be lured back into Hashtag is a hangover I'm nursing from a barbecue sandwiched in between the Clapton match and today's game. I've arranged to go with Ben and his five-year-old son Henry to see his first match, so there's no backing out. Ben preferred to see Maldon play Heybridge, but that match was rescheduled, or I got the date wrong. Henry is more disappointed that my daughter doesn't fancy coming along. It's an inauspicious start.

I was full of optimism for the new season. Hashtag had been rewarded for their efforts with a re-grading. Their academy series, which showed their open trials, was entertaining and introduced me to some of their new players, including winner Jake Lindsey. They also signed a few others who were more experienced at this level, including Steve 'Nutsy' Sheehan-Hart, whose nickname tells you what sort of centre-half he is.

After an opening day draw, Hashtag were knocked out of the FA Cup at the first hurdle and comprehensively beaten away on the Saturday. They did at least have a league point to their name, unlike Arsenal, but there were similarities in terms of players being absent and questions being asked about how young the squad was.

Hashtag did at least say they would allow those with last year's season tickets to use them this season, which was a lovely gesture and turned the worst-value ticket into just about the best. I would use mine for the first time on this overcast afternoon. There was a slight feeling that I was going out of obligation rather than fear I would miss any action, similar to how I felt going to Arsenal towards the end.

My season ticket helped me jump a queue for the one open turnstile. Then again, having the right change would also have secured an escort through what was described as the executive area. This turned out to be a bar, and I met Ben and Henry, who were no slower through the turnstile, with Ben pleased that under-12s only cost £1. We find a seat at the front of the main stand with kick-off approaching.

Hashtag are in their new blue and yellow kit. Brentwood are in their change strip of all orange. The colours are jarring in my delicate state. I'm also surprised by Brentwood's long history. I briefly lived there as a child, but I wasn't aware of the club, which was probably a result of them ground-sharing elsewhere under a different name. There had been a Brentwood club who reached the quarter-final of the FA Cup in 1886, losing to eventual winners Blackburn Rovers. Another incarnation had performed well in the Southern League before they amalgamated with Chelmsford City. The current club started as Manor Athletic in the 1950s and only became Brentwood Town in 2004. They had won a smattering of local trophies, as well as plaudits for Brentford's win over Arsenal due to Twitter users mixing up their names.

No mix-up for Henry in who he is going to support. He is there to cheer on the blues of Hashtag. There is even some cheering from a small group of Hashtag fans behind the goal, who have songs for a few of the players. Henry has plenty of questions as the game kicks off. Does one team have more players than the other? Has anyone scored a goal? Brentwood nearly do, as they cut the ball back from the byline and the shot is blocked.

I ask him if there are any players he likes. He picks out Lee Hursit, shortly after he has a swerving left-footed strike saved spectacularly by the Brentwood keeper. Ben says there isn't anyone who has caught his eye that he doesn't like. Hashtag continue to build up the play in Brentwood's half. After deciding he is going to support the blues, Henry is concerned whenever Brentwood counter.

Hashtag win a dubious corner, which was just a 'shit shot' according to a visiting fan behind. Ben is relieved no more is said in front of young ears. The referee rectifies his mistake by awarding a soft free kick soon after the corner is taken. But there is nothing soft about a challenge from Hashtag captain Ross Gleed just before half-time. He goes for a fifty-fifty ball at chest height and takes out an opposition player. There's a chorus of disapproval from behind us and the visiting team surrounds the referee. Nutsy is immediately on the scene, trying to stop the Brentwood players reaching the referee. It's no use, and Gleed is sent off once both players are treated by their physios. Also seeing red are Henry's trousers, when he drops his hot dog during the fracas. While Gleed will be apologising to his team-mates, Ben will have to explain himself to his wife after a classic 'Don't tell your mother' treat.

Hashtag hold on until half-time and Henry has more questions. 'Who is the fastest player?' I point out a couple of Hashtag players to watch. Ben is affronted that the conversation is more technical than the ones we have at a game. He then asks who the most aggressive player is. I don't deem it worthy of an answer, so Ben suggests, 'It's the goalkeeper, isn't it? They're always angry.' Before I launch into an impassioned defence on behalf of the goalkeepers' union, I suggest we do a lap of the pitch.

We find a spot behind the goal Hashtag are attacking. Ben suggests we should stand at the other end where he expects most of the action to be. I point out that Henry can join in and make some noise for the home team and encourage him to bang on the back of the stand. Ben instinctively wants to put a stop to it until I point out that it's very much encouraged at football.

The home fans are nearly silenced when Brentwood's Tom Richardson is in on goal. Anthony Page, who stops the initial drive with an outstretched hand, smothers the ball before Richardson can tuck away the rebound. Hashtag haven't given up on creating chances themselves and bring on Jesse Waller-Lassen. He links up well with Jake Lindsey and they combine to create some space in the box. A cross is blocked at short range. There's a muted appeal for handball and the referee awards a penalty. I'm uncertain my explanation that his hand was in an unnatural position was clear for Henry, let alone Ben.

The visiting team aren't convinced it's a penalty either and after a break that represents the majority of time Waller-Lassen has been on the pitch he steps up to take the spot kick. Ben lifts Henry up to see the action. Waller-Lassen places the ball into the net in front of us to make it 1-0. Henry is pleased to have seen a goal. The Hashtag fans celebrate and there's another excuse to bang on the back of the stand, which Ben hopes isn't a habit Henry takes home with him.

Hashtag have a good half an hour to hold on. Brentwood look purposeful coming forward and keep the play mostly down the opposite end of the pitch. Their goalkeeper wanders out of his penalty area, much to Henry's dismay. Ben reassures him it's fine, much in the same way I had to explain to my mum that goalkeepers shouldn't stay rooted to their goal line. One game going on near the goal line at our end is a version of the Eton wall game, being played by some younger supporters against the hoardings, making their own entertainment when Hashtag aren't on the attack.

Just as anything goes in those early versions of the sport, a Brentwood foul in midfield is unpunished and Daniel Ogunleye turns a defender to break through on goal. He slams the ball into the bottom corner to make it one apiece. Soon after, a misplaced pass in Hashtag's overrun midfield leads to a chance for Richardson. His effort cannons off the bar. Henry is concerned. The game is slipping away from Hashtag.

Brentwood's full-backs get forward again. A cross causes some uncertainty, particularly amongst those of us watching from the other end of the ground, and Ogunleye bundles home to give Brentwood the lead. It's a vindication of Ben's experience in watching a team he expects to lose over Henry's hope that the action will be in front of us. Brentwood look to press home their advantage and hit the bar again, before being awarded a penalty soon after. Richardson steps up to take the kick. Ben predicts he will go left. Then changes his mind and says right. No hesitation for Richardson as he sends it down the middle to make it 3-1.

Brentwood have a chance to add a fourth at the end, but Richardson overruns it before back-heeling the ball to a team-mate who can't get a shot away. There is to be no fairy-tale comeback. It's a harsh lesson for Henry that your team doesn't always win, and for Hashtag that teams will punish you at this level. Ben does at least have a plan: that he can take Henry to see a different team in blue and pretend it's the same one. It's less clear what Hashtag can do to turn things around.

Just as Arsenal have gotten off to a poor start, both they and Hashtag should have enough quality to move up their respective tables. There are fundamental concerns about both sides and plenty of opinions on social media. It's the usual mix of the sensible all the way through to the outrageously ill-informed. In Hashtag's case they do seem to lack pace at centre-back and miss the direct running of Josh Osude up front. George Smith continued his goalscoring duck in my presence, but the reference to him sitting deeper than his hairline was a tactically astute, if a little harsh, observation. The most outrageous were the calls for manager Jay Devereux to go and for Spencer to spend some money.

Some armchair fans expected Hashtag to race through the leagues, as if it were a game of *Football Manager*. There were plenty of rival teams' supporters willing to knock the club for not doing so. It was this reaction that put my back up and made me feel more a part of the club. I had been to the game. I saw first-hand what they were trying to do and how hard the league would be. I felt more informed than those armchair pundits. It was the 'us against the world' siege mentality, which teams often talk about.

The game itself was poor. The result was disappointing. At best, it was a bit of fresh air to clear the hangover. It wasn't the carnival atmosphere of watching Clapton a couple of days ago, despite a similar-sized crowd of 352 in attendance. I will go again, as the story of this club remained one to follow, but had I just fallen into the habit or was there something more to it? I couldn't say.

As for Henry, his favourite bit was when the blue team scored and he didn't like it when the orange team scored, which is the level of analysis most fans can give after a game. He was drawn into the contest, but football would remain below farms, dinosaurs and space in his interests for now.

Chapter 21

I've seen carthorses
better than you

THE LAST thing I need right now is to throw another team into the mix. I watched Brightlingsea Regent away at Enfield Town last season and was keen to check out one of their home games. This was mainly because I could combine an Isthmian Premier League game with a trip to the seaside. There are some good sides at this level and their opponents, Lewes, were also going well in the league and caught my attention for other reasons.

The Rooks are a fan-owned club from Sussex and the first to offer equal pay to their men's and women's first teams. They also generated some media attention for installing beach huts for use as executive boxes, which are at one end of their evocatively named Dripping Pan ground. I am meeting one of their 1,400 owners, a former Arsenal fan, and colleague of Vicki's at the Football Supporters' Association, Richard Irving.

Before meeting Richard, I arrive early to go for a stroll along the seafront. It is a glorious September afternoon. The sun glistens on the sea and plenty of families are making use of their beach huts. The town is well kept, with neat flowerbeds and an assortment of Victorian houses.

This all feels a little too genteel for a day at the football. Nearer to the ground, it's both comforting and disturbing to see a burnt-out car and someone complaining 'this place gets more like Jaywick by the day'. There is a lone flag in Regent's colours hanging from a window as I turn into the road leading up to the Taydal Stadium. Home fans aren't waiting to ambush any visitors; instead there are just a couple of car park marshals, who wave hello.

I pay £12 and clack my way through the turnstile gate, before paying another £2 for a programme and spending the rest of my change on raffle tickets. The sun is beating down and the Brightlingsea team are doing their stretches as near to the shade of the main stand as they can. I walk a lap of the ground. Regent goalkeeper Charlie Turner is peppered with crosses from the goalkeeping coaches. There's an odd assortment of covered areas, with some smart terracing to one side of the goal, if two steps can count as terracing. On the far touchline is another turnstile, subs' benches, scaffolding for a TV gantry that's not being used, and scaffolding that is being used as a small stand. This must be the stand that the club purchased off eBay when they needed extra capacity to meet ground grading requirements. It's worrying to know such items exist on eBay, as it will tempt me to look for them late at night, and if I thought collecting a kayak would be difficult, I dread to think how I would get a stand home.

I turn into the shade of the covered terrace behind the other goal. It's painted in neat blocks of black and red, like much of the ground, and leads me to the changing rooms, refreshment kiosk and clubhouse. I sit under the cover of the main stand and watch the contrasting styles on display in the warm-up. Lewes are playing a small-sided game. The Regent defenders are belting the ball down the touchline from one half of the pitch to the other, with several going out of play and requiring the need for an alert of 'heads!'

I go to the bar to meet Richard, who is with a small band of away supporters, which includes chairman Stuart Fuller. They have come by taxi from Colchester, preferring the pubs on offer there to the ones in Brightlingsea. Richard explains away games are more enjoyable for the volunteers, as they don't have various duties that take them away from watching the football with a beer. Richard is no longer Lewes's away match secretary, which is part of someone's full-time job. Otherwise he would arrive an hour before kick-off to get the team sheet from the manager and exchange it with the opposition. He now volunteers with his wife on directors' hospitality for home games.

We stand behind the goal Lewes are attacking. I feel like we should be watching cricket in this heat and we continue to talk about Lewes, fan ownership and problems with the modern game as the match gets underway. At least we won't miss any action, because unlike cricket, it isn't happening far away in the middle. Razz Coleman De-Graft gets to the byline in front of us and cuts the ball back. Joe Taylor, a big mobile number nine, shoots. The small band of away supporters expect the net to bulge, but it's a let-off for Regent, as the ball bobbles wide.

I ask Richard who are the Lewes players to watch and he names most of the front six, who have experience higher up at Leyton Orient and Bromley, with a couple of others following the new manager over from Cray Wanderers in the summer. He expects them to win comfortably today and I can't say I've seen anything from Brightlingsea that would suggest otherwise. I express my surprise that Regent have been operating at this level for the last five seasons. In a town of 9,000, with only 183 people in attendance today, it's a remarkable achievement. Richard suggests they must either be in a good catchment area for players, or someone somewhere must be putting a lot of money in to keep them going.

Money in football is a topic that is never far away, and I'm keen to understand the benefits of fan ownership. Richard tells me about his role at the FSA providing support to fan-owned clubs, helping them run sustainably and providing community-run clubs with a guiding hand. The key principles for these types of clubs are to be not-for-profit, sustainable, and not run as vanity projects.

I ask whether this could ever work at a club like Arsenal. Richard sees it as a bottom-up approach. AFC Wimbledon, Exeter City and Newport County are paving the way for fan-owned clubs in the league. He has high hopes for AFC Wimbledon, who, if they were to reach the Championship, would show others what is possible. To compete in the Premier League would require a change in the law.

The FSA have been involved in the Independent Fan-Led Review of Football Governance, chaired by Tracey Crouch MP. The interim report notes the critical social, civic and cultural role clubs play in their local communities and that they are not ordinary businesses. It flags up the need for protection, including from club owners. It also acknowledges that clubs should not be immune from the ordinary financial controls, checks, balances and behaviours that are good practice in any multi-million-pound company but too often can be absent across the game.

Among the recommendations is the establishment of a new governing body covering financial regulation, corporate governance and ownership aspects of the game. Mechanisms to protect heritage assets such as grounds have been mooted, with ideas including a golden share, more fan engagement with club boards and greater transparency.

Richard supports these recommendations and points out that Lewes's accounts are available online. On the pitch, they look to open their account. Razz gets in behind the left-back again. He crosses low, and it's helped on for Ollie Tanner to put Lewes in front.

I ask where Richard sees Lewes's natural ceiling if they are operating sustainably. He says this level, or maybe even the one below, is about right, based on home crowds of around 500. The club is ambitious after a brief taste of the National League not long ago.

The team have designs on adding to their lead and Joe Taylor lays it square to Taylor Maloney to make it 2-0. The away following take it in their stride and the small band of Regent ultras give us a rendition of '2-0 and you still don't sing'. I might have cause to cheer if my raffle tickets come up, but the lady walking around with the winning numbers doesn't have any of mine.

The half-time whistle goes and the away fans head for the bar. I check the big screen in the smart clubhouse to see Arsenal have the lead against Burnley. Richard doesn't give it a second glance as he gets a round in. I'm impressed that they have polypins of beer from the local Colchester brewery, but the Lewes contingent aren't enthralled with it, no doubt spoiled by the Harvey's brewed locally to them.

We take up a position behind the other goal for the second half. We are shaded, as if we are in a beach hut on the seafront. Instead of watching the ferry crossing to Mersea Island, we are watching Ollie Tanner crossing low into the penalty area. A lone Brightlingsea fan is taking as long as a paddle-boarder to swap ends and starts a chant. Richard notes it's hardly West Ham's Inter City Firm taking the North Bank.

There's some ferocity on the pitch as a Regent defender boots the ball into a prostrate opponent after he's fouled. It doesn't spill over and I ask Richard why he stopped supporting Arsenal. His one-word answer is 'Kroenke'. Richard tells me his dad watched Arsenal since the 1940s and took him to his first games. He became a shareholder and owns a flat in the old ground. When Kroenke completed his buyout, he bought up the shares of the many independent shareholders, like Richard, and with it a big part of his identity. What was a small slice of a club Richard cared about deeply became just another tiny part of the American's business portfolio; a number on a spreadsheet somewhere. Lewes look to increase their figures on the scoresheet, as a cross comes in to Taylor. He shoots straight at the keeper's legs.

Richard's last Arsenal game was in 2017 and he got into Lewes after moving to the area. We wonder how many other Arsenal fans have drifted away and who is going to replace them, as they price younger supporters out. So long as the TV money keeps rolling in, Kroenke is unlikely to worry about so-called 'legacy fans'. Watching a game on TV is a passive experience and you miss so many of the little things that add to the matchday experience. We see straight away that a long goal kick is going to land between Joe Taylor and Regent's keeper just outside the box. The flag doesn't go up. Taylor challenges the keeper with a high foot. No sign the ref is going to award a free kick. The ball breaks to Taylor. The keeper is in no-man's land, and Taylor slots it past a recovering defender to make it 3-0.

The Regent fans continue to get behind their team, but their side is well beaten. Lewes are given plenty of time in the box and it's only Charlie Turner keeping the score down with a series of saves. Regent centre-back Chris Ribchester attempts to stem the tide, but Ollie Tanner is too quick for him and takes a crack to the shin for his troubles. It's a clumsy tackle and a definite yellow, but the sound as much as anything sees a red card produced. Ribchester trudges off. A Lewes fan tells him 'I've seen carthorses better than you'. Ribchester glares at him, but leaves it at that.

Richard remembers he hasn't checked in on the *Futbology* groundhopping app to record his attendance. He asks if I'm on there and whether I will just continue going to different grounds if I don't find a team. I can see the appeal, but want to avoid feeding my more obsessive tendencies, after already wondering how close I am to visiting all the grounds in Essex.

Lewes go close to adding a fourth goal. Sub Iffy Allen goes for goal when Taylor is better-placed. Soon after, he scuffs a shot. Not long after that, Taylor dummies and Maloney bags his second of the afternoon to add some much-deserved gloss to the victory. The full-time whistle goes. The Regent fans are still singing, while Richard and the Lewes supporters are hoping their taxi returns to collect them.

This is the second time I've seen Brightlingsea and both times I've done the equivalent of flirting with the waitress on a date. They are a good little club operating at a decent level, and much like Wivenhoe, if I lived locally, I would happily support them. It's great to see them offering free season tickets to local schoolchildren and I hope they can build their small but loyal following.

I may even be tempted to watch a few more games here, but I don't think they are the club for me.

As for their opponents, I can also see the appeal of people from far and wide wanting to get involved in a fan ownership scheme and the team did their bit with a good attacking display, but my interest in them is perhaps from more of a groundhopper's perspective, rather than wanting to become a long-distance fan.

I may not have found a new team, but I enjoyed the game and take a leisurely stroll back to the car, treating myself to an ice cream on the way. On the drive home, I pass Colchester United's new ground next to the A12. This is the closest league ground to where I live and a convenient drive, yet it's never appealed to me in the way their old Layer Road ground did. I will of course need to pay it a visit if I'm going to visit all the grounds in Essex, but I'm more enthused about the inconvenient trip to Harwich & Parkeston's old ground, or visiting the less salubrious towns along the Thames Estuary.

I'm left wondering whether the team I support should be fan-owned. The ability to own part of a club builds a sense of belonging. It was part of Richard's bond with Arsenal, even if then-chairman Peter Hill-Wood avoided answering his question at an AGM. At least he didn't get the apocryphal 'Thank you for the interest in our affairs' response. We were under no illusions that things were perfect before Kroenke's time. The patrician owner appears long gone and the real kicker when I was trying to understand if fan ownership is better was when Richard said: 'It's not as if private ownership is doing well; look at the number of league clubs going into administration.' With that in mind, it's great the FSA exists to help supporters' groups get involved in running their clubs and avoid the traps others fall into.

Since several fan-owned clubs are transparent with their book-keeping, I rather uncharacteristically take it upon myself to go through Lewes's and Clapton's accounts the day after the game. Now I'm by no means an accountant or good with figures, but, still basking in the glow of being at a game, I am prepared to go down various rabbit holes looking into the teams I'd recently seen. Lewes were clearly the bigger operation, with a £527,000 turnover, making a £159,000 profit. They had significant expenses in relation to the upkeep of their ground, whilst Clapton were only paying around £8,000 a year for pitch hire. Lewes' total wage bill comes to £322,000, so I estimate a player's average salary to be £137 per week. Clapton only pay travelling expenses, being at a level just above that where players are paying subs. Lewes command greater matchday revenue, given the minimum ticket pricing at their level, with Clapton only asking for donations. Clapton appeared to make significantly more than Lewes from merchandising, no doubt aided by their away shirt sales. Overall, the margins were fine and the need to find new ways to bring money in was ever present.

One thing that struck me as noteworthy was that Lewes received around £200,000 in directors' loans. They had converted some to donations and others were partially repayable in the unlikely event of reaching the FA Cup second round, or selling a player for more than £10,000. They made these pre-Covid and they were the difference between turning a profit and posting a loss. It begged the question of how sustainably Lewes were being run. There was nothing at all untoward about these arrangements and smaller private donations totalled £98,000. It showed that even well-run clubs could be reliant on one or two individuals to keep them afloat, or help them grow. There would always be the temptation for clubs to live beyond their means, or want to keep up with others, and this shows the need for the sort of regulatory reforms the FSA supports.

This was far more due diligence than anyone ever needed to choose a football team. It showed that despite the game recapturing my imagination, I would never be far from the economic realities that spoiled my enjoyment of top-flight football.

Chapter 22

You're shit, but your bird is fit

IT WAS time to spice things up in my relationship with Hashtag. Maybe a change of scenery would rekindle some of that initial spark. It was time to go away with them. Witham on a wet Tuesday night isn't anyone's choice of setting for a romantic mini-break, but with football the romance is often in the gritty setting and maybe I was getting drawn into the groundhopping side of things. Hashtag would be looking for their first away points of the season, having recorded their first win in a shock 3-0 victory over Maldon & Tiptree. The Tags were still languishing near the foot of the table, after a series of poor results either side of the Maldon game.

Witham had started the season well, but didn't interest me as a club, or indeed a town. It was looked upon as the poor relation to Chelmsford, where people only seemed to move because it was cheaper, albeit still unaffordable. Witham is mainly famous for having a lone ultra following their team and being the constituency of former Home Secretary, Priti Patel, who disappointingly isn't the lone ultra.

I went into the game thinking about my ex. Arsenal had won the north London derby at the weekend and there were some pangs of regret at not being there. Watching highlights of a committed display, seeing the photo of Arteta celebrating a goal, and videos on social media of fans celebrating after the game, showed passion. Despite the ills at the top of the game, I couldn't deny the drama and feeling that accompanied the greed and soap opera surrounding it all.

The other big news story was a national petrol shortage, which led to several postponements in non-league. For once I have a full tank and remember to check the game was on before making the short hop to Witham. Any hopes of people being put off driving and bagging a car parking space at the ground are dashed, and as the clock ticks towards kick-off, I crawl along the lane to the ground and back out again.

I park nearby and trot back up the lane to join a long queue to enter the Simarco Stadium. This sounds like a Serie A venue, but is a ground in the corner of extensive playing fields at the edge of a sprawling 1960s estate, backing on to a railway line. Simarco are a logistics firm and clearly don't have any input into the turnstile operation, as everyone is waiting at the lone open turnstile, while others lie redundant. A supervisor shouts out it is cash only, which reduces the queue by a couple of people who have to go back down the lane to the nearest cashpoint. Someone jokes from behind, 'Do you accept crypto?'

I pay my £8 entry, £2 for a programme, then another £2 for golden goal tickets, which part of me worries will somehow increase the chance of it finishing 0-0, a result that I would readily accept, being more interested in seeing Hashtag get some points than being entertained. The entertainment is in the jeopardy of not knowing what will happen. I take a seat in the far stand on the halfway line, my equivalent of picking a cinema seat in the middle of the back row. The pitch is framed like a screen, with the dimly-lit stand contrasting with the bright green pitch beneath the floodlights.

The action gets underway and it's a frantic start. The cinematic version of the game would open with lots of close-ups showing pained expressions as players strain every sinew to get to the ball, cutting to a shot of the ball at someone's feet, before it's passed away hurriedly, and a sliding tackle comes crunching in. There would be motivational calls from the captains, jump cuts to fans imploring their team forward and some sort of moment of high drama. In reality, it was more like a badly directed battle scene. Tackles were flying in, the ball was pinging about, players were all shouting at once. Those sitting nearby were just chatting amongst themselves, and there was no obvious narrative to follow.

Off screen, or behind some pillars if you prefer, Hashtag work the ball into a crossing position. The ball enters the frame at stomach height for the Witham keeper, who curiously punches, clearing the danger in an unorthodox manner. Less unorthodox was a crunching tackle from a Witham defender, which fired the ball off the wall of the clubhouse back into the penalty area, such was its ferocity. The first touch from the resulting Hashtag throw also pings towards the clubhouse.

I try to capture this passage of play on film, knowing it won't make any highlights package, but as soon as I take my phone out, the game lapses into a series of long balls into the corner and hoofed clearances. I'm then easily distracted by passing trains, and a steady stream of supporters shuffling past to go for refreshments. It's a young crowd with the odd group of players' relatives cheering on their man, so I restrain myself from calling for a foul on a Hashtag player and for them to kick a Witham player in the shins, after he's opted for the child-sized-shin pad-and-rolled-down-socks look.

Before the break, Hashtag have a couple of half-chances. The Witham keeper is almost caught in possession before clearing. Then a Witham defender makes a superb recovery tackle as Toby Aromolaran, fresh from *Love Island*, looks to score. Now, under normal circumstances, a player missing pre-season to feature on a reality TV show would draw my ire, but it was a move that would set him up financially in a way eighth-tier football never would. There couldn't be any complaints that the players at this level were earning too much money, or not putting in a shift. In terms of quality, it was a case of getting what you pay for. I expect things to settle down in the second half at least.

The referee blows for half-time and a calm descends. The pitch empties. There's no more imploring team-mates, just a bunch of substitutes having a half-hearted kick-about, and someone in the crowd announcing he's going to get a sandwich and a pink monster. I flick through the programme, spotting some reasonably priced hospitality deals and the ground regulations in full. There's a potentially unreasonable regulation referring to anyone 'whose presence within the Ground is, or could (in the Club's reasonable opinion), constitute a source of danger, nuisance, or annoyance to any other person.' And if I've avoided annoying anyone, I'm not sure whether recording a snippet on my phone falls foul of the impenetrable regulation 19 on filming.

I hear a tinny radio version of 'Eye of the Tiger' drift across the pitch, which gives the song a less uplifting quality. Were it a film soundtrack, it would point towards an equally poor second half. I remember to check my golden goal times, expecting to find times that have since passed. I'm relieved to find there will be some added drama for me around 56 and 76 minutes. Elton John's 'I'm Still Standing' then comes on, which I take as a good omen.

Hashtag kick off the second half and go direct with a raking ball into the channel for Harry Honesty to chase. It's a departure from their usual approach and, having struggled to detect any patterns in play until this point, I'm pleased to spot a tactical change. It's hardly up there with Jonathan Wilson's analysis, but for much of the time this level seems to have more in common with under-10s all running after the ball than overlapping centre-backs and inverted tea ladies. It's with some satisfaction that the highlights afterwards show Dev's half-time team talk boiling down to 'Keep things simple and don't overplay it.'

Early in the second half, I realise I didn't check the exact time they kicked off. It must be close to 56 minutes now. Witham have a corner and I wonder whether I would choose £45 over Hashtag's chances. It's telling that I would sooner Hashtag stay on level terms, which they do. That said, the prospect of £45 doesn't keep me on the edge of my seat for the next 20 minutes either. The main moment of excitement is when a ball sails over the bar towards the railway line and I try to work out whether it made it to the track. My guess is that the ball didn't quite make it up the embankment, so I won't see what happens if a train were to run it over.

The next thing I notice is how far apart the dugouts are from each other. They are level with the 18-yard line at each end of the pitch. Unable to think of any other examples further apart, I decide this must be some sort of record and a nightmare for fourth officials. I look for a fourth official and realise they don't have them at this level. Despite my mind wandering, I am enjoying the game. The ground is more atmospheric than it appears from a passing train. It's fully enclosed, with some small terracing and quite a few fans. There are moments when the play is immediately in front of me. There are chances, as Joni Vukaj snatches at a cut-back and a defender on the line stops his bobbling effort. Home supporters become animated about the award of a throw-in. There's enough to get the Hashtag fans singing 'It's the Hashtag boys making all the noise' to which a lone Witham fan replies, 'No you ain't.' Unfortunately, the lone Witham ultra isn't in attendance to create any more atmosphere. There are 371 in the crowd, though.

It looks like home fans will have something to cheer as their stocky number nine, Greg Akpele, holds off his man and gets away a shot at Anthony Page in the Hashtag goal. Page saves awkwardly with his foot, in the manner of someone distractedly passing a ball back to a group of kids in a playground, while pushing their own child's swing. He collects the ball, and the kids did at least say 'Thank you' to me for a dreadful pass off my shin, which has played on my mind since.

One kid sat along the row from me collects the ball more comfortably than Page, as a clearance is belted at him. A defender apologises, but the lad is delighted with his work and getting to touch the ball. He tells his mates that is the highlight of the game so far and it's one of the few things I've noted as we approach the 76th minute. Witham have another corner around this time and the kids prove less likeable with their umpteenth appeal for VAR after a routine free kick is awarded.

I decide to make my way back round to the exit and stand behind the goal Hashtag are attacking for the last ten minutes. I find myself stood next to injured defender Nutsy and a small entourage. There's concern as Witham attack. There's more concern when he mentions the players 'don't talk much' on the pitch, which is a fatal mistake at this level. Hashtag break and Honesty is in. There's no one to pass to, so he takes a shot. It sails well over. Nutsy's entourage bemoan Hashtag's attacking options. They do have the wind on their side, as a cold blast feels like it will blow the corrugated metal stand over.

It's far more than a gust of wind that takes Aromolaran down in the box soon after. Hashtag have a penalty. I'm tempted to film the key moment. It's not the ground regulations stopping me, more the worry I might jinx it, as the irrational thinking common of so many fans takes over. Kris Newby steps up and makes no mistake in putting the Tags in front. I form a belief that Hashtag score a disproportionate number of goals when I've gone to stand behind the goal they are attacking; the sort of superstitious thinking a fan develops.

I move along the terrace behind the goal, passing a jubilant group of Hashtag superfans, and stand near the corner flag. Again, I'm in the right place for the action, as this is where Hashtag keep the ball. They do a decent job of it and even create a couple of chances. Newby blasts a shot straight at the keeper. Then Flood and Debell almost bundle their way through before running it out of play. Hashtag slow the game down as Aromolaran is subbed off, to chants of 'You're shit, but your bird is fit' from a group of home fans behind the away dugout.

Witham have the chance to get the ball into the box and despite my increasing superstition and emotional investment in the team, I am nerveless. Just as calm is

Page, who comes to gather the ball. 'How long?' goes up a panic-induced cry from a team-mate. 'Two minutes,' comes the reply. About two seconds later, the referee blows up and I look to beat the rush out of the exit gate. I'm caught up in a scrum of kids looking for selfies with Spencer, who is commentating from a small booth. It's not been a classic and the production team will have a job pulling any highlights together. The Tags have secured a valuable three points, and I am buoyed by the result. I return to the car with a spring in my step, which is helped when I see a police van blocking the lane to the ground and having to reverse back to let everyone else out, while I have a quick getaway.

Chapter 23

Hope you've got a strong neck

FOR MOST football fans, planning which games to go to is a simple case of looking at a single team's fixture list and keeping an eye out for postponements and rearranged kick-offs. As I've taken an interest in several clubs, I'm scanning several fixture lists and always on the lookout for different opportunities to watch a game. There are often several games that take my fancy and then I need to factor in family commitments. My next match is a case in point. An opportunity arose when I needed to go into the office for work and I looked to see if Clapton Community, Fisher or Ilford were at home. Ilford are hosting Clapton (non-community) and Cricklefields is on the way home. Then Mrs C asks me to get back early as she has plans. Her plans are cancelled as I'm about to head home and before I know it, I'm off to the game again.

I'm pleased to be seeing Ilford and giving them some support. The official attendance for a recent match against White Ensign was 26. This was despite Ensign striking up a friendship with Rangers on Twitter. After Leigh-on-Sea-based Catholic United congratulated Celtic on the signing of a former player and received an influx of support, Southend-based Ensign sought to do the same. Playing on their naval links, they generated a lot of online interest and some merchandise sales, but it hadn't translated into increased attendances.

Ilford's results had been mixed. They were languishing towards the bottom of the table, but had snatched points late on in two of their most recent games. An incident that seemed to typify their luck and cast them in my mind as some sort of heroic underdog worth rooting for occurred in their FA Cup qualifier. Up against Barking from the league above, they won 2-1. Soon after, messages appeared that the result was being looked into. Barking reported Ilford for fielding players without international clearance. These players had played in the competition in previous seasons and Ilford protested they had acted in good faith, going on what previous clubs had told them. A replay was ordered and Ilford lost 2-1.

I last saw Clapton being comprehensively beaten by Hashtag, and now, having seen their rival breakaway team, Clapton Community, I was keen to see them beaten again. Both sides were close to the relegation places, and I hoped to see Ilford lift themselves further from the drop zone. The programme noted that these clubs must have faced each other in excess of 400 times, with attendances of around 4,000 commonplace for the fixture. Both were grand old non-league teams, but like the boarded-up Cauliflower gin palace nearby, both had seen better days. With that option for a pre-match drink ruled out, I go straight to the ground.

The turnstile operator apologises for the slow card machine. There isn't a queue behind me to make it a concern. The machine eventually takes my payment and the operator asks if I know where I'm going. I confidently reply that I've been before and then realise I haven't been to the bar. A sign points left to the toilets and straight on to the bar. I assume this means up a fire escape and need Ilford chairman/manager, Adam Peek, to point me in the right direction, as he bemoans the cost of something or somebody.

Walking into the bar is like walking into the wake of a distant and unpopular relative. It's eerily quiet, despite a couple at one table and a pair of older blokes at another. There is nothing on tap, so I settle for a bottle of Doom Bar for a very reasonable £3. I take a seat by a large picture window, where I have a view of the pitch. Ilford are warming up with some running drills, during which a player somehow falls over.

I recognise the photographer from my last game here and he introduces himself as the vice-chairman to the two older blokes, who must be Clapton officials. They talk about how they are just trying to keep their old clubs going. The conversation turns to the Clapton ultras and an anecdote about how they abused an accountant friend who was loosely involved in the acrimonious split. One of the group declares, 'Anti-fascists are fascists. If you don't agree with them, they shut you down. Just like that lot blocking the roads. Or vegans. It's a case of I'm right, you're wrong.' Now I might not agree with those opinions, but I did at least respect their viewpoint and the need for more civility. These seemed like people who were genuine in their concern for keeping two grand old non-league clubs going.

The conversation didn't change my feelings towards either Clapton club, but it threw some shade on things. Non-league was like an HBO box set you want to binge watch, with its feuds, rivalries and battles to survive. The more I looked into these teams, the more interesting it was becoming. The Premier League in contrast was more like a latter edition of an action movie franchise, becoming ever more preposterous to the point of self-parody, with the latest news being the controversial takeover of Newcastle United going through, and more billions being thrown at the game.

No astronomical figures tonight, as I count no more than 12 fans in the crowd. The teams come out of the tunnel, making their own noise to get themselves going. I get myself another Doom Bar and buy a copy of Michael Foley's *History of Ilford Football Club 1881–2000*, and settle down with my notepad, imagining I'm some sort of booze-soaked old football hack, but looking more like I'm doing some accounting. I flick through the programme and spot several roles requiring volunteers, including stadium announcer, which sounds like it would be fun. I imagine all the witty and edgy remarks I could make to become the Cyril the Swan of announcers until I realise I would mangle many of the squad's surnames worse than Paul Merson on *Soccer Saturday*.

Another supporter comes in to find the bar is now unattended. 'I hope you've got a strong neck,' he says. 'You'll need it to see all the long balls. Route one stuff. Dog and Duck. It's shit.' Ilford's first ball does indeed go over the top and is collected comfortably by the Clapton keeper. 'Is that Barlow playing?' he asks. 'I've no idea,' I reply; there is no announcer to read out the teams after all. He helps himself to a coffee and pays up when the barman returns.

I ask the supporter how come he's here if it's so shit? He explains he runs the shop downstairs and was the assistant manager until he got fed up with 'all of the shit', which he refrains from elaborating on. I now recollect seeing him on the bench at the Saffron Walden game, only he looks a lot younger without the matchday stress. We try to work out who is in the side today. The pacey wingers I'd seen before aren't playing and it's Clapton's left-winger who is nearly in. He asks if I'm a scout, which I've long been expecting someone to ask given I'm in possession of a notebook at matches. I explain what I'm writing and he asks if I've actually seen any decent football. We discuss the Saffron Walden game. He then asks me the sort of question I get from my father-in-law, seemingly simple to see if I'm with it, but one I can't help thinking is set to trip me up. 'There's three types of passes. You know what they are?' I'm thinking of good, shit, and am struggling for a third when he answers himself: 'Forward, backwards and sideways. It's a simple game. They just need to keep it simple.' As if to prove his point, Ilford give the ball away again.

I ask why such a historic name in non-league, based in a good location, is struggling. He mentions that they don't use an entrance gate that leads on to a main road, that people don't want to watch a struggling team and that they don't pay the players. I ask if that matters at this level; no one is getting enough to make that big a difference. It turns out there's always teams willing to pay that bit more. Some players will use a team like Ilford as a shop window, but most aren't any good at this level.

The former assistant manager provides another damning assessment, saying, 'I was told as a player, if you end up having to play at this level, you've had it.' The Ilford keeper clears into touch trying to find a team-mate and the assistant manager in him comes out as he yells, 'For fuck's sake, just play it long down the middle.'

I suggest there can't be much money coming in to improve things on the playing front. The former assistant and barman lament the fact that £7,000–£8,000 a year goes on rent for the pitch. They point out that £3,000 was spent on a Veo box to record the games. Not much is happening to record right now. The Clapton number seven might like to watch back a tackle in the box he feels was a penalty. A wry laugh from the former assistant manager suggests it was close.

Approaching half-time and Clapton get forward down the right. The linesman flags for a foul and the referee plays advantage. The cross comes in. There's a free header for a Clapton forward. The keeper gets down, but it squirms under him and into the net. 'One chance, one goal. Typical,' says the barman.

A second chance presents itself to Clapton from a corner soon after. A low cross isn't dealt with. A Clapton forward gets a foot on it to direct the ball goalwards, but with little power. Another forward is unmarked at the back post to sweep it in for 2-0. The whistle blows for the interval and I go downstairs to the refreshment kiosk and have to explain that I am coming back for the second half, as the former assistant manager says goodbye as if I'm leaving and he can't blame me.

The kiosk is closed, so I go back to the bar. Dinner will have to comprise crisps, a Snickers and a hot chocolate, since they sold the last Doom Bar while I popped out. It looks like the buffet for the committee is just a plate of crisps as well, which has appeared on the table the Clapton contingent are sitting at. The Ilford photographer/vice-chair comes in and asks if we are warm enough, before opening one of the floor to ceiling windows, so he can take photos during the second half. While those in the bar ready themselves for the second half, a Clapton potshot from distance pings off the crossbar.

The photographer/vice-chair complains there wasn't a single highlight to capture in the first half. It might get worse as a Clapton forward controls a cross-field ball perfectly with the outside of his left foot and is in on goal. He takes his time and then the chance is gone, as a defender slides in. It's soon the Clapton defence's turn to be stretched, as the Ilford number 12 breaks down the left. His cross is cleared. The ball is played back in over the top. Me and the photographer/vice-chair are convinced it's a penalty, the former assistant manager less so.

After that flurry of activity, conversation turns to whether they should set up a vets' team. The barman is roped in. I'm asked if I'm old enough. The photographer/vice-chair is more interested in planning to use the long-jump pit to practise his bunker shots and the goalmouth for playing out of the rough. Another committee member joins us and is introduced to me as the author of the Ilford history book. He soon laments, 'I know they've been told to go long because of the state of the pitch, but they're losing every header.'

'C'mon Andre, pass the fucking thing,' exclaims the former assistant manager, as the Ilford number 12 cuts inside and is caught head-down in possession. Clapton quickly play the ball out to the left. A forward is in on the advancing keeper and dinks it over him for 3-0. There's much consternation about Andre's role. He's looked lively, but hasn't done the basics.

Ilford keep going and the photographer/vice-chair compliments a player's workrate. The club historian points out, 'He's chasing balls he should have controlled in the first place.' He has a keen eye for what players are and aren't doing. I'm barely able to detect any quality and Ilford miss a very presentable chance from a couple of yards out, which the keeper smothers. 'Just

231

£400 a week for a playing budget would make all the difference,' the club historian concludes. He's hopeful an exhibition about the club's history later in the month will generate some interest in the club and there's an in-depth conversation about the practicalities of blowing up an action shot of the team to cover a wall. Rather poignantly, he says: "We've got loads of stuff about our past, but the exhibition should also be about the club's future and we have got nothing on that.'

The only action from the pitch to distract from conversations in the bar is the constant shouting of the Clapton keeper. The photographer/vice-chair has had enough of him claiming for things going on in the other half and every other word being 'fucking'. He acknowledges that having a vocal goalkeeper to organise the defence is important and the Ilford stand-in hasn't impressed on that front. After the full-time whistle goes, he's keen to pick that up with one of the Clapton officials, saying there might not be any kids here, but it's not on. He's otherwise magnanimous in defeat. I spotted one lad with his dad, no doubt as unimpressed as I was watching this level of football as a kid.

As an adult, I felt differently. The game was dreadful, but watching from the bar with a couple of drinks, talking football with the former assistant manager and just being immersed in the game was a decent night out. It didn't get me any closer to making my mind up about Ilford as a team to follow. I feel like that decision will be made for me. If I attend much more often, I'm sure I'll feel compelled to volunteer in some capacity and keep the show on the road. I would be happy to do so with the right club, but I'm not sure that club is Ilford. Were they a passport to misery every other Saturday? Were they a club where I could make a difference? Or were they a lost cause? Would Mrs C think it a total waste of time when I could be at home with the family?

Chapter 24

We've got the best long-jump pit in the league

A RETURN to the office in my day job gives me the chance to catch midweek games in and around London without worrying too much about messing with Mrs C's plans. I spot Woodford Town are at home to Hoddesdon in the Essex Senior League on a Wednesday night. The Woods had only come to my attention as being a team languishing at the bottom of a league table I was becoming rather familiar with. More recently, they had moved back into Woodford after a 28-year absence and were playing at a new ground, Ashton's playing fields. They attracted around 800 fans for their first game back and were often getting crowds of 500 in a league where most teams did well to hit three figures. The Woods fans also had a reputation for creating a bit of atmosphere.

On the pitch, the team were improving and sitting comfortably in mid-table, but not yet showing any evidence of Brazilian flair to match their club colours.

Tonight's opponents, Hoddesdon, were another lower-mid-table team, albeit with the distinction of being the first winners of the FA Vase. I had so far missed out on seeing any games in what is a national competition for teams at this level and below. Nor had I seen any in its sister competition, the FA Trophy, for teams competing in the fifth to eighth tiers of the game. These competitions and their forerunner, the FA Amateur Cup, generated much prestige in the non-league game and it was good to see another team listed on the roll of honour.

I take the Central Line out to Woodford, which means the ground is within easy reach of both my office and home in Essex. I exit the tube station and follow Snakes Lane downhill, and pass under a bridge carrying the M11 overhead. I pass the site of Woodford's old ground, which is now a playing field. There's no trace of the old stands and it's only the gasometer I had seen in old photographs that confirm this was the former location. It also turns out this incarnation of Woodford Town differs from the one I'm watching tonight.

I approach the ground and there's a 1930s brick pavilion, which I assume belongs to Wood Green and Essex Ladies Athletics Club, who share the site. This is a name I had seen accompany the leading athletes in many local races I'd run, but their only real claim to fame was for being the club Sally Gunnell belonged to. I take the bend round the track somewhat slower in the dark and hurdle a kerb before finding a lone turnstile. A queue builds as someone tries to pay by card. Two old boys don't seem to mind, but one of them quips they might need a telescope to see across the athletics track to the pitch.

When I reach the front of the queue, I pay the £7 entry and £2 for a programme. I look for some form of half-time draw, but find the only competition on offer is a 'spot the ball' picture in the programme. I need to email my guess for the chance to win two pints at the next match. I'm not inclined to drink anything before the game I'm at, so I pass on the opportunity and go for the classic combination of burger and hot chocolate from the catering van. This is accompanied by some 'classic banter' from a group of lads who, in amongst jibes insinuating relations with one of their mate's girlfriends, appreciate the set-up here with the clubhouse and regular Friday night fixtures. Although they also say the standard of football is rubbish long-ball stuff.

There's one option to view the game from and that's in the stand running along one touchline. It's only a handful of rows deep and doesn't provide much elevation to see over the long-jump pits and running track in front. There is a shed end, but unlike Chelsea's, this one is just storage for athletics equipment. A small group of Woodford fans with drums start up a rendition of 'C'mon the Woods' to the tune of 'Auld Lang Syne' and the game gets underway.

As the band move on to 'And it's Woodford Town, making all the sound', it's Hoddesdon making the early running. They get a low shot away, which the

Woods' keeper, Rasmus Kriisa, does well to hold. 'All you need is Town' to the tune of 'All You Need Is Love' accompanies a tricky backpass, which Kriisa shanks for a throw-in, suggesting some composure is also needed. I lose my composure as Mrs C phones to ask why I haven't fixed a broken drawer, during which time Hoddesdon fail to break the deadlock.

Contrary to the banter lads' opinion, Woodford are looking to play out from the back and choose their moment for a ball over the top, rather than send it long every time. As they look to spring the offside trap, I get another call from Mrs C. She appeals for me to tell her where the kids' toothpaste is located, as the Hoddesdon defence appeal in vain for offside. The attack comes to nothing and I hope the game picks up if I'm going to get grief for missing a difficult kid's bedtime for it. There's a chill in the air, too. The game is disjointed. The samba drumming from the Woodford fans feels like I'm listening to a group practising in a nearby community centre; it's so distant from what's happening on the pitch.

A hopeful cross comes in from Hoddesdon. It's cut out, but falls to the visitor's number nine. He takes his time to compose himself. A couple of defenders get back into position, but he curls the ball around them and into Kriisa's net. There's a smattering of applause. I'm impressed that the home fans are so sporting as to acknowledge an ordinary finish until I spot the white and black scarves on a handful of visiting fans. I'm less impressed when I realise the team sheet pinned to the clubhouse wall, which I had photographed, didn't put the numbers against the names of the Hoddesdon players.

Woodford's number 12, Chaynie Burgin, a tall, ungainly forward, looks to respond straight away. He wins a corner. The ball is swung in towards Alex Reed in the Hoddesdon goal. He can only pat the ball down for Woodford's captain, David Agboola, to smash into the net. It's 1-1, and that's how the half ends.

Mist rolls off the River Roding behind the far touchline. The Woodford fans don't have a version of the 'Mull of Kintyre' song often heard at Charlton and Forest. An announcement reveals there's only 181 in attendance tonight, one of the lowest crowds they've had since moving in, so the atmosphere generated by the five diehards is even more impressive. They take a break during the interval and it's the roar of the M11 that could almost lull you into thinking there's a giant terrace obscured by the fog.

Traffic is on the mind of some of the old boys nearby, who complain about the recent Insulate Britain protests. The band gets into gear ready for the second half with another rendition of 'C'mon the Woods', but the team make a spluttering start and it's Hoddesdon who look to get in the driving seat. A ball to the near side finds a player clearly offside. He's allowed to proceed and sends in a low cross. Kriisa is slow to get down to it and can only palm the ball back into an attacker's path, but the shot is blocked.

The stadium announcer tries to generate some excitement when he introduces a substitute. A penalty for the home team soon after does far more to lift everyone's spirits. Burgin blasts his kick past Reed, who appears to have as much chance as a small child in stopping the hosts from taking the lead.

With their noses in front, Woodford are more confident in playing the ball out from the back. They string together a dozen or more passes and progress to the edge of the Hoddesdon box. This is something I haven't seen in non-league and really is like watching Brazil. Until it's cleared. Woodford try again, but this time it's more 1990 vintage Brazil, as someone slips over before they get out of their own half.

The home fans are happy enough. The old boys approve of the new set-up, saying all you need is your own ground with a bar in the clubhouse and you're sorted. The diehards sing to the tune of 'We've got the whole world in our hands' about how they've got the best of various things in the league, including long-jump pits. Some of the Woods defending isn't the best as a full-back hacks at thin air, letting the ball through on goal. It rolls harmlessly to the keeper and could have been mistaken for a deliberate dummy were it by a Brazilian player, but clearly wasn't. Woodford look more purposeful coming forward, trying to spring the offside trap. Their number 10, who isn't listed on the team sheet, resembles Alex Song both in appearance and the frustrating tendency to carry the ball well for a bit and then try an over-ambitious through ball. This draws much less ire than it would at the Emirates. An away fan loses his patience and storms past to stand level with the 18-yard line and implore his team forward. 'Keep it going,' he repeats, with his blood pressure building up more than any Hoddesdon attack.

Momentum is killed every time a ball goes out for a throw-in, across the running track and long-jump pit. Keep-it-going-man continues his tirade, threatening 'I'm not walking back there' as if his presence nearer the Woods goal will help Hoddesdon. A lone ball boy inexplicably helps them get the ball back quicker, not showing any of the gamesmanship you would normally expect. One player is more wily. Woodford have a throw. A Hoddesdon player flings the ball back in frustration from close range. The defender ducks and lets it travel on to the running track, leading to a small kerfuffle and more time added on.

Time ticks by and some fans drift away. Hoddesdon's number seven has a first-time shot across the keeper. It brushes Kriisa's fingertips, clips the post and goes wide. It was a chance out of nothing and shows the game isn't over. Far from it, as the referee gives some players another long talking-to. The diehards adapt 'Whole world in our hands' to 'We've got 15 minutes' injury time.' The game rumbles on. I edge towards the exit, and the band sing 'Here till midnight' to 'Guantanamera' as I pass. I feel compelled to stay and see the outcome. A supporter runs past shouting 'Is this a cricket match?' trying to get the band to start up a song. He gets a series of bemused looks, the sort of which I fear should I ever try to start any song. The band goes with 'Five-day football match' before the referee finally pulls up stumps and calls it a day.

I head back to the tube station reflecting that Woodford tried to play a bit more than others I'd seen in this league. The support was the best in the league and the crowd numbers might translate into a promotion push at some point. The future looked bright for the Woods. It was good to check them out, but there wasn't any real connection. I'm not sure they were ever in serious contention to be a team I would follow. I was interested in taking in some of the good feeling associated with their return home. Maybe groundhopping would become a feature of my football watching after all. A small snippet of a club's history, the picture of a stand, talk of a vociferous atmosphere, a game taking place at a convenient time. All these things could lure me to a non-league game.

Chapter 25

Just because he squealed, you don't have to give it

WHEN LOOKING for other post-work fixtures in London, I notice Arsenal have a league game where tickets are on general sale. I'm tempted to go back and see if any feelings linger. Arteta's side seems to be taking shape, with homegrown players coming through and some more likeable characters in the squad. It's only when I see the cost of the ticket I decide I would rather use the money for my next half a dozen non-league games instead.

I do travel to north London for a game between Wingate & Finchley and Worthing in the Isthmian Premier soon after. I couldn't honestly say I was auditioning Wingate. I had seen they had a nice old stand full of character, but so did Enfield Town, and that alone wasn't enough. It intrigued me to see if I would still enjoy the game on its own merits and I did. This was down to table-topping Worthing putting in a display that suggested Enfield Town, or Lewes, would do well to overhaul them in the race for promotion to the National League South. They ran out comfortable 3-1 winners and I left perhaps closer to becoming a non-league groundhopper than anything else.

Keen to get back on track and continue my quest to find a team to support, I arrange to go to an old favourite, Saffron Walden. It's a wintry Saturday afternoon in November and I'm meeting my dad, in what must count as an annual tradition after we saw them play Ilford at the same time last year. This afternoon's opponents are Clacton, who I saw edge out Ilford earlier in the season. The visitors are sitting in mid-table going into the game, whilst Walden are hoping to keep pace with Walthamstow at the top of the table.

I get to the ground about ten minutes before kick-off, showing I must be some sort of regular who knows the route and all the parking options near the ground. My dad is waiting for me and we head to the old grandstand to take a seat as the players finish their warm-up. The Clacton management team are talking to someone in the stand who plays for another club and appear to be enquiring about his availability. Jason Maher is not far away, listening in. I rustle up some loose change for the fifty-fifty draw, which might help the club fund any new signings.

The current team come out in their usual red and black stripes. Clacton are in their home strip, which appears to be a discarded design for an early 2000s Great Britain rugby league strip of white with random flashes of red and blue. The teams gather round the centre circle. The referee blows his whistle and the players applaud, before realising it's supposed to be a minute's silence and stop abruptly.

The game gets underway. Clacton go long. I sagely tell my dad they can be a threat from the long ball, with Mekhi McKenzie getting on the end of them. Clacton look to press. 'Relax!' comes an urgent and unconvincing plea from one of their defenders. Chairman Stuart Vant walks past in conversation with someone, not looking too relaxed himself. He's not had a chance to do the announcements over the tannoy, and he is unhappy the Clacton officials have put their Veo camera up without asking first.

The game is hurried. Maher implores his team to clear their lines. Clacton complain about every other decision. McKenzie scuffs a shot that's easily saved even after the keeper stumbles. Both sides rush clearances, looking to get it forward early. Gavin Cockman plays a couple of well-weighted passes. One is back-heeled into the path of a Walden forward. There's a gasp from the crowd. The forward treads on the ball and the danger passes.

Walden defender Matt Hurley treads on an opponent's ankle with a late tackle, to prompt more complaints. Hurley is lucky not to be sent off and is a rare example of me witnessing decisions even themselves out. The referee goes back to book him some time later, as the recipient of the tackle stays down. This gives a visiting fan nearby a chance to impart his tactical advice, 'Charlie, pull the trigger,' which presumably refers to shooting on goal rather than escalating things in a niggly game.

Things escalate in the use of the word 'fuck' stakes. There's a strained 'fuck' as someone stretches for the ball, an exasperated 'aw fucking hell' as a Walden chance flashes wide, and several loud shouts of 'fuck off' when a Walden forward flicks it over the keeper and is taken out. The referee points in the vague direction of the penalty spot to cheers from the stand, which turn to 'fuck off' when it becomes clear he's given a goal kick. Even the fifty-fifty ticket seller was upset by the decision. The referee turns another penalty appeal down when the ball appears to be handled on the line from a Walden corner and I'm disappointed to note my dad is the person to say: 'VAR is needed on that one.'

There's a brief respite in the hectic proceedings as a player goes down with cramp, which gives my dad a chance to update me on the health of a relative. Walden's Michael Toner is keen to update the ref on his performance. 'That's not a chat,' is his view after being shoved in the back. Both teams line up to contest a goal kick. Every ball is an intriguing battle, with each one keenly fought for. Neither side can gain an advantage and the half ends goalless.

Like all good dads going to the football with his son, mine has brought snacks. He gives me a flapjack from a multipack and has one himself. The burgers didn't impress him last time out. With no queue for refreshments to take our minds off the encroaching cold during half-time, I decide to pop out of the ground to move my car, as the parking will run out before full time. I can see there are spaces in the car park at the ground and the turnstile operator is happy to re-admit me. He says it's a good job as the wardens are 'pretty hot on it when it's a market day'.

For the second half, we move to the other stand behind the dugouts. 'You just want to see if the manager loses it again,' says my dad. I confess to finding the goings-on in the dugouts entertaining. There are many things that can be fascinating to watch, whether it's the grace and athleticism of someone like Thierry Henry, or as is more likely at this level, the passion, commitment and industrial language aimed at officials. Maher's passion stands out and I can hardly mock someone for getting so irate when I've silently made the same gestures playing *Football Manager* at 3am. As we take our seats, Maher is asking someone in the crowd about horse racing, which only adds to his 'proper football man' credentials.

Maher's enquiries to the linesman about a decision soon after the restart are less cheery. 'Sorry, I couldn't see. I haven't got my glasses on,' is the lino's deadpan retort. Maher spots another infringement the officials don't, with another penalty shout for a shirt-pull, and tells his forward, 'Go down, you're too honest son.' Cockman gets in on the act and rounds on the linesman, who is quick to reply, 'I need to borrow your glasses, Gav.'

One thing that Maher doesn't want to see is a floater. Walden are awarded a free kick in a dangerous position. You could say they had finally got a decision go their way, but given the sheer number of decisions, even the best ref was going to get plenty wrong today. Maher has seen his charges get plenty wrong in trying to float free kicks up and over the wall in training, and commands Toner to blast one. He does and the keeper tips it over.

My fifty-fifty ticket ends up being just above the winning number. My dawdling must have cost me. Maher is equally reproachful about his side's apparent laziness. He flits between berating his team and Darrell the linesman, at one point resembling an indignant penguin flapping his arms against the standard-issue manager's coat. 'Just because he squealed, you don't have to give it,' he rages, as another free kick stalls Walden's momentum.

Maher has even more reason to complain when Clacton are given a free kick in a dangerous position after a rare foray forward. Charlie has the chance to pull the trigger unimpeded. It's a straightforward shot for James Young in the Walden goal, but he fumbles and the linesman on the far side signals a goal, when it was far from clear the ball had crossed the line. Walden look to respond straight away. Cockman sends in a teasing cross. Players charge on to it. Someone goes down. There's a hint of a nudge and a penalty is given at last. After some deliberation on who should take the kick, Toner steps up and fires home the equaliser.

Walden have the bit between their teeth and with less than a quarter of an hour remaining are looking for all three points to keep the pressure on Walthamstow. They throw caution to the wind and leave themselves open at the back. Walden have a let-off when a Clacton goal is chalked off for an offside. They keep looking to get forward, but Clacton hold firm. They send a long ball through to McKenzie, who turns his marker, bursts forward and slips a left-footed shot past Young to make it 2-1 to the visitors. There is stunned silence among the crowd of 211, apart from a small pocket of away fans. 'Sea, sea, seasiders!' they chant.

Walden look to turn the tide, but frustration bubbles over. Cockman escapes the sin bin for backchat and adds a shout of 'Rah! fuck off' to his next long throw. Clacton defend it and clear to McKenzie, who calmly puts it away for 3-1. Straight from the kick-off, Walden send the ball wide to Cockman. He bursts into the box and slams a shot past the keeper at his near post to pull it back to 3-2. We've had six minutes of added time already. Both benches are manic. Walden want just one more chance to salvage a point. Clacton clear, but commit a foul in the Walden half. 'We've played 53 minutes this half!' the visiting manager appeals. Young scuffs his kick. Cockman tries to keep it alive, but the whistle blows for full time.

It's been an exhilarating final 15 minutes. I'm disappointed that Walden have lost in a manner reminiscent of one of Arsenal's flimsy title challenges being derailed by a plucky visitor hitting them on the break and holding out. It's not put me in the same dark mood for the rest of the weekend, though. As

I say goodbye to my dad and set off home, I'm quite buoyed by the fact I've seen the two most entertaining games in our traditional father–son fixture. Saffron Walden Town is a club that remains in the running for my affection, and whatever happens I can see myself making time to get along to Catons Lane in late autumn for a proper football experience.

Chapter 26

Come on Oliver!

ONE TEAM I wasn't expecting to come back into the reckoning was Chelmsford City. Out of the blue, my next-door neighbour sent a group WhatsApp message to say his lad was playing for their academy side in the FA Youth Cup, against Exeter City. Now, if one thing is going to draw me into a team, it is a community connection. I can't say I'd seen Oliver play in the street since he was a nipper. If he had, he would most probably have been run over, given the amount of traffic. I often saw him on his paper round when out on my morning run, and the prospect of cheering on a team with a real local connection, watching alongside some of my neighbours, was just the sort of football experience I was looking for.

The FA Youth Cup is a national competition for under-18 teams and features all the top league clubs. Arsenal have won the competition seven times and featured players such as Pat Rice and Jack Wilshere in their winning teams. The top clubs wouldn't be entering the competition until the next round, but League Two Exeter would represent tough opposition. They were reputed to be a full-time outfit, whilst the Chelmsford side had spent their day studying for their A-levels. That said, the Grecians would have spent most of their day on the coach drive from Devon.

My drive is much more straightforward, albeit rather hurried. Mrs C only returns from work 15 minutes before kick-off, so I race across town to get to the ground on time. I find one of the few remaining parking spaces and a steward points me to the shorter of the two queues for a turnstile, with cash payments working better than scanning pre-paid tickets. I pay £5 entry and head to the main stand just in time for kick-off.

There's a decent crowd, which is all relative, of course. When I was one of 60,000 watching Arsenal, a crowd of 244 would seem insignificant and barely worth the effort, especially when *Grandstand* would insist on going through games in the Scottish lower divisions, attracting similar numbers, before showing the league tables. But 244 at a gig, or in a pub, is lively. This feels like an event. There are quite a lot of youngsters, watching their mates from college play. I find the group from my road huddled together at the front of the stand.

The match gets underway and both sides look to pop the ball around rather than punt it long, which makes it stand out from a lot of what I've been watching lately. I find it hard to place what level this would be the equivalent of in the men's game, as I could imagine the more grizzled, stocky veterans of the Essex Senior League out-muscling what appear to be two slightly built teams. Chelmsford's centre-backs look comfortable on the ball in the way everyone wants modern defenders to be, but would make Mekhi McKenzie look like Didier Drogba if he didn't already based on what I'd seen of him.

Oliver wins an early header as both teams look to assert themselves. It soon becomes clear that he is up against Exeter's most threatening player, a winger that has him for pace. He does well to show him down the outside and put pressure on the cross. Chelmsford's keeper is equal to it and assured in his handling. Everything is technically neat and following the coaching manual, but it's not altogether clear where any creative spark will come from. A Chelmsford winger tries to cut inside, but he is well marshalled, and the home team can only fashion a couple of half-chances.

Exeter continue to threaten down Oliver's flank, but can't find an opening. They win a cheap free kick on the opposite wing. The ball is swung in towards the keeper and only the faintest of touches is needed to make it 1-0 to the visitors. 'Heads up, Chelmsford,' comes the cry from several parents who fear the worst. A second is bundled home soon after, to confirm those fears. The scorer's name is read out and a cry of 'Who?' comes from the back of the stand with no hint of irony.

Chelmsford can't create any chances before the break, and at half-time we all go down towards the players' tunnel. A few of the blokes are keen to advise Oliver to get tighter and foul his man at every opportunity. I would usually be a whole-hearted advocate for this approach, but given Exeter have had more joy from set pieces than anything they've been able to deliver from his flank, I'm not convinced.

I ask neighbours Viv and Chris if they've been to many games over here. They say they haven't, but they used to go to the old ground a fair bit, the smell of the burgers being the main thing they recall. Ralph chimes in, saying we're lucky the burger van isn't open tonight, as it absolutely stinks. We bemoan the state of the current first team and Oliver's mum is apologetic that the academy side don't seem to be playing as well as they usually do. It's not as if they've played badly, but it's going to take something special to get back into this tie.

A slick one-touch passing move early in the second half carves open the defence, and the ball is slotted home. Unfortunately, it's Exeter making it 3-0 to go into complete control. 'Heads up, Chelmsford' is the forlorn shout from a few of the parents. Oliver's mum is less inclined to embarrass her son than my mum was at my games. She restrains herself from shouting at the team. I still recoil at the thought of my mum's tactical advice, which consisted of ways to avoid getting cold from standing in goal covered in wet mud.

Exeter keep Chelmsford at arm's length, as the parents hope for a consolation goal. A last-ditch tackle sends the ball out for a corner when the Grecians play the ball through. It's harshly adjudged to be a foul and a red card by the referee. The centre-half trudges off to appreciative applause. The double jeopardy decision of penalty and red seems unfair. Oliver appeals to the referee and his mum implores him not to get involved, mainly to avoid the fine that would come with a yellow card. Exeter dispatch the penalty for a flattering 4-0 scoreline, which is how it ends.

Oliver's mum is full of apologies to those who have come. I've no regrets about going. It's not like I've been invited to watch someone perform am-dram, where at best I'll be bored and at worst I'll cringe through fluffed lines. Or in the case of Ben's appearance in a Shakespeare comedy, both. This has been a much better evening. It's more satisfying to watch opponents actively trying to thwart one another, rather than impenetrable dialogue made worse by bad acting. There's food for thought as to what level players will end up in and how many will drift away, along with the support of those who came tonight.

The game may not have convinced me to get along to watch City more often myself, but it showed that so long as I lived here, I would always keep an eye out for their results. I was keen to see them pull away from this season's single relegation spot, which they were fighting it out with against local rivals Billericay and Braintree. I even expect to be tempted back to the occasional match, particularly where there are more of those little things that make the club a more prominent part of the local community.

One consequence of a cold night at the Gulag is that it hastened the onset of a terrible cold. This didn't develop into pneumonia and my Herbert-Chapman-like demise, but it prevented me from my planned post-work trip to see Romford v Heybridge Swifts the following night. Swifts ran out 7-0 winners, and after seeing them win 5-0 before, I wondered if witnessing them chalk up another thumping win might have seduced me. Deep down, I knew they weren't the team for me. I had already passed up several opportunities to cycle the near-perfect distance to one of their home games. Close enough for it to be a convenient mode of transport, but far enough away to make all the faffing with kit and exertion worthwhile. I also realised I had a clear preference for Hashtag over Heybridge, feeling mild disappointment when the result of their meeting went in Swifts' favour.

Chapter 27

Fifty shades of Grays

IN THE week spent at home following the Chelmsford game, the main sporting story I follow is the 101-mile run ex-rugby league player Kevin Sinfield completes in support of his former team-mate and friend, Rob Burrow, to raise funds for Motor Neurone Disease. It's a prime example of sport's transcendent appeal that touches on raw human emotion and I can't help but be drawn into it. At the same time, Hashtag United do their bit for the Movember charity, with a 24-hour football match. I'm not sure my four remaining YouTube followers make me enough of a creator or influencer to put myself forward for a playing slot, even in the early hours of the morning, so I settle for donations to both causes.

It's Hashtag who I go to see next, with a short trip to the Len Salmon for their home game against Grays Athletic. The drive doesn't take much longer than getting across town to see Chelmsford City, who are at home in the FA Trophy. This is a trophy Grays won twice in two seasons in the early 2000s. They also reached the heights of the fifth-tier National League at the same time. They stayed at this level until 2010, when relegation coincided with the expiry of the lease on their ground. Forced to ground-share and unable to afford to play at that level, they were placed in the eighth tier, where, despite a spell in the league above, they find themselves now.

The current club became fan-owned in 2016 and are now pushing for both a move back to Grays and a promotion play-off place. There was a lot of talk about them moving to Thurrock FC's old Ship Lane ground, which was abandoned in 2018 after the club folded when their chairman stepped down because of health reasons, and a new buyer couldn't be found. Some had even speculated that Hashtag could buy this ground, but the issue seemed to be due to planning permission rather than reticence on Grays' part.

It is a cold, blustery day, with the remnants of Storm Arwen buffeting the trees around the ground and anything not fixed down inside of it. I receive a warm welcome at the turnstile, as I finally swap last season's season ticket for this season's one. I make my way to the shelter of the main stand, where there is a mix of older away fans, players' relatives and a few home supporters. Once the game is underway, a larger group of away supporters make their way behind the goal Grays are attacking and put up their flags, including one bearing the phrase 'Fifty shades of Grays', which suggests recent years have been mildly erotic torture for them.

Grays left-back Macaulay Joynes is being tormented early on. The wind is sending the ball his way with the regularity of someone administering a spanking. 'Macca, Macca, Macca!' go the cries from his teammates like some sort of safe word, as they give him the option of a ball infield. Hashtag's Anthony Page sends a clearance through to the corner flag before drilling a half-volleyed kick into Toby Aromolaran's path, but even on the ground the ball scurries away to the corner.

While Hashtag struggle not to over-hit passes, Grays have difficulty clearing their lines. One clearance loops back over the defender's head. Goal kicks are blown my way in the stand. It's hard to judge the flight of the ball, as it moves like one of those plastic balls you buy at the seaside, so I'm relieved when it either sails over the stand, or swerves to someone next to me. Both goalkeepers are doing well to handle the ball in the circumstances, although Hashtag do little to work Danny Sambridge in the visitors' goal.

Grays create the better chances. The wind holds up the ball for them to get in behind and put the ball in the box between keeper and defender. Chances come and go, as the ball flashes across the box. One header clips the post. One through ball holds up enough to leave Page in no-man's land and it's flicked past him. A combination of Ross Gleed and the wind stop it crossing the line.

Hashtag haven't taken advantage of the conditions going forward, until Aromolaran slaloms his way through a bevy of defenders. He carries the ball all the way to the edge of the box until he is body-checked. There are complaints from the defending side and complaints about their continual complaints from the bloke behind me. There's no booking and criticism for there being no bookings to stop their complaining. The free kick comes to nothing and the half-time whistle soon blows.

I decide to get myself a hot chocolate to warm up. There's a £5 minimum spend on card and I've no cash. I would need to buy five hot chocolates, or an entire meal deal, such is the value on offer. To warm up, I go to the bar. I check the scores in the Premier League. There are only four games taking place, after European fixtures midweek, with little of interest in relation to Arsenal, so I go back to reclaim a seat well covered by the roof.

It's advantage Grays in the second half, having the wind behind them as players inevitably tire. Playing into the wind had helped them in the first half as the ball held up, but it would only take one potshot to be caught right. Hashtag will need to concentrate at the back. Seeing how the teams cope with the conditions is something to savour. I would like to see more Premier League matches played in conditions like this, or with a sloping pitch, or on a quagmire, maybe as a punishment for clubs who resist the fan-led review. The FA Cup will sometimes throw up such an opportunity against a much lower-ranked side, but I'd like to see two equally matched sides having to adapt to the conditions, in the way a wet Paris–Roubaix is a unique challenge to racing cyclists.

Hashtag start the half brightly and Geoffrey Okonkwo is on his bike to get across to prevent Aromolaran from getting on the end of a Kiernan Hughes-Mason through ball. Momentum swings in Grays' direction and Gleed has to throw himself in front of a shot from the edge of the box, after another cross causes concern. Hashtag struggle to get out of their own half. Even a mis-controlled touch from a forward with their back to goal blows back towards the Tags goal.

There comes a point in most non-league games, where you realise what started out as something that could feel like just a kick-about in a park has taken on far greater significance. The grievances stack up, a few pushes in the back go unpunished, players are more annoyed with the ref and each other, the crowd wants to see a goal, or a yellow card at least. There's more intensity to the game. In the stand it only goes so far as the bloke behind me saying, 'You're having a laugh, you need your eyes tested,' when a Grays old boy complains about a decision.

Grays win a corner. They swing the cross all the way over Page to the back post. Okonkwo is unmarked and directs it into the net for 1-0, which he celebrates with a jig. Hashtag remain penned in their own half. A few youngsters not yet in their teens go down that end to get behind the team. Emboldened in a group, they taunt the visiting fans with 'Can you hear the Grays sing?' The older Grays fans are as uncompromising as their team and come back with 'Who the fucking hell are you?'

The referee signals for an advantage when the ball breaks to Luke Hirst after a cynical foul on Hughes-Mason. New signing Hirst has looked lively, but now finally has a sight of goal. He hits it into the side netting. He's then flagged offside, which begs the question: where was the advantage then? Not for the first time, I join the bloke behind me in shouting at the referee. I make a mental note that it's Hashtag who compel me to shout at referees the most, which must indicate who I'm subconsciously becoming a supporter of. Humming along to songs at Clapton may be another sign, but that could just be because their songs were catchy.

Hashtag can't catch a break today and it ends in defeat. I hurry back to my car and turn the heater on. While I warm up, I check some other scores. Chelmsford City lost to lower-league opposition in the FA Trophy in front of a crowd not much bigger than the 228 at Hashtag. It's less gloomy for Hashtag, but their lack of goals leaves them not far above the relegation places. Just over 48 hours later, Hashtag are at home again to another side in the play-off mix, AFC Sudbury. I can't make it as Mrs C is working late and neither can I watch it at home, as midweek games are now behind a paywall. Naturally, I miss a 3-2 win, with a stoppage-time winner, which still stirs those familiar emotions of pride, joy and relief.

Chapter 28

He fell over, Barcelona

THE FOLLOWING Saturday I'm unexpectedly given the opportunity to go to a game. Clapton, Fisher, Ilford, Saffron Walden and Hashtag are all away, so this will either show who I really want to see, or be a decision based on the easiest drive. I don't fancy travelling to some far-flung part of London for the first two, and Hashtag would involve driving through Southend on a Saturday afternoon in the lead up to Christmas. That leaves Ilford and Saffron Walden, who are both a 30-minute drive away. Ilford are clear of relegation danger and Walden have drifted out of title contention in the Essex Senior League, so neither game has much riding on it. At Ilford, I would be just about the only away supporter, which doesn't appeal to me. In the end, the fact Walden are playing on the Essex side of the Herts border, ticking off another new ground in my adopted county, and at a ground with what appears to be a larger car park, is enough to swing it.

I arrive in Takeley, and the car park is full. The overflow car park is true to its name and overflowing, both with cars and deep puddles. I try several cul-de-sacs until I find one without parking restrictions and hope the residents aren't the sort who take exception to people they think are looking to avoid parking charges at nearby Stansted Airport.

I rush to the ground, crossing a bridge over the old railway line, and see the pitch from the road. The thought briefly crosses my mind that I could see most of the game for free, but £7 entry, including a free programme, is hardly a fortune. I've enough change for a few fifty/fifty tickets as I pass the vendor on the way to the main stand. Some signs printed on number plates indicate the home and away sections and I sit on the away side of the aisle.

I flick through the programme and spot one of the usual features, containing some history about the visiting team, which always starts in a neutral tone before it becomes clear someone from the visiting side has written it. I'd not seen this account before, so am intrigued to learn that Walden's ground used to have a more pronounced slope. They fell foul of ground grading requirements and were denied promotion, spent money reducing the slope, got into financial difficulty and dropped down the leagues, even pulling out of men's senior football at one point, before becoming supporter-owned.

As I try to get my head round this, along with the usual potted history covering various league and cup competitions that no longer exist, Kylie's 'Can't Get You Out Of My Head' stops abruptly on the tannoy. This isn't a prompt for someone to read the teams out, it's just left to buzz in the background. The teams enter the field anonymously, so I have to work out the Walden team from who I can recognise. I also spot the distinctive look of the WAGs who sit down nearby with their young children. One of the entourage remarks that the pitch looks in good condition. I suspect if they found their skin in that state they would need to trowel on the foundation. Their kids clamber all over the stand, clearly not interested in daddy's exploits, although to be fair very little happens early on.

Unlike some of the tackling on the pitch, the children aren't out of control. The play is a jumble of soft free kicks, backchat when consecutive decisions go the same way and little in the way of football. Walden gift a presentable chance to Takeley, but the side-footed effort seems to be deadened by the long grass before Walden keeper James Young falls on it.

One of the WAGs keeps warning her kid to watch a floodlight pillar they are about to walk into. Tears are avoided and Walden avoid conceding anything in the box with a well-timed tackle. The kids continue to totter around the concrete steps and avoid a clattering fall, whilst those on the pitch are felled with increasing regularity. James Solkhon is quick to reprise what must be his catchphrase of 'That's embarrassing, ref' as well as helpfully suggesting to the referee that he 'Don't let them talk to you like that' as both teams aggravate one another.

In amongst the dross, I think I spot something reminiscent of Bergkamp's turn and finish against Newcastle, only the pirouette is born out of a mis-controlled first touch that clips Ollie Miles' heel and puts him in on goal. He curls wide and one of his team-mates mutters that he's a 'fucking useless cunt'. It seems like Walden have a new forward every other week and some appear to have won their place in a raffle. No such problems for Takeley, as their number nine slips it past Young for 1-0 and celebrates with a front flip.

There was a hint of offside about the goal, but when Walden hit back to level soon afterwards, I am more surprised to see the flag go up. My view through the throng outside the tea bar isn't ideal and I'm no neutral, so I don't protest. Walden keep up the pressure and the net bulges once again, only it's the one protecting passing traffic. Walden do grab an equaliser before the interval, as a long cross into the box is chested down for Miles to hit first time and make it 1-1.

To keep warm during the break, I decide to do laps of the pitch. A group of teenagers with muddy knees attempt to continue their kick-about on the main pitch, before they and the subs are told to keep out of the sandy goalmouth. I'm briefly involved in the subs' passing drill, as I side-foot a stray ball back. I have another momentary flutter of excitement as the first number of my fifth/fifty draw ticket is read out, but my time spent getting parked means the other numbers are too low. The ground is neither charming, nor full of any less obvious rugged charm, although the tea bar does serve tea in proper mugs.

I'm tempted to carry on my stroll throughout the second half to stay warm and get some exercise. I feel I should stand with the Walden fans gathered behind the goal they are attacking, but something holds me back. The film *ID* comes to mind and I imagine I'm an undercover police officer, infiltrating a hooligan gang. This is far-fetched, especially when a stray ball from the teenagers' kick-about that hits them doesn't provoke so much as firm words, let alone violence. There has been little noise from the away supporters and the silence makes me realise it takes years of going to games, seeing the same people week after week, until you are one of them. To prove myself, I decide to take the Takeley end and sit in a spare seat on the home side of the aisle.

Several other supporters have moved around in the interval and I now have two contrasting commentary options, with a proper geezer to my left and two pre-teens to my right, which would make interesting red button options for a televised game. The pre-teens work as a classic commentary duo. 'Oh, great ball,' purrs the lead commentator, who is instantly preferable to Clive Tyldesley. The co-commentator sets out his credentials: 'His touch was rubbish there. You should have seen me the other night. I rolled two players, did a step-over past one, then megged another,' which I don't recall Danny Murphy or Jermaine Jenas ever doing. They even come up with catch phrases: 'On your bike', as Takeley counter, and 'He fell over, Barcelona' whenever anyone goes down.

Niggly fouls and backchat to the officials persists, and the geezer is keen to broadcast his views on the officiating. At first the lino needs glasses, then he's told, 'Don't let him talk to you like that, call the ref over.' Then he admonishes the ref for a decision, before he tells a player, 'Let the ref ref the game.' Which the referee does by taking double the time the Takeley keeper has wasted to run over to him and book him for time-wasting.

Based on the way I've angled myself to face the goal Walden are attacking, they must be on top, although they create no decent chances. One attack produces an Aubameyang-like miss from close range, before Takeley break and win a free kick on the edge of the Walden box. A low shot is blocked, before falling to a Takeley player to tuck home for 2-1.

Miscommunication in the Walden defence results in a Takeley corner. The initial cross is cleared and a looping header is sent back towards the goal. Young dives and the ball somehow drops over him and into the net, like a glitch in a computer game, for 3-1. Things go from bad to worse when Solkhon is given his marching orders soon after to give the ref some peace.

Walden continue to play on the front foot and I hope for another grandstand finish. Chances come and go, with the ball ricocheting around the box, but the match fizzles out after a contest had broken out for a while. Solkhon comes back on, after it emerges he had been sin-binned rather than sent off. The sting has gone out of the game though. It's less niggly and the post-mortem starts in the stands. Another blow is dealt as Takeley break and a shot is curled left-footed into the bottom corner of Young's goal for 4-1. A bigger cheer goes up from a few home fans when they hear Liverpool have scored a late winner. The geezer shrugs and says, 'You can't win 'em all.' On the way out, a home fan declares it was the best game of the season.

I check the other results to see if it was the best game I could have seen. Clapton, Fisher and Ilford all lost in lower-scoring games, but Hashtag won 4-3 after being 3-1 down and scoring a last-minute winner to make me regret my choice of game. Maybe it shows a fondness for Hashtag, or a sense that something is always going to happen in their games. But perhaps it was a lack of connection with Walden away from their home ground. The result didn't really matter, and that was telling. I wasn't dejected the way I would be if I was more keen on them and maybe it revealed that Walden are not the team for me. Sure, I would continue to follow their results and get along to the odd game, but I wasn't going to be a supporter.

Chapter 29

It's just like watching Arsenal

BY NOW, I have without doubt rediscovered my
obsession for football. Why else would I be spending
a Friday night in December watching a youth team
game? It's not any old youth team game though, as I
will be watching Arsenal's under-18s in the FA Youth
Cup. Almost a decade since the last time I went to
an Arsenal game, I'm seeing them play at nearby
Colchester United.

Now, this may look like the equivalent of trying to
get back with an ex, and you may read this willing me
not to do it. All the reasons I stopped going to Arsenal
are still valid, but I figured I can be mature about
the situation and still have some sort of relationship
with the Gunners. This isn't me getting back together
with them and is very much an opportunity to tick off
another Essex ground on the cheap.

I will, of course, be wanting Arsenal to win. I
still look out for their scores and even watched their
frustrating 3-2 defeat to Man United on Amazon

Prime, by virtue of a subscription Mrs C forgot to cancel. That defeat, along with another away to Everton a few days later, punctured some of the optimism that was building. I was hoping the academy team would be a source of renewed optimism. The U23s had been doing well. The U21s had progressed in the Papa Johns Trophy against league opposition. Now it was the turn of the U18s. They would include highly rated prospects Charlie Patino and Omari Hutchinson, who had also featured in those older age group teams.

Tonight's opponents Colchester started out in non-league before being elected to the Football League in 1950. Apart from a brief spell in the early 90s, they have remained a league club and are currently playing in the fourth tier. Their academy side wasn't expected to be any match for Arsenal, so it was an excellent opportunity for local fans to see an Arsenal side in the flesh in the same way I remember being taken to see the reserves play Charlton's reserves.

Colchester's Community Stadium is a convenient drive from Chelmsford, being just off the A12 with a large car park, which, along with the £8 tickets, made going to the game appealing. The ground is smart, but the four identikit stands lack the charm of their old Layer Road ground. I fondly recalled watching a game in the tightly packed stands there. The home fans mercilessly barracked a former player and a young mascot slipped over *à la* John Terry in a half-time penalty shoot-out. A night out in town afterwards was less charming when the nightclub's response to someone being sick on the dancefloor was to crank up the smoke machine, so a girl slipped over like a mascot taking a half-time penalty.

I approach the turnstile and am asked by a steward whether I'm here for the game or a Covid vaccination. Thrown by the question I don't think to ask whether I could have a booster before kick-off, so am directed away from a tent next to the turnstile and into the ground. I head straight to the refreshment kiosk underneath the stand. It's all breeze blocks and pre-cooked burgers. They have added some old photos, including their famous FA Cup giant-killing over Leeds United, and have pies on sale as well. I opt for my old favourite from a league ground, the balti pie, and a molten brown substance purporting to be hot chocolate, for dinner.

I sit in one of the many spare press seats, partly for somewhere to rest my notepad, partly because the folded-down rests offer some protection from the icy wind, which is coming in through the corners of the ground. The Arsenal team is announced, and I instinctively clap. The game gets underway, Arsenal look composed on the ball and I almost miss the first action reading a text message from Mrs C: 'Have you fed the cat?' I'm typing 'Yes' when the Colchester keeper paws an Arsenal effort over the bar.

Arsenal look to impose themselves. They mimic the first team, trying to play out from the back. Colchester stop them playing through the midfield. 'Double pivot,' their manager calls, so they drop back into shape. Patino drifts past players. Hutchinson looks tricky, but gets brushed off the ball and almost makes me want to be the one to say he's too small to make it. Norton-Cuffy looks to burst forward from right-back. Even the centre-backs are vocal and appear commanding, until Taylor Foran is caught on the ball by Colchester's big number nine Samson Tovide, who bursts clear, but fires wide. It's a warning.

There's no caution for a foul on Arsenal's other centre-back, Zac Awe, when a foot is left in on him after he over-runs it. There's a sense that Arsenal are getting rattled. Colchester create a couple of chances to give the crowd a lift. Arsenal give them further encouragement by trying to play out from a goal kick and losing possession. They then concede a soft penalty, which captain Ryan Lowe converts to give the hosts a 1-0 lead at half-time.

I almost lose any sense that this will prompt a response from the Gunners when their keeper drops a cross at the feet of a Colchester forward, who directs it more towards the corner flag than the gaping net. Patino tries to carry the ball forward, but is brushed off it too easily. He keeps showing for it and looking to drive forward, but Colchester stop him by fair means or foul. Either way, he looks to grab hold of the ball when he goes down, in the time-honoured tradition of playground fancy Dans the world over. Hutchinson is also getting on the ball more and more and getting past players in the box, before going down too easily for the liking of those behind me. They're not impressed with either player, having heard good things. You can see they would have a good highlight reel, but both are overplaying it and Arsenal create very little.

Colchester break up the play and Tovide continues to menace Arsenal's centre-backs. He's a willing runner and even more willing to leave a foot in, stop a quick restart and engage in the general sort of shithousery that Arsenal teams always seem to struggle against. A nearby child asks if there's going to be a yellow card soon. Tovide wins a free kick near the corner flag. They send in the kick and the Colchester number nine heads home unmarked to make it 2-0.

Arsenal create a couple of presentable chances, but blaze them over. The clock ticks down as time is taken to retrieve the ball from the empty stand behind the goal. The Gunners try to press forward, but Colchester break and finish a flowing move to make it 3-0. In stoppage time, things could get worse. United break with four on one, but a dubious offside call goes in Arsenal's favour. It doesn't matter as the hosts have earned a shock victory and the entire squad runs on to the field to celebrate at the final whistle.

It's hard to get too worked up about an academy fixture and I feel much the same way as if one of the non-league teams I'm fond of had lost. I sense that despite having some promising young players, Arsenal will continue to make the same mistakes and be the source of a low level of frustration, but won't be something I will get too worked up about. The set-up at Colchester also leaves me cold, and not just from the wind. The 10,000-seater stadium is smart enough and would be the envy of a club like Chelmsford, but it feels like a soulless thing to aspire to. There will always be a dream to move up the leagues, but there is something comforting about remaining in the lower reaches of the football pyramid with its ramshackle grounds and quirky appeal.

Chapter 30

Left-over sandwiches

THE FOLLOWING day I'm off to watch Clapton Community. Mark is keen to return with a group of us to celebrate his birthday. In the end, only Phil and I join him, as others have the sort of excuses you would expect of a particularly uncommitted Sunday team. Christmas shopping needs doing. Christmas lights need putting up. In-laws need visiting.

To get us in the festive spirit, I make some mulled beer to keep us warm on the terrace: ruby red ale, cognac, cinnamon sticks, orange, sugar and honey, simmered for the time I have between remembering to do it and having to leave to catch the train. Not wanting to wait until we're on the terrace, I share the elixir out on the platform, apologising for the lack of star anise or cloves. Phil is glad not to have bits to fish out. The day is underway.

We head to Hackney Wick before going on to Walthamstow, as Mark is keen to check out the brew pubs in Queen's Yard. It's all old factories covered in graffiti and bench seating. We are the first ones in the bar, as if we're on a lads' weekend in Europe. We have time to sample several beers from the excellent Howling Hops Brewery and put the world to rights on the latest scourge of modern football: fan tokens and NFTs. Talk of fans being ripped off leads Phil to wonder why we are still paying nearly £6 a pint when the beer we are drinking is brewed in the next room and there are no transport costs. That doesn't stop us buying a couple of cans to take to the match.

We arrive at the Wadham Lodge Matchday Centres by taxi, just in time for kick-off. Clapton Community are on the main pitch today against AVA, who are a Romanian heritage side playing only their third season in senior football. I put a note in the bucket for entrance donations to cover us, pick up a programme and am given a note reminding us that the venue has asked for there to be no use of pyrotechnics or glass bottles brought in.

We head to the terrace where the fans are mostly gathered. Play has just gotten underway, but a lengthy stoppage for an injury gives us time to find a spot behind the goal before play resumes. Rather oddly, the fans have congregated behind the goal Clapton are defending, not following the usual non-league tradition of standing behind the goal they are attacking and swapping at half-time.

I've not brought my notebook, as I'm planning to just enjoy the day and go on how I feel about the experience. Besides, I don't want to encourage Mark and Phil to go all Saint and Greavsie on me, trying to come up with something I will quote them on. It's rather subdued on the terrace as well: more like being in a lively bar, with small groups talking, drinking Tyskie. One group share a flask around. Mark and Phil move on to an 8.5% DIPA.

Cheers break out when Dean Buoho puts Clapton ahead from a corner early on. Josh Adejokun adds another from close range to put the Tons in control shortly afterwards. Everyone is in a relaxed mood now, as Clapton look to be back on track after a few bad results that saw them drop from the top of the table. Phil thinks AVA look the better side and have a couple of players who look capable on the ball, but they can't create any clear-cut chances, so it remains 2-0 at the break.

At half-time player-manager Geoff Ocran comes back on to the pitch to talk to the fans. He publicly thanks a couple of the volunteers and asks everyone to dig deep for the Christmas toy collection – not something that would be part of Mikel Arteta's process. It shows that the club is about much more than what happens on the pitch.

The atmosphere gathers some momentum in the second half. The singing builds to a crescendo. Mark gets to join in singing 'Tons just wanna have fun'. I try to bang the metal wall behind me to the tune of the songs, but my complete lack of rhythm lets me down. Noah Adejokun is put through on goal. The keeper forces him wide. He composes himself and, from a tight angle, curls it into the corner of the net directly in front of us, and the crowd celebrates. Phil and I bang a simple tune on the wall and get a few 'Claptons' from those around us. It's a jovial atmosphere and adults drinking beer on a terrace is far from being the public order issue those against a trial in league games are warning about.

The main issue is that it requires a trip to the toilet block, back by the turnstiles. It's raining persistently, as I walk along the sodden touchline. I notice the linesman has thick gloves, jogging bottoms and whatever else he can fit under his kit to keep warm. The leaden skies mean the light is fading even earlier than expected. The 2:00pm kick-off to avoid having to switch on the floodlights doesn't look like being enough.

I walk back to the terrace and I can hear the sound reverberate from under the metal roof. There's a cosiness back on the terrace, as we watch the game conclude. Clapton run out 3-0 winners in the gloom and we head to the bar. *Soccer Saturday* is on TV. I notice for the first time that Arsenal are also 3-0 up against Southampton. Phil notices the bare thighs on display amongst a women's hockey team who are having post-match drinks and a buffet. The hockey team kindly offer us a left-over platter of sandwiches, which are much appreciated since we've neglected to eat anything. Mark declares that he has found his non-league team, impressed by both the experience and the inclusive nature of the club on his two visits. We noted that the atmosphere was a bit more subdued than last time, but Phil still enjoyed himself.

I suggest that some fans might have foregone this afternoon's game to travel to Plymouth for an early kick-off in the women's team's third-round FA Cup tie the next day. Their cup run had really captured the imagination of Clapton's fans, who have been going in increasing numbers and creating the same fervent atmosphere. As someone rightly pointed out, if you believe in what the club stands for, then you should offer the same support to both men's and women's teams. If the game hadn't been in Plymouth on a Sunday, then I would have suggested we went to that one instead.

Clapton's run in the women's FA Cup highlighted the disparity in prize money between the men's and women's competitions, with Clapton having to crowd-fund their travel costs. The prize money was even less than the FA Trophy or Vase competitions. Surely the FA should direct funds to grassroots football and encourage the widest possible level of participation, rather than offer what amounts to some more pocket money to Premier League clubs in the vain hope it stops them putting out reserve teams in the men's FA Cup.

Before we settle into becoming a second-rate *Sunday Supplement* panel of beer-soaked hacks, it's time to return to Queen's Yard for more craft ale. The consensus is that we had a good night, although no one can recall much. Mark's review of the day was 'Clapton won, we got some leftover sandwiches and then it's a blank.' The prospect of free sandwiches must be why he started talking about becoming more involved in the club and joining the committee. Phil remembered little between the DIPA and Mark falling asleep in the curry house at the end of the night, apart from what might have been a fantasy when a girl in hockey shorts brought him sandwiches.

The day has been the perfect mix of sport and a social occasion, which will be recalled with fondness like a day at the cricket, or a big win at the horses. Our memories of the game will boil down to little more than Adejokun finishing from a tight angle and general bonhomie on the terrace, but sometimes that's enough. The match created a warm feeling that the resulting hangover didn't entirely diminish. For Mark it could lead to more, in the same way a day at the races led Phil to buying shares in a racehorse. For me, it's been a great day out, but I don't see myself wanting to do that every week. Being a passive spectator at the Emirates must have become too ingrained in me. It feels more like somewhere to go as an occasion.

The one occasion we will look out for is the Tons return to the Old Spotted Dog ground, which looks nearer to happening after planning permission for new changing rooms was granted. This requires more crowd-funding and we're all keen to contribute. More than just being an occasional outing, it makes us think about causes linked to the game we want to support.

Some Clapton fans lead the way again, offering to help those trying to resurrect Leyton FC, and bring back football to their old Hare and Hounds ground, after they folded in 2011. Those running the campaign were only looking for signatures to a petition at this stage, so that's an easy cause to support. I also think that

I should watch the women's team of whoever I decide to support. I had already watched highlights of Arsenal women in the same way I followed the men's team on YouTube these days. Seeing them avoid defeat against Spurs in a game they dominated gave it an elevated sense of importance. The standard of play was more impressive than FA Trophy or Vase level. Further down the women's pyramid in the fourth tier are Hashtag, who are covered by my season ticket. Further still in the seventh tier are Clapton, who acquitted themselves well against second-tier Plymouth the following day, but exited the cup with heads held high.

Chapter 31

How long, ref?

BEFORE I'M able to get to a Hashtag women's game, I have an assignment to cover the men's team. At some point during the day out watching Clapton, I offered my services as a contributor to the *Outside the 92* website, and they were keen for me to cover Hashtag games. I got off to an inauspicious start when a trip to Brentwood Town was called off due to the weather. Still keen to see a game, I went to see the Maldon derby between Maldon & Tiptree and Heybridge Swifts, which itself was abandoned at half-time due to floodlight failure.

With festive fixtures coming thick and fast, it wasn't long until I was at the Len Salmon Stadium on New Year's Day to cover Hashtag v Basildon United. My pre-match research consists of finding out Basildon's nickname and looking through their squad list. Armed with the fact that their nickname is the Bees, I think of all the bee puns I can conceivably work into a match report. The only player name I recognise is Bertie Brayley, who played for Chelmsford, Braintree and just about every other club in Essex. Brayley is almost as old as the club themselves, who began life as a junior team when the new town developed.

I take a seat close to the press box to get a look at the team sheet. Spencer takes a seat behind me in the commentary position and is joined by a Hashtag superfan from America, Professor Chibs, who is on co-commentary. Spencer runs through his usual advice and does some intro pieces to the camera. I glean that Luke Hirst is up against his former club, where he is still top scorer, which I make a note of for my report.

Hirst is involved early on. Hashtag defender Harry Haysom cuts out a long punt forward. Kiernan Hughes-Mason ferries the loose ball on to Jesse Waller-Lassen. He looks up and dinks it over the defence for Hirst to run on to. He gets there before the keeper and chips the ball over him on the half-volley to make it 1-0 after 11 minutes, which I've dutifully noted.

I try to concentrate on the game more than I usually would, but in amongst the long balls from Basildon I find myself trying to think of a neat way to compare how their keeper's impressive beard resembles a beard of bees, and how to deal with Paul Shave, who is both bald and bearded. Luckily, Gabriel Piorkowski is busy, industrious and whatever other adjectives can be associated with a bee. He lets a sweet shot fly towards Anthony Page's goal and stings his palms.

Hashtag are on top. Carlos Flood carries the ball forward. Waller-Lassen pulls the strings in midfield and Bantick has a couple of half-chances. The half ends and I'm able to sit comfortably, knowing Hashtag look secure and I should have a relatively straightforward match report to write, provided it doesn't all kick off in the second half.

When the second half gets underway, Basildon present Hashtag with an early chance inside their own penalty area. The Bees gift-wrap the ball in a jar to Bantick. He squares to Waller-Lassen, who fires home to give the Tags a comfortable 2-0 lead. Less comfortably, Paul Shave soon contests a decision against his team. A mum with her two kids does an admirable job of telling her oldest that he didn't hear a swear word, with the sort of outright denial even a politician would blush at. Eventually, she concedes he might have heard something, but he's not to use it himself.

The lad takes Shave's lead in questioning the referee's decisions, appealing for several fouls. Again his mum is on hand. Putting a stop to any nonsense, she points out there wasn't any contact. Along with my mum's intolerance towards play-acting, there's a potential answer to refereeing shortages, if only the FA targeted the sort of Don't-be-so-bloody-daft-and-don't-come-crying-to-me mums that can often be found on the touchline.

This doesn't make the match report, as Brayley hitting the post for Basildon seems more relevant, along with a few of Flood's runs, which give me some justification for giving him my man of the match award. Professor Chibs also selects him as official man of the match before the game concludes.

At full time there's a scrum to get past the tunnel entrance and if I were a proper journalist, I would look to get a word with Spencer or a player, but I don't fancy joining a group of 12-year-olds waiting for high-fives and looking like I somehow want one as well. Instead, I'm thinking of pun-laden headlines.

To underline my newfound seriousness in following Hashtag, the report is published and I'm back watching them 48 hours later, away to Barking. It's a drive through endless east London sprawl to reach their Mayesbrook Park ground, which adjoins a modern sports centre and athletics track. The football ground is a bit more run down from the outside. A hodgepodge of fencing gives way to a turnstile through what appears to be an old shipping container. There's a function room off to the right, where an event is taking place to raise funds to build a statue to commemorate former Barking player Jack Leslie. He was due to become England's first black international in 1925, but was de-selected once the selection committee realised the colour of his skin.

Those selected to play in today's game are listed on a board, handily placed on the way through to the terrace. I emerge behind one of the goals and make my way along to a low grandstand on the touchline, with four rows of seating. I take up a position near halfway and check into the *Futbology* app, having succumbed to the lure of knowing how many grounds I'm racking up.

Despite there being nothing too special about this ground, I feel a distinct thrill in watching a game somewhere new. There's the pleasure of spotting any historic features, in this case a couple of sets of old turnstile gates in amongst the outside bar tables. There's the chance to come across eccentric fans, although I don't think the kid doing laps of the ground on an e-scooter really counts. And of course, there's another football match to watch.

My pre-match research reveals Barking's nickname is the Blues, which is disappointing from a punning perspective. At least there's the possibility of using 'barking mad' if there's controversy, or 'barking up the wrong tree' if something bizarre happens involving the row of trees on the opposite touchline. Of more use, I find out this is Hashtag manager Jay Devereux's former club. There's also the familiar tale of a ground move and mergers, with other Barking teams in their formative years and latterly with East Ham United, before they folded and Barking reformed in 2006.

More information is forthcoming over the excellent tannoy, as they read out the teams and there's a change from the posted team sheet. Clearly, if I end up getting drawn more into groundhopping, I'm going to develop a niche interest in the quality of tannoy. For some it's the availability of a printed programme, or cup of Bovril, but for me, knowing the teams and the winner of the fifty-fifty draw is all important.

The game is important for Hashtag too, as they look to make it six wins in a row. They get off to a good start, as Harry Haysom sends a long ball wide to Lewis Watson, who puts in a cross and Sam Bantick heads home unopposed inside the first five minutes. 'Another cheap goal again' is the verdict of one of an older family of Barking fans to my right.

Barking look to bite back, playing the ball into the inside-left channel, but Steve Sheehan-Hart and Harry Haysom deal with the threat. Play stays over on this near side, as the Tags use Bantick for an out ball. The family of Barking fans coach their left-back, who is getting stuck in. The midfield turns into a dogfight, with recent Hashtag signing Lewis Watson acquitting himself well and getting a bloody nose for his trouble. Another Hashtag player goes down under a challenge from forward Charlie Heatley. 'That's just how he tackles ref,' protests a Barking fan, before he commits another foul and receives a booking.

A ball from a kid's kick-about enters the field during another break in play. An irritated Barking keeper boots the extra ball into the trees lining the perimeter, which would almost give me a reason to shoehorn in 'barking up the wrong tree' if it had affected the game. One man who is affecting the game is Bantick. He goes in late on his marker, which outrages the home support, although not as much as when he appeals for a foul throw at every throw-in. Bantick continues to gee up his team-mates and show for the ball. He gets on the end of one long ball, cuts inside and squares to Hirst, who slots it past a defender on the line to make it 2-0 on the stroke of half-time.

I use the break to write up the first part of my match report, confident the story will be another Hashtag win. Bantick has just edged ahead of Haysom and Watson in the man of the match stakes with his goal and assist. My only concern is that he might pick up a red card. Early in the second half, he doesn't endear himself any further to the home crowd when he leaves a second ball kicked back on to the field, after it had sailed over the stand behind the goal.

Hashtag are happy for the clock to run down in the face of a Barking side that keep battling. Hashtag full-back Matthew Wooldridge finds some space to burst forward and lets a shot fly from distance. The Barking keeper can only paw it into the path of Luke Hirst. He cuts the loose ball back for Bantick to get his second, seal the win, and the somewhat less prestigious honour of being my man of the match.

Barking keep working hard. Hashtag pick up a couple of bookings. A ball breaks to Jess Norey in the box and he slips it under Page to reduce the deficit. My headline could be in jeopardy, especially since I'd seen Barking were involved in a 3-3 and a 4-4 in recent weeks. The Hashtag players are concerned, asking the ref and lino 'How long?' at every stoppage. Sheehan encourages Wooldridge to jog slowly over to take a throw, which the referee doesn't like and Sheehan unconvincingly tries to explain that he's injured. Barking still get a few hopeful balls into the box, but can't fashion an effort on target. The final whistle blows and Hashtag run out 3-1 winners and move into a play-off spot.

I'm pleased with the result and doing match reports gives me a reason to go to more games. It's not the volunteering with a club that I had in mind, but it's great to have something that keeps me involved and promotes the non-league game in a small way. Perhaps my team has been chosen for me. I'm sure to be sympathetic in my reporting and Hashtag will continue to be a great story to report on.

Chapter 32

Equality FC

LUCKILY *OUTSIDE the 92* didn't expect me to cover every game, which was just as well given my availability was likely to be as patchy as Abou Diaby's. Before I returned to Hashtag, I had a birthday treat to enjoy. My parents booked an executive beach hut to watch Lewes v Merstham. It was a chance to watch a game with all the family and take my kids, Ruby and Ivan, to their first game.

They punctuate the journey down with cries of 'I don't want to go to the football, it's boring.' As soon as they are inside the beach hut with a tray of chips and complimentary lollipops, the tune soon changes. The adults present are just as happy with their Harvey's beer and the elevated view. A few minutes in, while the game still has Ruby and Ivan's full attention, Lewes win a free kick at the other end of the ground. The home supporters are still making their way to the far terrace when Ollie Tanner curls a sumptuous left-footed shot into the top corner. My kids aren't sure what just caused a cheer, but have been drawn in. There follows plenty of explaining what throw-ins are, why players are down injured, and what substitutes are. Ruby then tracks players with numbers she likes and says one is good at kicking, just as he sends the ball out of the ground. She is concerned about what will happen if it's lost, presumably well aware of how much match balls cost. She is also concerned when the Lewes keeper leaves his area after the Rooks clear following a spell of Merstham pressure.

The volunteers at the ground show their concern for us, popping in to check all is okay and selling us raffle tickets. Luckily, Ivan isn't screaming 'Poo poo!' at the top of his voice, which he has been doing on and off for no particular reason. I tell him if he wants to make some noise he can shout 'C'mon Lewes!' which he does before adding to his repertoire with 'I don't like you Lewes.' This is where being able to keep them penned in comes into its own. As the half draws on, they occupy themselves with colouring books and we see the ball break kindly to Joe Taylor, who finishes emphatically for 2-0.

Half a match satisfies Ruby and Ivan, presumably confident the result is a foregone conclusion and Lewes will move up to second in the Isthmian Premier. Midway through the second half, Lewes are awarded a soft penalty. Ruby is keen to watch it right in front of us, but Ivan is happy just to watch my video of Joe Taylor sending the keeper the wrong way for 3-0.

We let the mostly contented crowd of 879 drift away, finish our drinks and take the kids down to the pitchside. The stud marks in the turf and the teams 'being told off' by their managers fascinates them, and they enjoy running up and down the terrace. They both agree they like football and want to go again. A photo of the Lewes women's team captured Ruby's imagination and I suggest taking her to a game. I point out the 'Equality FC' advertising board to Mrs C explaining the Rooks' equal pay initiative to get her approval, but she's more interested in another hoarding claiming Lewes to be the centre of the cosmos, which I can't explain.

On the way out, I check how Saffron Walden are getting on in their FA Vase tie with Loughborough Students. Kick-off was delayed to allow a bumper crowd of 760 in and the match has gone to penalties. Part of me wishes I was there. I willed them on, in hope of another home tie in the next round. Twitter updates are jumbled before there's confirmation they are out. I'm disappointed for Walden and surprised at my continued strength of feeling. I regret not being there, but it doesn't detract from the incredible football experience at the Dripping Pan.

It feels just as good as a trip abroad to watch football with the lads, especially with my parents babysitting, so Mrs C and I can explore the old town. Pride in the club is evident in the number of scarves we spot, as well as many businesses advertising forthcoming matches with the club's unique posters for both men's and women's fixtures. We have a couple more pints of Harvey's in the Lewes Arms and Mrs C admits she can see why I like non-league football. She says, 'It's like going to festivals – when you're young you want to go to the big ones with tens of thousands of people, but when you're older, it's nicer to go to smaller, intimate ones.' We've all enjoyed ourselves. I suggest taking Ruby to a Hashtag women's game, although I think a lot of the appeal for her was the beach hut and not sitting in the cold on a hard plastic seat.

First, I decide to check out Canvey Island's Park Lane ground by myself. Hashtag women play here in the fourth-tier National League Division 1 South East. It's a Wednesday night, so not one for Ruby, being on a school night. Hashtag are facing Billericay Town in a top-of-the-table clash and local derby. It's the first women's game I've seen in person. I passed on a one-sided international many years ago with my dad and brother at The Valley. They were both scathing about the quality of goalkeeping, even accounting for the fact they saw me ship double figures most weekends.

I knew the game had moved on from then, having seen internationals on television, and it intrigued me to see what the standard was like in the lower leagues. I wasn't about to be swayed by blooper videos that occasionally cropped up on YouTube, as you can find those for any league, and some men will knock the women's game no matter what. I walk into the ground past a sign telling me sea level is just above my chin and both sides are engaged in technical warm-up drills. Some players are well below sea level, but the game has moved on from seeing a short, un-athletic girl shoved in goal like a playground game.

The game is also moving on from teams being called 'ladies' to 'women'. I kept having to remind myself of this, after being accustomed to the Arsenal programme reporting on Arsenal Ladies winning all before them. I didn't want to become the elderly relative confused by the socially acceptable term for things just yet. One of the Hashtag fans has trouble themselves, cheering 'Let's go, ladies.' His friend corrects him: 'You can see they're women, why don't you just say Hashtag?' There was a decent-sized crowd in and the game was being streamed live on YouTube.

I wasn't at all tempted to stay at home and watch the game in a warm living room. I want to be out in the elements, watching the game as it should be watched. I'm also adding to my tally of grounds visited. Hashtag start on the front foot and play some neat exchanges on the edge of the box. It's the sort of tentative early probing that doesn't get you hooked watching on TV, in much the same way as I've struggled to get southern friends to watch rugby league beyond the opening passages of play.

An intriguing battle develops between Hashtag's Malika Apindia and Town's Kerry Stimson. Apindia is strong and fleet of foot, with a significant height advantage, but Stimson's pace and positioning prevents the Tags from creating any clear-cut chances. The one that falls to Gem Abela is pushed over the bar by Alex Baker at full stretch.

Some of the Hashtag fans behind Baker's goal jeer her goal kicks in the traditional, albeit less sweary, manner. At first, I'm reminded of reports of a Clapton women's game where their opponents, not used to playing in front of a crowd, complained about the shouts from the fans. After hearing Baker berating a defender, I'm less concerned she will be upset and more worried she might turn on the spectators.

Hashtag struggle to create chances and Billericay pose a threat on the break. A cleverly-worked short corner leads to a shooting chance on the edge of the area for Town, which is blocked. There seems to be less of an imperative to just lump it into the box. Although I do worry I might be about to watch my first nil-nil in two seasons, it's far from dull as both sides are looking to play. One good move, or one slip, could swing the balance of play and the title race.

Early in the second half, a through ball from Hashtag causes confusion between Baker and Stimson. After being so composed until now, they see the ball break to Apindia, who rolls it into the unguarded net for 1-0. The visitors launch an immediate response. Town up the tempo, but Hashtag match them. They appear to have weathered the storm when the ball goes out for a Billericay throw-in near halfway. The visitors keep possession and switch it to the left. Logan O'Shea is unmarked in the penalty area and curls a shot into the top corner, giving Imogen Riches no chance, to make it 1-1.

Both sides battle hard to take the initiative, but cancel each other out. The physio is on a few times and the ball leaves the ground several more times over the low stand on the far side. There's another break in play when Hashtag win a free kick in a wide area. Captain Grace Gillard comes over to send the ball deep into the box. It's in a difficult area for Baker and her defence. An onrushing Katharine Nutman strokes it home to restore the Tags' lead, with a little under ten minutes remaining.

Billericay win a set piece of their own and look for another quick response. The ball into the box almost embarrasses Riches. She can't get there and it flashes across the goal. Hashtag compose themselves. By my watch it's almost full time, so I make my way towards the exit and stand on the corner terrace. Hashtag make their own way there to hold the ball near the corner flag. I'm in the right place for a late bit of drama. The Town players concede a foul in frustration. Hashtag fake a free kick, so the referee stops play for encroachment. They repeat this several times right in front of me. Frustration grows. A Town player is booked. The challenges become more robust. Gillard keeps asking how much longer. I'm shaking. Although that's because the terrace is exposed and we've played a lot longer than I expected. Finally, the whistle blows and the Hashtag bench runs on to the field in celebration. You can see what it meant in those dying moments and those little vignettes make a live game such a visceral experience – albeit one I dash away from to reach the warmth of my car.

On the way out, I catch a glimpse of a TV in the clubhouse and see that Spurs beat Leicester with two stoppage-time goals, which dampens my mood in the same way the Walden result did leaving the Lewes game. I feel a certain fondness for both Lewes and the women's game, and I'm keen to bring Ruby along once it's warmer. The point a Clapton fan made about supporting both men's and women's teams is spot on. Anyone who is a fan of the sport should support the women's game. The standard tonight has been decent. It's always tempting to place it somewhere in comparison with the men's game, but like the youth team football I've seen, it's best to judge the game on its own merits. Tonight, I've seen a top-of-the-table clash and found an absorbing contest.

It's notable that some of the teams I've been drawn to, such as Clapton, Hashtag and Lewes, are all strong supporters of the women's game, which perhaps says something about those clubs and is something else that makes them worth supporting. I can hardly ignore the fact that Arsenal women have long been one of the country's best sides, so I add them to the list of clubs I could take Ruby to see and let her decide which she likes best. Although when I offer to take her to another game, she asks if they have beach huts and isn't interested when I say no.

Chapter 33

We go again

ANOTHER CLUB who are strong supporters of the women's game is Dulwich Hamlet. Phil and I were supposed to see their men's team play Chelmsford City nearly two years ago. Our rain check led me towards Hashtag and I suspect it's now too late for me to become a Hamlet fan. I remained keen to check them out, as their credentials as a community club had seen them grow in popularity, attracting sell-out crowds of over 3,000 at Champion Hill. We had to buy our tickets in advance and plan a pub crawl for afterwards in preparation.

Phil wasn't full of love for our hometown club, having watched City the previous week. His day started badly trying to get the bus driver to part with tickets for him and his son to travel across town, which took an eternity on a Saturday afternoon. Scanning tickets at the gate went no better, and neither did getting drinks. A long queue for the main bar would have been relieved by the can bar, but having been told to use that, he found it didn't open until half-time. The game itself was a drab goalless draw.

We debated which end we should stand in, as we had some pre-match drinks. This included mead from Gosnells Meadery under the arches at Peckham Rye. Phil was keen to check it out, adopting a 'when in Rome' approach, and I am glad we did. My only previous experience of mead was a sickly sweet example of the honey-based drink as a punishment shot while playing *Pro Evolution Soccer*. Gosnell's finest was a revelation. Their range went from a simple fizzy perry-like refreshment through to a much stronger concoction mixed with cider and winter spices.

After the meadery and a couple more pubs, we arrive at the ground just before kick-off. A steward directs us away from three moderately busy turnstiles to another supposedly quieter one on the other side of the ground. Some five minutes after kick-off we eventually get into a packed Champion Hill. We decide not to join the snaking queue for the main bar and try the corner bar near the away fans. The queue stretches all the way to the penalty area. It is at this point we decide we will support the visitors.

I shuffle towards the corner bar, as City make more assertive progress towards the Hamlet goal. I see Charlie Sheringham, son of the former Spurs striker, lay a perfectly weighted ball off to Danny Imre. His cut-back goes into the area and the next thing I know, the net is rippling and the away supporters are cheering. City have the lead.

Sometime later I have drinks with which to celebrate. Later still, I find out Dara Dada was the player to turn it in.

Hamlet, who are in the play-off mix, are stung into action and cause a few scares for the City defence before a cross is headed home to make it 1-1. The celebrations from the home end feel rather muted. The lack of atmosphere surprises Phil and me. We saw a drummer on the way in and can't hear him, so perhaps the acoustics of the uncovered terracing aren't helping. Either way, we're being drawn to the noisier away support around us.

At half-time we swap ends to stay among the City fans. There's the practical aspect of needing to do some more queuing for the toilets and bar on the way round the ground. We also can't escape the fact that we identify more with the older Essex blokes in the away end. Most of the home support seems to be much younger than us and we pick out all kinds of northern accents. Phil, despite advocating our trip to the meadery, isn't a fan of students or hipsters, particularly if they're not creating much atmosphere.

We're drawn into the singing. The CCFC chant is easily done, as I could just as well be signing about Clapton Community. 'Wheel 'em in, wheel 'em in, wheel 'em in' is catchy and traditional. City are on the front foot, which helps our mood. A low ball into Crystal Palace loanee Imre is dispatched for 2-1 and we're celebrating wildly enough to still just about retain the contents of our pints.

The singing continues with a mixture of local pride, – 'City of Essex!' and mocking the opposition – 'You're only here for the catch-up.' It's great to be part of a noisy away following. The cheers increase when City are awarded a penalty. Sheringham steps up to take the kick. The keeper goes the right way, but I'm not given a reason to curse a member of the Sheringham family again, as he does just enough to beat him. Phil is keen to make it known to the keeper that he should have saved it. I refrain from joining in with Phil's goading as part of the *omerta* that even lapsed members of the goalkeepers' union abide by.

The game finishes 3-1 and we make our way from the ground to the Brick Brewery Taproom. We expected more from the home side both in terms of the team performance and the experience. I had heard some murmurings from home fans that Dulwich had gotten too popular and facilities needed improving. I couldn't blame people for succumbing to the appeal of non-league football, wanting to be part of a progressive club, and helping that club grow. There was a worry that what had drawn me to Clapton and Hashtag could go the same way. Therein lies the paradox of being a non-league fan. Naturally, you want your team to do well, but doing well moves you further from what you like about the experience.

The experience of following City away was more surprising than the pre-match mead. A combination of promising team performance, craft beer, and being part of a small band of away fans from the same city made for a great day out. The ease with which I was drawn into the singing took me aback, and although I always knew I would have a soft spot for the Clarets, I didn't expect them to come back into the reckoning for my full-time support.

A team who had drifted out of the picture was Fisher, because of a lack of midweek fixtures. When they eventually had one, it coincided with a tube strike, torrential rain and the possible outbreak of World War III. I couldn't tempt anyone else along, but looking for an after-work distraction I found another route to the ground and bagged a seat in the main stand. I was joined by several groundhoppers, who made themselves known by their notepads, smug satisfaction knowing this game wouldn't be rained off due to the artificial pitch, and checking into the *Futbology* app. Since I had my own notepad out and had already checked into the app, I was clearly one of them; so much so that I heard my name read out when one of them looked to see who had checked in. I was identified as an Arsenal fan because of the number of games I had logged with them. There were also hoppers from York and Gala Fairydean, which was instantly confirmed as being in Scotland.

More supporters take cover in the stand and have to shuffle back a row upon realising the roof doesn't protect the front seats from the elements. There are a few more northern accents among the newcomers. It's a night for those committed to logging grounds, and those accustomed to far worse weather. The downpour puts me off going to the bar, so I will find out if much of my warm feeling towards Fisher stems from last watching them in August with a beer in hand.

There isn't anything to watch as 7:45pm comes and goes. There's no tannoy in operation. The hoppers say this is because of neighbouring flats complaining about the noise, despite the higher decibel level coming from the main road behind us. A volunteer comes round to tell everyone of a 15-minute delay, due to the linesman being stuck in traffic. Talk turns to how you never used to hear players screaming, even if they broke their leg, surprise at the resurgence of the non-league game, and of course the situation in Ukraine. Although their concern with current affairs was far more parochial, worrying about the impact of immigrants rather than the existential threat of a nuclear conflict.

The game kicks off 20 minutes late, and it takes the teams a while to get going. The only movement of note is when one hopper asks a group of lads to move from the hatched area in front of the stand, so we can see the goal Fisher are defending. I expect them to have to defend a fair bit, with opponents Sheppey sitting second in the league and looking good for promotion to Step 4.

There's a stoppage for an injury, which promises to make it an even later finish. When play resumes, there are few chances for the forwards to finish. A ball is played into a Fisher forward, whose number I can't make out, with a defender close at hand. He can't get the ball out of his feet and the defender does enough to deflect a scuffed shot out for a corner. The northerners complain about the quality of the finish and one hopper reminds them if they could finish, they wouldn't be playing at this level. The corner comes to nothing.

One northerner asks where Sheppey is located. The hopper uncharitably, but somewhat accurately, describes it as the arsehole of the Thames Estuary and speculates there must be some dodgy chancer putting money into the side for them to be in second. There's further speculation on how little Fisher must get, but at least they put in some committed tackling, with one block sending the ball out of the ground and 'On the bus back to Rotherhithe'.

The visitors are awarded a free kick. 'Top right' calls one northerner. 'Third tree from the left' is the wizened prediction of the hopper. The strike is heading towards the top right, before dipping and being spilt by the keeper. A forward follows up and can only balloon it into the trees, so both parties are satisfied with their predictions.

Approaching half-time, Fisher will be satisfied they've kept the visitors quiet, apart from one schoolboy fan who has been particularly vocal and warrants one hopper to question whether it's past his bedtime. The Fish win a corner. It's sent towards the near post and is bundled home by centre-half Sam Fitzgerald to make it 1-0. The half ends soon after.

Someone comes round to announce the winner of the raffle. 'Amir S,' he calls. 'Yes, you are here!' comes the retort, but no sign of Amir. The persistence of the raffle ticket seller reassures me I probably didn't win on my previous visit. The hoppers talk animatedly about their plans for the week. There's mention of Ilford's game tomorrow evening. I'm tempted to go to that one myself, until they express concern that it might be rained off, but then note the pitch isn't exactly conducive to good football even in August.

The second half gets underway and straight away Sheppey bundle in a corner for an equaliser. An award of a penalty immediately follows when Tommy Taylor in the Fisher goal takes down a forward, who beat him to a through ball. Taylor is lucky to avoid a red card, but cannot stop the penalty, which turns the tide in favour of the visitors, who make it 2-1.

The second half drifts along. Fisher are floundering as they can't sustain any concerted pressure on their opponents. The Fish win a free kick out in the deep. It's launched into the box and Fitzgerald gets a foot on it and places it into the bottom corner to net the equaliser. This prompts a late flurry as Fisher search for a winner. They get a corner in stoppage time. The ball sails into the box and the referee emulates Clive Thomas and blows the final whistle. Those in the stand are left fuming, even though the kick was over-hit. It ends all square.

The 147 in attendance disperse into sodden streets. I'm pleased to have taken my mind off world events and spend the journey home composing a match report with all the fish puns I can think of. I don't feel as enamoured with Fisher as I did on my previous visit. The lack of sunshine, or trip to the Mayflower, played a part in that, but also things have gotten more serious with other clubs in the meantime. I hesitate to rule out the Fish entirely, as I will swing by and catch a game or two given the proximity to my office, but I don't count myself as a supporter.

Chapter 34

Who are ya? Who are ya? Who are ya?

THIS ALL leads to the inevitable question of who *do* I support? My brother suggested I should do a big reveal with a tattoo of my chosen club. That feels like it would tempt fate and things would soon turn sour; besides, I'm too much of a wimp. Things almost turn sour with Hashtag when I see them sign a fan token deal, which I disagree with. I nearly throw my lot in with Clapton Community, but listening to Spencer's justification, I could see where he was coming from. I'm reminded that Spencer and Hashtag could always do something that I disagreed with and the club wasn't at the stage where I felt like a fan had the right to question the founder.

The other way I considered a big reveal was to hire a minibus and invite my mates to a game and keep it a secret until we arrived. I would have been too tempted to make it a Clapton game, as there's a proper sense of occasion watching the Tons and I know my mates would have enjoyed the atmosphere. But the cost of a minibus to and from London would have been prohibitively expensive and I'm not entirely sure Clapton are the one either.

If this were a dating show, I would be forced to choose. I've grown to like two very different clubs for very different reasons. Hashtag remain a great story to follow and, as their correspondent for *Outside the 92*, I will continue to follow it. They are a conveniently local team and the highlights videos keep me hooked. Clapton are the team who embody collective joy, a community you can feel a part of, where going to a match feels like a special occasion and it means more than a game of football. Like Hashtag, it's entirely possible I may disagree with the club's views at some point in the future and no club is going to be perfect.

Most fans can instinctively pick a side when two teams face one another. Through a combination of distaste for rival teams, perceived slights over the years and occasional begrudging respect for the odd team or individual, there's often a way to tell who you are secretly rooting for in the most innocuous of fixtures. The fact Hashtag are several levels above Clapton means there isn't an opportunity to see how I feel in the heat of battle.

Perhaps I need a half-and-half scarf to show my support for both clubs. These much-maligned garments are made for tourists to commemorate going to a game, when no right-thinking fan would want to wear something with a rival team's name on it. I'm old enough to recall an earlier tradition of half-and-half hats, showing friendships between teams. I recall seeing Arsenal-Celtic ones popular amongst Irish fans. I could even make my own Hashtag-Clapton scarf by joining my old Arsenal home and away scarves, if only I could find them. This would rather neatly capture some residual fondness for Arsenal themselves, which I don't think I can ever get away from. At a push, the home colours could also represent Chelmsford City, who I will continue to look out for.

I think a lot of fans have more than one team and that is the real taboo. Plenty of those going to non-league games display their allegiance to a Premier League club. Many more will follow the fortunes of several clubs in their local area, or follow teams in other sports. That's often how other sports are consumed and means going to those events can be more civilised, albeit lacking the same passion. My brother asked whether I would celebrate a Hashtag goal in the same way as Arsenal beating Spurs and I don't imagine I would. For a genuine fan, the game is all-consuming, plans are made around it, the highs are celebrated wildly and the lows represent the depths of despair. My life has moved on from those levels of commitment.

I have rediscovered that I'm a supporter of the game once again, though. If money into club coffers is a measure, then I've supported several teams, while still spending less than on an Arsenal season ticket, with Hashtag and Lewes being the primary beneficiaries. If lending my voice to get behind the team is the measure, then Clapton and Chelmsford come out on top.

It's fair to say I will still follow the fortunes of several other teams from afar, with Saffron Walden, Ilford, Fisher and, of course, Arsenal, being teams I look out for. Seeing if all these teams can win on the same day is like hoping for an accumulator to come in, only without losing money every week. It feels like reverting back to childhood, when all aspects of the game were fascinating, from enjoying the occasion of an FA Cup Final regardless of who was playing, through to learning minor facts from magazines and sticker books about different teams.

Football needn't be taken so seriously – it should be fun. I see how my young nephew, Sam, is getting hooked on the game and he loves nothing more than getting a new shirt for a different team. When fanaticism for one team takes over, the fun can disappear. There can be highs and it can be an intense experience, but the sight of fans defending the indefensible when those associated with their club do something repugnant is far from edifying. Seeing clubs with thriving women's and youth sections is great too, especially as my own kids start showing an interest in the game.

At the heart of it all, the game of football is still unsurpassed for drama, beauty and enjoyment, and I'm glad the game is back in my life. You might say that's fine, but who do I actually support? If this were a murder mystery, I would round up Arsenal, Hashtag, Clapton, Chelmsford, Saffron Walden, Ilford, Lewes and Fisher in a room, before ruling them out one by one, until I reveal Dial Square were my new team in a surprise twist. I will not do that. Dial Square may have proven some of my initial misgivings to be unfounded, but they are not my team.

I have to be honest and say that there isn't one team I support in the way I supported Arsenal. Football is unpredictable. There's not always a neat ending. Draws can, and do, happen and this quest has ended in a draw. There are two teams where I go beyond being a follower; I am a season ticket holder at Hashtag and I became an owner of Clapton Community, which by most measures makes me a supporter of both teams. My Clapton ownership came about when I couldn't make any of their remaining home games and wanted to contribute to the club. I felt encouraged by the way their supporters are welcoming to those from far and wide. I'm sure they wouldn't mind if their latest owner had a clear conflict of interest, would provide limited financial backing and may well turn up in that half-and-half scarf. I may not renew my Hashtag season ticket, but that would only be based on it being more cost effective to pay for individual matches on the gate. Watching their away games is also more appealing to me.

I'm keen to travel to new grounds, be that with Hashtag or watching teams that take my fancy. As I continue groundhopping, it will draw me to other clubs, especially those with tales of woe, where a beloved local institution is facing uncertainty. If I ever move to a new area, I will want to check out the local clubs. I've essentially gone from leaving a loveless marriage to becoming a bigamist with a roving eye for nonconventional beauty. There is plenty of beauty waiting to be discovered in non-league and I urge anyone reading this to watch a local non-league team. You will find a warm welcome and will help a vital part of your community to thrive. You won't necessarily see any good football, but you will have a great footballing experience.

Epilogue

It's up for grabs now!

WITH THE all-important honour of my support being decided, around the same time of year the Premier League title is usually sewn up, there was the small matter of promotions and relegations to be decided across the leagues I've been following.

In the National League South, Chelmsford City went on a seven-match losing streak after I saw their win over Dulwich. Discontent with the owners led to the clarets4change group forming, to secure fan participation in the club's running. It was pleasing to see fans not letting the club wither and die. I watched the team get back to winning ways in a big six-pointer against local rivals Billericay, which went a long way to ensuring their place in Step 2.

On a whim, I saw the Clarets with Ben and Henry on a glorious spring afternoon. Talk on the terraces had turned to the county cricket team and people were even wearing t-shirts at the Gulag. A fine strike from Matt Rush settled the early nerves, before Billericay's direct approach forced an equaliser from a set piece. After we swapped ends at half-time, a steward instructed one fan who had taken a pint on to the terrace to down it, and other fans taunted the diminutive Billericay goalkeeper. He made the mistake of bragging about his league career, which only led to those fans looking it up online and taunting him further. They claimed the assist when he couldn't keep out a late Deon Moore strike. We ended up in amongst the celebrations, with Henry losing a shoe, but gaining more love for the game.

Billericay ended the season in the sole relegation spot. Chelmsford will face Dulwich Hamlet and Dartford again next season, as Hamlet fell out of play-off contention and Dartford lost their play-off eliminator. Dorking came out on top in the play-offs to join champions Maidstone in the National League.

In the Isthmian Premier, with alliteration as good as some of their football, Worthing were worthy winners. It disappointed me to see an equally attack-minded Lewes slip out of the play-off picture in the final few weeks of the season after a couple of notable defensive lapses. Cheshunt capitalised and surprised runners-up Bishop's Stortford with a come-from-behind 3-2 win in their semi-final. They faced FA Trophy holders Hornchurch in the final, after they overcame Enfield Town in a 3-2 thriller of their own, with former Chelmsford man Sam Higgins bagging a late equaliser.

I rounded off my season with this fixture to experience the thrill of a play-off final. I wasn't left disappointed, but the home fans were. Hornchurch couldn't muster another late comeback, with Higgins cutting a frustrated figure. It would disappoint the Urchins to remain at Step 3, in contrast to Brightlingsea Regent, who were delighted to pull away from the relegation places and stay in the division.

Hashtag came up short in their late bid for play-off glory in the Isthmian North. They kept their hopes alive with some impressive results, which included inflicting their only home defeat of the campaign on eventual champions Aveley. Some indifferent results against teams towards the bottom cost them, along with their slow start. Maldon & Tiptree were just as frustrated, if not more so, after the previous two seasons. They finished just below the Tags, but above neighbours Heybridge in mid-table.

Walthamstow deservedly claimed the title in the Essex Senior League, which was just reward after two curtailed seasons in which they had battled it out with Hashtag and Saffron Walden at the top. Walden went on a run of ten wins in their last 11 games to claim second and an inter-step play-off against Witham from the league above. It transpired that Mrs C didn't consider Witham to be a romantic destination for her birthday, so I missed their clash. Former Hashtag player Josh Osude, who scored a 95th-minute winner in Witham's last league game to avoid an automatic relegation spot, was on the scoresheet again in a comprehensive 3-0 win to deny the Bloods promotion. They would remain at Step 5 alongside the likes of Ilford and Woodford Town, who finished in the bottom half, albeit well clear of relegation. At the same step in the SCEFL Premier, Fisher also finished in lower mid-table.

At Step 6, in the Thurlow Nunn Eastern Counties First Division South, Wivenhoe made the play-offs, which may or may not have been thanks to the youth team players I stood with. They lost their semi-final against Buckhurst Hill, who were only just pipped to the title by Ipswich Wanderers, after they racked up over 200 points between them. It didn't seem to count for anything in the final, where they lost at home to Halstead Town. However, when the FA announced the league allocations, Buckhurst Hill found themselves elevated to the Essex Senior League anyway.

Clapton Community's promotion bid faded towards the end of the season. A run of poor results, including a game that was abandoned and awarded to the opposition after an altercation between opposition players and home fans, left them in third. With only one promotion place available to the highest-placed team with a suitably graded ground, this meant only NW London were promoted. The Clapton women's team also finished third, but were promoted.

Elsewhere in the women's game, Lewes justified more than their equal pay by remaining in the second tier up against the likes of Liverpool, Crystal Palace and Sunderland. Hashtag women narrowly missed out on promotion to the third tier, pipped to the title by a single point, with Billericay taking the sole promotion place. The Tags had the consolation of winning the County Cup, beating Billericay in the final. I didn't go to the final after feeling a little deflated that *Outside the 92* would not continue. This left open the possibility that my ties with Hashtag would loosen. Only time would tell how my feelings would continue to develop for the Tags, and others. I couldn't wait to find out, as I would once again look forward to August and the start of a new season.

Up the Tags! C'mon you Tons!